UNDERSTANDING
ENGLISH
GRAMMAR

UNDERSTANDING ENGLISH GRAMMAR

SECOND EDITION

Martha Kolln

The Pennsylvania State University

MACMILLAN PUBLISHING COMPANY
New York

COLLIER MACMILLAN PUBLISHERS
London

Macmillan Publishing Company
866 Third Avenue, New York, New York 10022

Collier Macmillan Canada, Inc.

Library of Congress Cataloging in Publication Data

Kolln, Martha.
  Understanding English grammar.

  Includes index.
  1. English language—Grammar—1950–   . I. Title.
PE112.K64   1986   428.2   85-4890
ISBN 0-02-366060-0

Printing: 2 3 4 5 6 7 8   Year: 6 7 8 9 0 1 2 3 4

ISBN 0-02-366060-0

PREFACE

THIS book has a simple purpose: to describe the rules of English grammar in a systematic way so that they will be understandable and accessible to the speaker and writer and reader of English. The purpose has not changed in this second edition of the book. The format, too, remains the same, with the basic sentence patterns as its focus. This edition does include substantial revisions in every chapter, in some cases fuller explanations and in others the introduction of new topics. All of the chapters on the sentence now conclude with a list of practice sentences, which the instructor will find helpful for homework assignments or for testing. This edition also includes three major new sections: an appendix on phonology; a complete glossary of grammatical terms; and a glossary of some of our common usage issues with grammatical explanations.

Understanding English Grammar does not describe or advocate one particular grammar theory. Its purpose is not to compare traditional grammar with new grammar or to explain the latest findings of linguistic research. Rather, its purpose is to describe and emphasize the systematic nature of the rules of grammar. To do so, it draws upon all of the theories, the old and the new, as each contributes to the understanding of a concept. It incorporates, for example, that visual aid of the traditional grammarian, the sentence diagram, along with the sentence patterns of the structuralists and the generative rules and branching diagrams of the transformationalists. This eclectic method takes advantage of all the theories, making use of whatever will help to illuminate the system.

The study of grammar is not just for English majors or for future teachers; it is for people in business and industry, in science and engineering, in law and politics. Every user of the language, in fact, will benefit from the study of grammar. The more that speakers and writers and readers know consciously about language, the more power they have over it and the better they can make it serve their needs.

Although *Understanding English Grammar* is addressed to native speakers of English, its method of sentence analysis based on sentence patterns makes it accessible to the nonnative speaker as well. The advanced student of English as a second language will find its systematic method of sentence expansion logical and practical.

The book begins with a description of the ten sentence patterns followed by the system for expanding the verb and ways of reordering or transforming the basic sentences; Part II deals with parts of speech, the classification of words; Part III shows how modifiers are added to sentences and how ideas are coordinated and subordinated. Part IV takes up some common questions about usage. Part V is a glossary of the grammatical terms used in the book. Conventions of punctuation and other standards of edited English, as well as important differences between spoken and written language, are treated logically and systematically as the principles of expanding sentences develop. Each chapter includes exercises to help reinforce principles of grammar, as well as questions to encourage discussion that go beyond the concepts covered in the text.

For many years the subject of grammar has been misunderstood. It suffers from poor public relations, both in and out of the classroom. Too often it is seen as something to take—an immunization shot for preventive purposes—or something to put up with, like a gloomy day. But far from being painful or dull, our language is alive; it is a living, organic, continually changing part of us. The more we know about the grammar of our language, the more we know about ourselves.

ACKNOWLEDGMENTS

Behind every second edition of a textbook lies a first edition that succeeded in finding an audience and filling a need; I am pleased that the first edition of *Understanding English Grammar* has had that success. I am pleased too that so many teachers who used the first edition have taken time to share their enthusiasm for the book's strengths and to offer suggestions for its improvement.

Especially helpful have been the careful comments of the following reviewers: Richard F. Thompson, Northern Virginia Community College; Connie Eble, University of North Carolina at Chapel Hill;

Joseph Sawicki, California State University, Fullerton; Muriel Schulz, California State University, Fullerton; Carol Croxton, University of Southern Colorado; R. Baird Shuman, University of Illinois at Urbana-Champaign; Lettie J. Austin, Howard University; Ann W. Sharp, Furman University; Dorothy Disterheft, University of South Carolina; Wanda B. Morgan, Moravian College; Edgar C. Alward, Westfield State College; Anne LeCroy, East Tennessee State University; John W. Schwetman, Sam Houston State University; Edward P. J. Corbett, Ohio State University; William H. Wiatt, Indiana University, Bloomington; Lee Little, Western Kentucky University. I am grateful indeed for their help.

I also wish to tell my Penn State colleagues, Ron Buckalew and Betty Johnson, that their encouragement through the years and their suggestions for the book have meant a great deal to me; and I appreciate Ron's help with the new appendix on phonology.

The reaction of students to a textbook is the real test, of course—the bottom line. My students have taught me many lessons during the past several years; many of the changes in this second edition are the result of that education. I would also like to acknowledge the help of two students at other schools, at opposite sides of the country: Judith Gallant Lech, a student of Professor Edgar C. Alward at Westfield State College, carefully critiqued major portions of the first edition and offered important suggestions, many of which I have followed; Howard Williams, a student of Professor Eugene Smith at the University of Washington, wrote a scholarly review of the sections on phrasal verbs, and that too has influenced this new edition. I am grateful to both of them and to their teachers.

I reserve special thanks for my editor, Eben W. Ludlow, whose advice and enthusiasm have kept me on course; and both my thanks and my apologies to his assistant, Tucker Jones—the thanks for her cheerful efficiency throughout the project, the apologies for addressing her as "Mr. Jones" way back when; my thanks also to Bob Hunter, who guided the book through the details of production with the right mix of patience and pickiness.

And, finally, I acknowledge the encouragement and support of a husband who, after thirty-five years of marriage, thinks of me as a woman who makes grammar exciting.

M.K.

CONTENTS

6 THE STRUCTURE CLASSES 122

7 PRONOUNS 147

PART III
EXPANDING THE BASIC PATTERNS 163

PART IV
USAGE 321

PART V
GLOSSARY OF
GRAMMATICAL TERMS 345

APPENDIXES

UNDERSTANDING
ENGLISH
GRAMMAR

I

SENTENCE
PATTERNS

IMAGINE a computer that is programmed to invent grammatical sentences for every occasion—a computer so ingenious that even with a limited storage of words it is able to generate an infinite number of grammatical sentences. The language component of your brain is just such a computer, a linguistic marvel that can go into action without a moment's hesitation, inventing sentences, putting together meaningful combinations of words, even putting together combinations that have never been heard before. In day-to-day situations your inventions tend to be fairly predictable: "Hi, how are you?" "Have you eaten yet?" "Sorry I'm late." "That was the funniest movie I've ever seen." "Coffee time!" But other occasions call for unique combinations, and you come up with such sentences automatically too.

Your linguistic computer has another job as well: to process the sentences you read and hear so that you can understand them. It does this just as automatically, usually with no difficulty, even in the case of strange sentences you've never heard or seen before:

> The rocking chair in my living room sat next to the woodburning stove, quietly contemplating the price of oil.

And, as you have just demonstrated, your computer can process a sentence and make sense of its ideas even when they're nonsense. The system underlying this computer-like ability of ours, this internal system that enables us to create and to process sentences, is the system we call grammar.

How shall we begin our study of grammar? First, imagine that we

1

are programming a computer to do what we as language users do—to generate grammatical sentences. We want the computer to be creative, as we are, to invent sentences on its own. How will we program it to do that? The obvious first step is to understand our own sentences. What rules do we follow? What are the parts of the system? How do they work together?

These are the very questions that linguists ask. Some fifty years ago when the structural linguists, also known as "new grammarians," began to ask such questions, they obviously weren't thinking about programming computers to produce sentences. They simply set out to describe the language in an objective way. Until that time, most descriptions of English grammar were based on Latin grammar. The new grammarians changed that practice, describing English on its own terms. They examined all of the components of English, beginning with the smallest unit—the meaningful sound, or phoneme—and then described how phonemes are combined into larger, meaningful units—morphemes—and then into words and, finally, sentences. This description came to be known as structural grammar.

Then in the 1950s a new generation of linguists took up the questions in a somewhat different way and added a few new ones: How can we account for this linguistic ability of ours? What rules do we follow in order to produce and process sentences? How does the system work? These are the questions of the transformational-generative linguists. They are still in the process of formulating answers.

The thread that runs through all of the answers through all of the years of asking questions is the idea of *system;* we put sounds and words and phrases and sentences together in a highly systematic way. This system makes up what we call the *rules of grammar*. It is this system of rules forming the language competence of native speakers that we will examine in the chapters that follow. We will begin the study of grammar with basic sentences—the sentence patterns; we will then look at the separate parts of the patterns; and finally we will examine the systematic way we expand and modify and combine them.

1

The Ten Basic Patterns

Linguists have shown that the number of possible sentences a speaker can produce is infinite, yet the number of basic sentence forms, or patterns, is decidedly finite—in fact, the total is very small. Ten **sentence patterns**[1] will account for the underlying skeletal structure of almost all of the possible grammatical sentences in English. The patterns are much simpler than most of the sentences that we actually produce in both speech and writing, but to understand those more complicated sentences, we must first understand the simple skeletons that underlie them.

Before looking at the ten patterns separately, we will examine one feature that all sentences share—the subject–predicate relationship. This binary, or two-part, division describes the sentence as a whole and many of its separate parts as well. The branching diagram represents any and all of the ten basic sentence patterns. An example of each pattern follows.

```
                        SENTENCE
              _____/          _____
          NP                              VP
       (Subject)                       (Predicate)
```

I.	The students	are upstairs.
II.	The students	are diligent.
III.	The students	are scholars.
IV.	The students	seem diligent.
V.	The students	became scholars.

[1] The words and phrases in boldface are defined in the Glossary of Grammatical Terms, beginning on page 345.

3

VI.	The students	rested.
VII.	The students	studied their assignment.
VIII.	The students	gave the teacher an apple.
IX.	The students	consider the teacher intelligent.
X.	The students	consider the course a challenge.

This list illustrates the two parts of every sentence: (1) the NP, or **noun phrase,** which functions as the **subject;** and (2) the VP, or **verb phrase,** made up of the main verb together with its complements and modifiers, which functions as the **predicate.** The subject, as its name suggests, is what the sentence is about—its topic. The predicate is what is said about the subject. The two parts can be thought of as the topic and the comment. This relationship underlies every sentence, including those in which the subject is unstated but clearly understood:

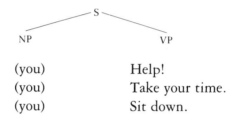

(you)	Help!
(you)	Take your time.
(you)	Sit down.

You may be accustomed to thinking of the subject of a sentence as simply a noun, rather than a whole phrase. But most nouns don't stand alone; there are some, in fact, that rarely do. Nouns are usually signaled by determiners, as in the foregoing examples—*the* students, *their* assignment, *the* teacher, *an* apple, *a* challenge. Further, nouns are often preceded and/or followed by modifiers: the *new* students; their *history* assignment; the *new* teacher *from Fresno.* The term *phrase* refers to any such group of words that acts as a unit within a sentence. The term *noun phrase* is also used in reference to a single noun or pronoun that fills an NP slot.

No matter what your experience with nouns and noun phrases, your intuition will often be sufficient for figuring out the two basic parts of the sentence. For example, if you were asked to divide the following sentences into subject and predicate, you could probably do so with no problem:

The county commissioners have passed a new ordinance.
The mayor's husband spoke against it.
The mayor was upset with him.
Several residents of the community spoke in favor of it.
The merchants in town are unhappy.
The new law will prohibit billboard advertising on major high-
ways.

Chances are that you made your divisions correctly—after these subjects:

The county commissioners
The mayor's husband
The mayor
Several residents of the community
The merchants in town
The new law

You were probably able to make those divisions on the basis of your
intuition. But if you want to check your intuition, one trick that can
help you figure out where the subject ends and the predicate begins is
to substitute a **pronoun** for the subject. The pronoun, you will discover, stands in for the entire noun phrase. You will also discover that
you use such pronouns automatically:

They   have passed a new ordinance.
He   spoke against it.
She   was upset with him.
They   spoke in favor of it.
They   are unhappy.
It   will prohibit billboard advertising on major highways.

Recognition of this subject–predicate relationship, the common
element in all of the patterns, is the first step in the study of sentences.
We should also recognize that this classification of sentences into ten
patterns is based on *variations in the predicates.* In the sample sentences
shown with the patterns the subjects are identical (*the students*); the
features that distinguish the patterns are in the verbs and the number

and kinds of structures that follow the verbs. So although the categories are called *sentence patterns*, a more accurate label might be *verb
phrase patterns* or *predicate patterns*.

The traditional grammarians classify verbs into three categories:
transitive, intransitive, and **linking.** We shall vary this classification
by adding the verb *be* as a separate category, as the structural linguists
do. These four classes, with variations in the structures that follow
them, will produce the ten basic sentence patterns.

In the list that follows, the ten sentence patterns are presented as
formulas, using symbols that represent, as far as possible, the *forms* of
the various elements in the sentences rather than using labels that
represent function. For example, instead of labeling the first slot *subject,* which is its function in the sentence, we label it NP, or *noun
phrase,* because that is the *form* that the subject usually takes. It is
useful to think of each part of the formula as a slot occupied by a
particular form. We cannot disregard either function or meaning in
discussing the patterns, nor do we want to. This description simply
emphasizes the importance of form in analyzing the language system;
we want to acknowledge how much the understanding of form contributes to the linguistic knowledge that we have as native speakers.

In the formulas, ADV/TP stands for *adverbial* of time or place,
ADJ for *adjectival.* The subscript numbers show the relationship between noun phrases: Identical numbers mean that the two noun
phrases have the same referent; different numbers denote different referents. **Referent** means the thing (or person, event, concept, etc.) that
the word stands for.

I.	NP	*be*	ADV/TP		The students are upstairs.
II.	NP	*be*	ADJ		The students are diligent.
III.	NP_1	*be*	NP_1		The students are scholars.
IV.	NP	V-lnk	ADJ		The students seem diligent.
V.	NP_1	V-lnk	NP_1		The students became scholars.
VI.	NP	V-intr			The students rested.
VII.	NP_1	V-tr	NP_2		The students studied their assignment.
VIII.	NP_1	V-tr	NP_2	NP_3	The students gave the teacher an apple.
IX.	NP_1	V-tr	NP_2	ADJ	The students consider the teacher intelligent.

X. NP₁ V-tr NP₂   NP₂ The students consider the
                            course a challenge.

THE CLAUSE

Before taking up the sentence patterns individually, we will consider the word *clause,* a word close in meaning to that of "sentence"—
so close, in fact, that Part I could have been called "Clause Patterns"
instead of "Sentence Patterns." Indeed, what we have been discussing
in this chapter—these ten patterns—are clause patterns. We will, in
fact, define a clause as a group of words with a subject and a predicate.

Then what is the difference between a clause and a sentence? All
complete sentences contain one or more clauses, but not all clauses are
complete sentences. In later chapters we will see sentences in which
clauses are embedded as modifiers; we will also see sentences in which
clauses fill NP slots. We call such clauses—those that are not independent sentences—**dependent clauses.** The sentences we are studying
in this chapter—the sentence patterns—are **independent clauses.**
Every complete sentence has at least one independent clause.

THE *BE* PATTERNS

The first three formulas state that when a form of *be* serves as the
main verb either an adverbial of time or place, an adjectival, or a noun
phrase will follow it. The one exception to this rule—and, by the way,
we can think of sentence patterns as rules that our internal computer is
programmed to follow—is a statement simply affirming existence: "I
am" or "Man is." Aside from this exception, Patterns I–III describe
all of the sentences in which a form of *be* is the main verb. (Other one-
word forms of *be* are *am, is, are, was, were, being,* and *been.* We will look
at the expanded forms of *be* and other verbs in detail in Chapter 2.)

PATTERN I: NP *be* ADV/TP

The students are upstairs.
The teacher is here.
The next performance will be soon.

The ADV in the formula stands for *adverbial,* a modifier of the verb.

The ADV that follows *be* is, with only rare exceptions, limited to *when* and *where* information, so in the formula for Pattern I we identify the slot as ADV/TP, meaning "adverbial of time or place." In the sample sentences *upstairs* and *here* designate place; *soon* designates time.

Notice that we are labeling this slot filler as an **adverbial** rather than simply an adverb. We do so because the adverbial information is often expressed by a structure other than a simple adverb; for example, it may take the form of a **phrase** (a group of words) or a **clause** (an entire sentence pattern). One of the most common adverbial structures is the **prepositional phrase,** a two-part structure consisting of a preposition—a word such as *in, out, up, down, over, under, between, for, from*—and a noun phrase, known as the object of the preposition:

> The students are <u>in the library</u>.
> The next performance is <u>on Monday</u>.

PATTERN II: NP *be* ADJ

The students are diligent.
The price of steak is ridiculous.
The play was dull.

Here the slot following *be* contains a **complement,** or completer of the verb—in this case, an adjectival, abbreviated ADJ. In the language of traditional grammar, this slot is the **subjective complement:**[2] The adjectival both completes the verb and modifies or describes the subject.

At this point you may be wondering how you can recognize a Pattern II sentence when you're not sure what an adjective is. To answer this question, look for a word that will fill both slots in the following frame:

> The ___ NOUN is very ___.

Only an adjective will fit. For example, when we insert the sample

---

[2] More specifically, the traditional label for the subjective complement in Pattern II (and IV) is *predicate adjective;* the traditional label for the NP in Pattern III (and V) is *predicate nominative.* We will use the more general term *subjective complement* for both adjectives and noun phrases.

subjective complements into both slots of the frame, we recognize the resulting sentences as grammatical; they are acceptable to a native speaker:

> The <u>diligent</u> student is very <u>diligent</u>.
> The <u>ridiculous</u> price is very <u>ridiculous</u>.
> The <u>dull</u> play is very <u>dull</u>.

There are a few adjectives that don't fit both slots—only one or the other—but most adjectives do; and any word that does fit both is unquestionably an adjective.

Besides adjectives, we sometimes find prepositional phrases filling the subjective complement slot in Pattern II sentences. Such phrases name an attribute of the subject, just as adjectives do:

> He is <u>out of his mind</u>.
> She is <u>in a bad mood</u>.

To figure out that such sentences do not belong to Pattern I, you can usually think of an adjective, a single descriptive word, that could substitute for the phrase:

> He is <u>crazy</u>.
> She is <u>cranky</u>.

Moreover, you can easily rule out Pattern I because such phrases do not supply information of time or place.

PATTERN III: NP₁ *be* NP₁

> The students are scholars.
> Professor Brown is my English teacher.
> The tournament was an exciting event.

The NP, of course, fills the subject slot in all of the patterns; in Pattern III a noun phrase following *be* fills the subjective complement slot as well. The numbers that mark the NPs indicate that the two noun phrases have the same referent. For example, when we say "Professor Brown is my English teacher," the two NPs, "Professor Brown" and "my English teacher," refer to the same person. The subjective complement renames the subject; *be,* the main verb, asserts identification or classification. We could restate the sample sentence:

The students are being identified as scholars.

or

The students may be classified as scholars.

Exercise 1: Identify the sentence pattern of each of the following sentences; then do a traditional diagram of each, like those you have seen next to the formulas. (See pages 25–27 for notes on the diagrams.)

1. His problem was a serious one. (Pattern **III**)   Np_1 be Np_1

2. Those joggers are out of shape. (Pattern **II**)

3. Their excitement is really contagious. (Pattern **II**)

4. Those pesky flies are everywhere. (Pattern **I**)

5. This vacation has been wonderful. (Pattern **II**)

6. The kids are being unusually silly today. (Pattern **II**)

7. The Smiths have been terrific neighbors. (Pattern **III**)

8. The horses are at the gate. (Pattern **I**)

9. The team is on a roll. (Pattern **I**) ✗ **II**

10. The final exam will be at four o'clock. (Pattern **I**)

THE LINKING VERB PATTERNS

Like *be* in Patterns II and III, linking verbs connect the subject to a complement that describes, defines, or identifies the subject.

PATTERN IV: NP   V-lnk   ADJ   students | seem \ diligent

The students seem diligent.
I grew sleepy.
The soup tastes salty.

In these sentences an adjectival following the linking verb fills the subjective complement slot; it describes or names an attribute of the subject, just as in Pattern II. In many cases, a form of *be* can be substituted for the Pattern IV linking verb with a minimal change in meaning:

I was sleepy.
The soup is salty.

Pattern IV is a common category for verbs of the senses; besides *taste,* the verbs *smell, feel, sound,* and *look* often link an adjective to the subject. And again, as with Pattern II, an adjectival prepositional phrase sometimes fills the subjective complement slot:

The fighter seems out of shape.

PATTERN V: NP₁ V-lnk NP₁

students | became \ scholars / The

The students became scholars.
My uncle remained a bachelor.

In this pattern a noun phrase in the subjective complement slot renames the subject: Only a few verbs fit this pattern; *become* and *remain* are the most common. *Seem* and *appear* sometimes take noun phrases rather than adjectives:

That seemed a good idea.
He seemed a nice person.
He appeared a good sort.

Again we should remember that the most common link between two noun phrases with the same referent is *be* (Pattern III).

Exercise 2: Identify the sentence pattern; then diagram the sentence.

1. The baby looks healthy. (Pattern _IV_)   Np V-lnk Adj

2. The neighborhood gang remained good friends. (Pattern _V_)

   Np₁ V-lnk Np₁

3. The piano sounds out of tune. (Pattern _IV_) Np_1 V-lnk   Adj

4. You look a mess! (Pattern _V_) Np_1 V-lnk Np_1

5. The chicken smells wonderful. (Pattern _IV_) Np_1 V-lnk   Adj.

6. The second rank seems out of step. (Pattern _IV_) Np_1 V-lnk   Adj.

THE INTRANSITIVE VERB PATTERN

PATTERN VI: NP V-int

students	rested

The students rested.
John slept.
The visitors from London arrived.

This formula describes the pattern of intransitive verb sentences. An **intransitive verb** has no complement—no noun phrase or adjectival—following. It's true, however, that such skeletal sentences are rare in both speech and writing; most Pattern VI sentences have information other than the simple subject and verb. You're likely to find adverbial information added:

The students rested <u>after their long trip</u>.
John slept <u>soundly</u>.
The visitors from London arrived <u>on schedule</u>.

In the discussion of "The Optional Slots," on page 21, you'll discover that such adverbial information can be added to all of the sentence patterns. However, because the adverbial is not required for sentence completeness, we will call it "optional."

You may have noticed that the diagram of this pattern looks a great deal like that of Pattern I, with no complement following the verb on the main line. But there is a difference: The adverbial in Pattern I is not optional; it is required. Another important difference between Patterns I and VI is in the kind of adverbials the sentences include. Pattern I requires a structure that tells where or when. The optional adverbial of Pattern VI, however, is not restricted to time and place information; it can answer other questions, such as why or how or how long. We can say, "John slept soundly" or "John slept for an hour" (Pattern VI), but we cannot say, "John was soundly" or "John was for an hour."

Intransitive Phrasal Verbs. **Phrasal verbs** are common structures in English. They consist of a verb combined with a preposition-like word, known as a **particle;** together they form an **idiom.** The term *idiom* refers to a combination of words whose meaning cannot be predicted from the meaning of its parts; it is a set expression, or formula, that acts as a unit. In the following sentence, the meaning of the underlined phrasal verb is not the meaning of *up* added to the meaning of *made:*

We <u>made up</u>.

Rather, *made up* means "reconciled our differences."

In the following sentence, however, *up* is not part of the verb:

We jumped up.

Here *up* is simply an adverb modifying *jumped*. The meaning of *jumped up* is the meaning of the adverb *up* added to *jumped*. The two diagrams demonstrate the difference:

Another way to demonstrate the properties of verbs such as *made up* and *jumped up* is to test variations of the sentences for parallel results. For example, adverbs can often be shifted to opening position:

Up we jumped.

But notice the ungrammatical result in the case of *made up:*

*Up we made.[3]

---

[3] The asterisk indicates a sentence that is questionable or unacceptable to the speaker of English—a sentence that most people would consider ungrammatical.

Here are some other Pattern VI sentences with phrasal verbs. Note that the first two include optional adverbials.

> We turned in at midnight.
> The union finally gave in to the company's demands.
> Tony will pull through.
> My favorite slippers wore out.
> The party broke up.

In each case the phrasal verb has a special meaning that is different from the meaning of its parts: Here *gave in* means "relented," *pull through* means "recover."

Exercise 3: Identify the sentence patterns; then diagram the sentences.

1. The fighter passed out in the first round. (Pattern ___) *Np V-int*

2. He came to in three minutes. (Pattern ___) *Np V-int*

3. The beef cattle grew fast during the summer. (Pattern ___) *Np V-int*

4. The hogs grew fat on their high-protein diet. (Pattern ___) *Np V-int*

5. We went to the game on Saturday. (Pattern ___) *Np V-int*

✗ 6. The fans went crazy after every touchdown. (Pattern ___) *Np V-int*

7. The hikers walked slowly up the hill. (Pattern ___) *Np V-int*

8. Sit down! (Pattern ___) *Np V-int*

THE TRANSITIVE VERB PATTERNS

Unlike intransitive verbs, all **transitive verbs** take one or more complements. The last four formulas classify transitive verbs according to the kinds and number of complements they take. All transitive verbs have one complement in common: the **direct object**. Pattern VII, which has only that one complement, can be thought of as the basic transitive verb pattern.

PATTERN VII: NP$_1$ V-tr NP$_2$

	students	studied	assignment

The students studied their assignment.
The lead-off batter hit a home run.
Claudia is eating dinner.

In these sentences the noun phrase following the verb, the **direct object,** has a referent different from that of the subject, as indicated by the different numbers in the formula. Traditionally, we think of the transitive verb as an action word: Its subject is considered the doer and its object the receiver of the action. In many Pattern VII sentences this meaning-based definition applies fairly accurately. In our Pattern VII sample sentences, for instance, we can think of *their assignment* as the receiver of the action *studied* and even of *dinner* as a receiver of the action *is eating*. But the definition isn't very accurate, and sometimes the idea of *receiver of the action* doesn't apply at all:

Our team won the game.
We enjoyed the game.

In both of these sentences, we would certainly be more accurate to say that *game* names the action rather than receives it. And in the sentence

Red spots covered her neck and face.

we are describing a situation rather than an action. So although it is true that many transitive verbs are action words and many direct objects are receivers, this meaning-based way of analyzing the sentence doesn't always work.

We can also think of the direct object as the answer to a *what* or *whom* question:

The students studied (*what?*) geometry.
Jason helped (*whom?*) his little sister.

However, the question will not differentiate transitive verbs from linking verbs; the subjective complements in Patterns III and V also tell *what:*

> John is a doctor. (John *is what?*)
> John became a doctor. (John *became what?*)

The one method of distinguishing transitive verbs that works almost every time is the recognition that the two noun phrases have different referents. We don't have to know that *study* and *hit* and *eat* are transitive verbs in order to classify the sentences as Pattern VII; we simply recognize that the two noun phrases, the one before the verb and the one following, do not refer to the same thing. Then we know that the second noun phrase is the direct object.

An exception occurs when the direct object is either a **reflexive pronoun** (John cut *himself*) or a **reciprocal pronoun** (John and Mary love *each other*). A **pronoun** (*himself, each other, I, me, he, she, it, they,* etc.) is a word that takes the place of a noun phrase. In these sentences with reflexive and reciprocal pronouns, the two NPs, the subject and the direct object, have the same referent, so the numbers 1 and 2 in the formula are inaccurate. In terms of the referents of the NPs, these sentences actually resemble Pattern V, the linking verb pattern. But clearly the purpose and sense of the verbs—*cut* and *love* in the case of these examples—are not like those of the linking verbs. Rather than institute a separate sentence pattern for these exceptions, where the difference is not in the verbs, we include these sentences in Pattern VII, simply recognizing that when the direct object is a reciprocal or reflexive pronoun the formula numbers are inaccurate.

Transitive Phrasal Verbs. Many of the idiomatic phrasal verbs belong to the transitive verb category, and like other transitive verbs they take direct objects. Compare the meaning of *came by* in the following sentences:

> He came by his fortune in an unusual way.
> He came by the office in a big hurry.

In the first sentence, *came by* means "acquired"; in the second, *by the office* is a prepositional phrase that modifies the intransitive verb *came,* telling where.

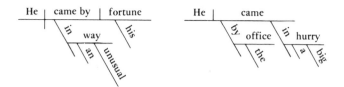

You can also demonstrate the difference between these two sentences by transforming them:

> By which office did he come?
> *By which fortune did he come?

It is clear that *by* functions differently in the two sentences.

The transitive phrasal verbs include both two- and three-word strings:

> I don't <u>go in for</u> horse racing.
> I won't <u>put up with</u> your nonsense.
> I will <u>look up</u> those words myself.
> Don't <u>bring up</u> past grievances.
> I finally <u>found out</u> the truth.

You can test these as you did the intransitive phrasal verbs, by finding a one-word substitute:

> I don't <u>enjoy</u> horse racing.
> I won't <u>tolerate</u> your nonsense.

Exercise 4: Identify the sentence patterns; then diagram the sentences.

1. The boys prepared a terrific meal. (Pattern VII) *Np₁ V-tr Np₂*

2. The dessert pleased everyone. (Pattern VII) *Np₁ V-tr Np₂*

3. The principal (passed out) the new regulations. (Pattern VII) *Np₁ V-tr Np₂*
   phrasal verb

4. The dog suddenly (turned on) its trainer. (Pattern VII) *Np₁ V-tr Np₂*

5. An old jalopy turned into our driveway. (Pattern VI) *Np V-int*

6. Help yourself. (Pattern _VII_) N_{P_1} V-tr N_{P_2}

7. My roommate finally took the law boards. (Pattern _VII_) N_{P_1} V-tr N_{P_2}

PATTERN VIII: NP_1 V-tr NP_2 NP_3

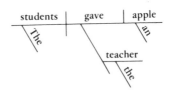

The students gave the teacher an apple.
The judges awarded Mary the prize.
The clerk handed me the wrong package.

In this pattern, *two* noun phrase complements follow the verb. Again, the three different subscript numbers on the three NPs indicate that the three noun phrases all have different referents. (When the referents are the same, the numbers are the same, as in Patterns III and V.) The first slot following the verb is the indirect object; the second is the direct object. Even though both Patterns VII and VIII use transitive verbs, they are easily distinguished, since Pattern VII has only one NP following the verb and Pattern VIII has two.

We traditionally define **indirect object** as the *recipient of the direct object* or as the person *to whom* or *for whom* the action is performed. In most cases this definition applies accurately. A Pattern VIII verb—and this is a limited group—usually has a meaning like "give," and the indirect object usually names a person who is the receiver of whatever the subject, NP_1, gives. As with Pattern VII, however, the most accurate way to distinguish this pattern is simply to recognize that all three noun phrases have different referents: In the first sample sentence, *the students, the teacher,* and *an apple* all refer to different people or things. Incidentally, in the third Pattern VIII sample sentence, a pronoun rather than a noun phrase fills the indirect object slot.

In the discussion of Pattern VII we noted that when the direct object is a reflexive or reciprocal pronoun (*myself, themselves, each other,* etc.) its referent is identical to that of the subject. The same system of identity applies in Pattern VIII when reflexive or reciprocal pronouns fill the indirect object slot, as they often do:

> Jill gave <u>herself</u> a haircut.
> We gave <u>each other</u> identical Christmas presents.

For these examples, the referent numbers 1, 2, and 3 do not apply to the three NP slots. *Jill* and *herself* refer to the same person; so do *we* and *each other*. In most Pattern VIII sentences, all three NPs have different referents, represented by the numbers 1, 2, and 3.

PATTERN IX: NP₁ V-tr NP₂ ADJ

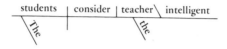

> The students consider the teacher intelligent.
> The teacher made the test easy.
> The boys painted their hockey sticks blue.

In this pattern the direct object, NP₂, is followed by a second complement, an adjective that modifies or describes the direct object; this is the **objective complement.** The relationship between the direct object and the objective complement is the same as the relationship between the subject and the subjective complement in Patterns II and IV. In Patterns II and IV the subjective complement describes the subject; in Pattern IX the objective complement describes the direct object. We could say, in fact,

> The teacher is intelligent.
> The test is easy.
> The hockey sticks are blue.

The function of the objective complement is twofold: (1) It completes the meaning of the verb; and (2) it describes the direct object.

When we remove the objective complement from a Pattern IX sentence, we are sometimes left with a grammatical and meaningful sentence: "The boys painted their hockey sticks." (This is now Pattern VII.) However, most Pattern IX sentences require the objective complement; the meaning of the first two examples under the Pattern IX formula would change without it:

> The students consider the teacher.
> The teacher made the test.

Pattern IX is a small class, with relatively few verbs, most of which appear equally often in Pattern VII, where they take the direct object only. Other verbs commonly found in this pattern are *prefer, like,* and *find.* Some Pattern IX verbs, such as *consider* and *make,* also commonly appear in Pattern X.

PATTERN X: NP$_1$ V-tr NP$_2$ NP$_2$

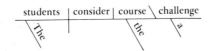

> The students consider the course a challenge.
> The students elected Barbara chairperson.
> They named their first daughter Kristi.

Just as both adjectives and noun phrases can be subjective complements, both adjectives and noun phrases also serve as objective complements. In Pattern X the objective complement is a noun phrase, one with the same referent as the direct object, as indicated by the numbers in the formula. Its twofold purpose is much the same as that of the adjectival objective complement in Pattern IX: (1) It completes the meaning of the verb; and (2) it renames the direct object. And again, we can compare the relationship of the two noun phrases to that of the subject and subjective complement in Pattern III:

> The course is a challenge.
> Barbara is the chairperson.

Exercise 5: Identify the sentence patterns; diagram.

1. The neighborhood kids drive my mother crazy. (Pattern ___IX___)

   Np$_1$ V-tr Np$_2$ Adj.

2. She considers them a menace to the neighborhood. (Pattern ___X___)

   Np$_1$ V-tr N$_2$ Np$_2$

3. Don't tell me my business. (Pattern ____) _VIII_

   $Np_1 \quad V\text{-}tr \quad Np_2 \quad Np_3$

4. The members of my bridge club prefer their coffee black. (Pattern _IX_)

   $Np_1 \quad V\text{-}tr \quad Np_2 \quad Adj$

5. I find Minnesota winters excessively long. (Pattern _IX_)

   $Np_1 \quad V\text{-}tr \quad Np_2 \quad Adj$

6. Professor Marsh assigned us six chapters for Tuesday. (Pattern _VIII_)

   $Np_1 \quad V\text{-}tr \quad Np_2 \quad Np_3$

7. The spring flowers along the mall make the campus really beautiful. (Pattern _IX_)

   $Np_1 \quad V\text{-}tr \quad Np_2 \quad Adj$

8. Cut me a piece of cake. (Pattern ____ _VIII_) $Np_1 \quad V\text{-}tr \quad Np_2 \quad Np_3$

THE OPTIONAL SLOTS

It is useful to think of the two or three or four slots in the basic patterns as sentence "requirements," the elements needed for sentence completeness. But, as you have seen in some of the sentence examples, we often add words or phrases that answer such questions as *where, when, why, how, how much,* and the like. Because the sentences are grammatical without them, we consider the elements filling these adverbial slots as "optional." You'll recall that in the case of Pattern I, however, the ADV/TP slot, the adverbial of time or place, is required. But a Pattern I sentence can include the optional adverbials, too, along with its required time and/or place adverbial:

> The fans were in line (*where?*) for tickets to the play-offs (*why?*).
> The plane was on the runway (*where?*) for an hour (*how long?*).

All of the sentence patterns can include these optional adverbials, which can come at the beginning or end of the sentence or even in the middle. And no sentence is limited to just one adverbial structure; we can have any number of adverbials in any sentence, providing information about time, place, manner, reason, and the like.

> I stopped at the deli (*where?*) for some bagels (*why?*). (Pattern VI)

> After midnight (*when?*) the subway is almost deserted. (Pattern
>   II)
> Mario suddenly (*how?*) hit the brakes. (Pattern VII)

No matter where they occur in the sentence, all adverbials are diagrammed as modifiers of the verb; the adverbs go on diagonal lines and
prepositional phrases on a two-part line below the verb:

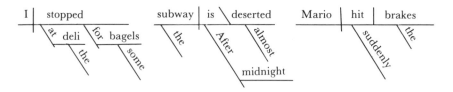

These and other forms of adverbials are discussed in detail in Chapter
8.

PUNCTUATION AND THE SENTENCE PATTERNS

There is an easy punctuation lesson to be learned from the sentence
patterns with their two or three or four slots:

DO NOT PUT COMMAS BETWEEN THE REQUIRED SLOTS.

That is, never separate—

* the subject from the verb.
* the verb from the direct object.
* the direct object from the objective complement.
* the indirect object from the direct object.
* the verb from the subjective complement.

For example, in the following sentences there is simply no place for
commas:

$Np_1 \quad V\text{-}tr \quad Np_2 \quad Np_2$

> The sportswriters considered the game between the Lions and the
>   Panthers one of the truly great games of the collegiate football
>   season.

Np₁ V-tr Npᵥ Np₃

The local women's club gave all the guests at the Marion County
Home for the Aged decorated Christmas trees for their rooms.
All of the discussion groups I took part in during Orientation
Week were extremely helpful for the incoming freshmen.

Np be Adj

So even though the noun phrases that fill the slots may be long, the
slots are never separated by commas. A pause for breath does not
signal a comma. In Chapter 9, where we will take up the expanded
noun phrase, we will encounter sentences in which punctuation is
called for *within* a noun phrase slot, but even in those situations the
rule stated above still applies: no punctuation between the required
slots.

The one exception to this rule occurs when the direct object is a
direct quotation following a verb like *say:*

He said, "I love you."

Here the punctuation convention calls for a comma before the quoted
words.

SUMMARY

These ten sentence patterns account for the underlying structure of
almost all of our sentences. When you can look at a sentence and
recognize that its basic elements form one of these patterns, you have
come a long way toward understanding the system we call grammar.

The traditional sentence diagram, which we have shown next to
each formula, offers a graphic representation of the pattern, a visual
aid to help you remember the patterns, to understand their common
features, and to distinguish their differences. On page 24, where all
ten diagrams are shown together, you can see the relationships among
them. For example, the two linking verb patterns closely resemble the
two *be* patterns, II and III, above them. Likewise, the intransitive verb
pattern, VI, placed at the left of the page, looks exactly like the main
line of Pattern I. Finally, the sloping line that separates the subjective
complement from the verb in the *be* and linking verb patterns, II
through V, depicts a relationship similar to that of the objective complement and object in Patterns IX and X, which are also separated by a
sloping line.

DIAGRAMMING THE SENTENCE PATTERNS

The be *Patterns*

I.   NP *be* ADV/TP   II.   NP *be* ADJ   III.   NP₁ *be* NP₁

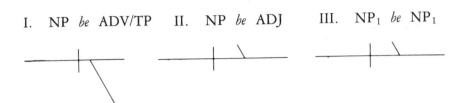

The Linking Verb Patterns

IV.   NP V-lnk ADJ   V.   NP₁ V-lnk NP₁

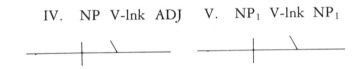

The Intransitive Verb Pattern

VI.   NP V-int

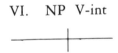

The Transitive Verb Patterns

VII.   NP₁ V-tr NP₂   VIII.   NP₁ V-tr NP₂ NP₃

IX.   NP₁ V-tr NP₂ ADJ   X.   NP₁ V-tr NP₂ NP₂

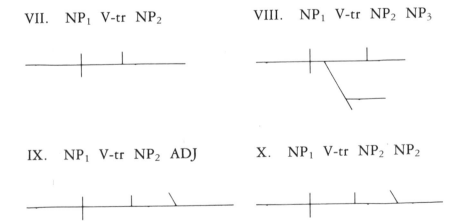

NOTES ON THE DIAGRAMS

The Main Line. Except for a few modifications, this method of diagramming follows the Reed and Kellogg system, which dates back to the late nineteenth century and traditional school grammar. The positions on the main horizontal line of the diagram represent the slots in the sentence pattern formulas. Only two required slots are not included on the main line: the adverbial (see Pattern I) and the indirect object (see Pattern VIII). The vertical line that bisects the main line separates the subject and the predicate, showing the binary nature of the sentence. The other vertical and sloping lines stop at the horizontal line:

The Noun Phrase. The noun phrases we have used in the sample sentences are very simple ones; in our examination of the noun phrase in Chapter 9 we will identify a wide variety of words and word groups that can modify and expand the noun. But now we will simply recognize the feature that all noun phrases have in common—the **noun head,** or **headword.** This is the single word that fills the various NP slots of the diagrams; the modifiers slope from the noun headword, which always occupies a horizontal line.

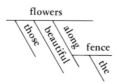

The Verb Phrase. The complements are set off from the verb itself:

1. The subjective complement follows a sloping line. Note that the line slopes in the direction of the subject to show their relationship:

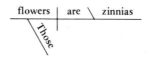

2. The direct object always follows a vertical line:

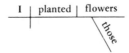

3. The objective complement is set off from the direct object by a line that slopes toward the object:

I | consider | zinnias \ beautiful

4. The indirect object is placed below the verb. We can understand the logic of this treatment of the indirect object when we realize that it can be expressed by a prepositional phrase without changing the meaning of the sentence:

The students gave the teacher an apple.
The students gave an apple to the teacher.

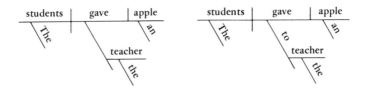

5. Adverbs are placed on sloping lines below the verb; they are modifiers of the verb:

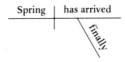

The Prepositional Phrase. The preposition is placed on a sloping line, its object on a horizontal line attached to it. The prepositional phrase slopes from the noun or verb it modifies. When the prepositional phrase fills the subjective complement slot, it is attached to the main line by means of a pedestal:

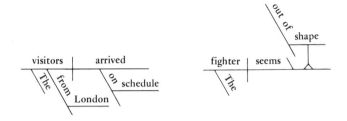

Punctuation. There are no punctuation marks of any kind in the diagram, other than apostrophes.

(Further details on diagramming are presented in Appendix C.)

SENTENCES FOR PRACTICE

To recognize the underlying sentence pattern, first identify the boundaries of the various slots: subject, verb, direct object, indirect object, subjective and objective complement. You'll discover that some of the sentences include optional adverbials, those words and phrases that answer such questions as *where, when, why,* and *how.* Remember that the adverbial slots can come at the beginning, middle, or end of the sentence. Diagram the sentences.

1. In the evening Chicago's skyline is a beautiful sight. *Np, be Np,*

2. After the picnic the teacher rounded up the kindergartners for the long return trip. *phrasal trans. verb Np, V-tr Np₂*

⁊ 3. My uncle is moving to Arizona for his health. *Np be Adv/TP*

✗ 4. Yesterday Rosa bought herself a lovely knit coat at Macy's. *Np, V-tr Np₁ Np₂*

5. She made up her mind almost instantly, after only five minutes. *Np, V-tr Np₂*

6. The asparagus in our garden grows really fast during June. *Np V-int*

7. Our grocer calls asparagus the Rolls Royce of vegetables. *complement to A.O. Np, V-tr Np₁ Np₂*

8. During his second term, Ronald Reagan became the oldest president in our country's history. *Np, V-link Np,*

9. At first glance the streets of Washington, D.C., seem very confusing. *Np, V-link Adj.*

10. The colors on my antique quilt have stayed beautiful through the years. *Np, V-link Adj*

11. According to the afternoon papers, the police are looking into the sources of the reporter's information.

Np, V-tr Np₂

12. Our art history class was at the museum for three hours on Tuesday afternoon.

Np₁ be Adv

Np₁ Vtr Np₂ Adj

13. Sometimes I find modern art very depressing.

14. We often have Chinese food on Saturdays.

Np₁ Vtr Np₂

15. For most of the morning the kids have been in a very grumpy mood.

Np₁ be Adj

QUESTIONS FOR DISCUSSION

Denotes skip

1. Here are some pairs of sentences that look alike. Think about their sentence patterns; diagram them to demonstrate their differences.

The teacher made the test hard.   *Np₁ Vtr Np₂ Adj*
The batter hit the ball hard.   *Np₁ Vtr Np₂*

My husband made me a chocolate cake.
My husband made me a happy woman.   *Np₁ Vtr Np₂ Np₂*

We set off through the woods at dawn.   *Np₁ V-int*
We set off the firecrackers at dawn.   *Np₁ Vtr Np₂*

2. The following sentences are either Pattern I or Pattern II; in other words, the prepositional phrases following *be* are either adverbial or adjectival. What test can you use to distinguish between them?

The mechanic is under the car.   *Np₁ be Adv*
The mechanic is under the weather.   *Np₁ be Adj*

The teacher is in a bad mood.   *Np₁ be Adj*
The teacher is in the cafeteria.   *Np₁ be Adv*

The students were in a frenzy.   *Np₁ be Adj*
The students were in a riot.   *Np₁ be ~~Adv~~ Adj*

3. The verbs *seem* and *remain* are usually linking verbs. Can you use either of them in transitive or intransitive sentences?

4. Very few verbs are restricted to a particular category or pattern. Although *taste* and *grow* and *feel* commonly act as linking verbs, they can fit into other patterns as well. Identify the patterns of the following sentences:

The cook tasted the soup.
The soup tasted good.   *Np₁ V lnk Adj*

I felt the kitten's fur.   *Np₁ V-tr Np␣*
The fur feels soft.   *Np V-lnk ADJ*
The farmers in Iowa grow a lot of wheat. *Np₁ Vtr Np␣*
The wheat grows fast in July.
We grew weary in the hot sun. *Np₁ Vlink Adj*
She acted tired.   *Np₁ Vlink Adj.*
She acted brilliantly. *?*   *Np₁*

5. The verb *go* is traditionally classified as an intransitive verb. Write a sentence in which a form of *go* is used as a linking verb.
   6. People commonly say, "I feel badly," ⟶*linking verb* when discussing their physical or mental condition. Using your understanding of sentence patterns, explain why this is sometimes considered an ungrammatical sentence. Assuming that "I feel badly" is indeed questionable, how do you explain the acceptance of "I feel strongly about that"?
   7. What is unusual about the following sentence? Think about the sentence pattern:

The waitress served me my coffee black.

8. In most Pattern VIII sentences the indirect object refers to a person. Can you think of a sentence in which the indirect object is an inanimate object? A car, perhaps? Or a math book?
   9. We have seen sentences in which prepositional phrases function as subjective complements. Can they be objective complements as well?
   10. In one of the sample Pattern VIII sentences a pronoun serves as the indirect object. Is it possible to substitute a pronoun in all of the NP slots of Pattern VIII? *NO*

John gave Mary a gift.
He gave her a gift.
John gave Mary ____.

11. One way to distinguish particles from prepositions in some sentences that look alike is to test the words for movability:

Joe turned on the light.
Joe turned the light on.

Joe turned on the bridge.
*Joe turned the bridge on.

I will look <u>up</u> the words.
I will look the words <u>up</u>.

I will look <u>up</u> the hall.
*I will look the hall <u>up</u>.

It is also interesting to discover that our use of pronouns is determined to a certain extent by the position of the particle:

Joe turned <u>the light</u> on.
Joe turned <u>it</u> on.
Joe turned on <u>the light</u>.
*Joe turned on <u>it</u>.

Try the same kind of substitutions in the following sentences:

He brought up an unexpected topic.
The suspect made up a phony alibi.
The police eventually found out the truth.

Now formulate rules regarding movability and the use of pronouns that can help us recognize phrasal verbs.

12. A sentence is **ambiguous** when it has more than one possible meaning. You can illustrate the two meanings of the following sentences by diagramming each in two different ways. Think about sentence patterns and the referents of the noun phrases.

Herbert found his new bride a good cook.
Sandy called her mother.

13. Consider the sentence pattern of the following sentences:

He took the loss of his job hard.
He takes the job seriously.

Do we need to change the formula for Pattern IX to include adverbs as objective complements?

14. Consider the following sentences:

The roast weighs five pounds.
The roast cost twenty dollars.

Because the slot following the verb is filled by an adverbial, we classify these sentences as Pattern VI, as intransitive verbs. But some linguists include such verbs in the "midverb" category. Explain their rationale for doing so. Could you also make a case for including them in Pattern VII with the transitive verbs instead of in Pattern VI?

Expanding
the Main Verb

In Chapter 1 we recognized the sentence as a binary structure:

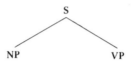

We also suggested that this feature applies to many of the separate parts of the sentence as well as to the whole. The two-part division of the verb phrase shows up clearly: The left branch is the verb itself and the right, the complement(s) and/or modifiers:

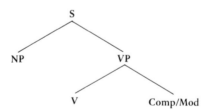

Most of the verbs used in the sample sentences to fill the left slot in the VP are single words: *are, is, studied, gave, consider, became.* We call such verb forms the simple present or simple past tense. But the verbs we use in our everyday speech and writing are often expanded forms that include additional verb forms called **auxiliaries:**

The students <u>have been</u> unhappy.
John <u>may become</u> a scholar.
The teacher <u>has given</u> us too much work.
The baby <u>is sleeping</u> upstairs.

The students <u>should elect</u> Barbara chairperson.
The students <u>will study</u> tonight.

Such expansions suggest that we can carry our branching diagram one step further; we can divide our verb into the auxiliary and the main verb:

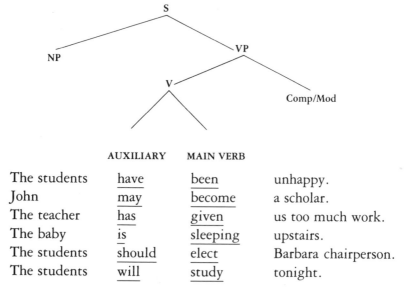

	AUXILIARY	MAIN VERB	
The students	<u>have</u>	<u>been</u>	unhappy.
John	<u>may</u>	<u>become</u>	a scholar.
The teacher	<u>has</u>	<u>given</u>	us too much work.
The baby	<u>is</u>	<u>sleeping</u>	upstairs.
The students	<u>should</u>	<u>elect</u>	Barbara chairperson.
The students	<u>will</u>	<u>study</u>	tonight.

These six auxiliary/verb combinations represent only a small sample of the possibilities for expanding our verbs. With little or no effort our linguistic computer can come up with many other two-word variations—and with three- and four-word strings as well:

The students <u>will be studying</u> all afternoon.
The baby <u>has been sleeping</u> all morning.
They <u>should have been studying</u> harder.

We have still only scratched the surface.

In this examination of the verb, we want to understand the system underlying our ability to expand it as we do; we want to discover all of the verb's possible expansions and to recognize the variations in meaning they can convey. Using *to eat* as our example, we will first look at some of the ways in which we use this verb in everyday situations. (In labeling a verb, we traditionally use the **infinitive** form, which consists of the present tense, in this case *eat*, preceded by *to*, known as the "sign of the infinitive.")

I <u>eat</u> an apple every day.
I <u>ate</u> one this morning.
I <u>have eaten</u> an apple every day this week.
I <u>should eat</u> oranges as well.
My sister <u>eats</u> the seeds and all.
I <u>am eating</u> a peach at the moment.
I <u>had eaten</u> all the grapes by the time you arrived.
I <u>have been eating</u> junk food all evening.
I <u>was eating</u> both candy and pretzels last night.
I <u>will eat</u> only two candy bars today.
I <u>might have eaten</u> only one yesterday; I forget.
I <u>may be eating</u> a gourmet dinner at Carol and Jim's tonight.

This partial list of the possibilities includes all of the forms of the word *eat* itself: *eat, ate, eats, eaten, eating*. (The only verb in English with more than five forms is *be*, with eight: *be, am, are, is, was, were, been,* and *being*.) Anyone familiar with a foreign language will appreciate the simplicity of this small set of only five. A speaker of French or Spanish, instead of adding auxiliaries to express differences as we do, can simply add a different ending, or inflection, to the verb. French verbs, for instance, have more than seventy different inflections to express differences in person, number, tense, and mood.

A speaker of English uses only two different forms (*eat, eats*) to express the present tense in first, second, and third person, both singular and plural:

	SINGULAR	PLURAL
1st person	I eat	we eat
2nd person	you eat	you eat
3rd person	he eats she eats it eats	they eat

The speaker of French uses five forms in the present tense; in only the first- and third-person singular are the forms alike:

	SINGULAR	PLURAL
1st person	*je mange*	*nous mangeons*
2nd person	*tu manges*	*vous mangez*
3rd person	*il mange*	*ils mangent*

The speaker of English uses only one form to express the simple past tense:

	SINGULAR	PLURAL
1st person	I ate	we ate
2nd person	you ate	you ate
3rd person	he ate	they ate

Again, the speaker of French uses five, all different from the first set. In fact, for the various tenses and moods the speaker of French uses fourteen such sets, or conjugations, all with different verb endings.

THE FIVE VERB FORMS OF ENGLISH

Before looking at the system for adding auxiliaries, we will name the five verb forms so that we can conveniently discuss them, using labels that reflect our emphasis on form rather than meaning. (The traditional names are shown in parentheses.)

1.	eat	the base form	(present tense)
2.	eats	the -*s* form	(3rd-person singular)
3.	ate	the -*ed* form	(past tense)
4.	eating	the -*ing* form	(present participle)
5.	eaten	the -*en* form	(past participle)

A comparison of *eat,* which is an irregular verb, with the regular verb *walk* will provide the rationale for the labels -*ed* and -*en:*

1.	base form	eat	walk
2.	-*s* form	eats	walks
3.	-*ed* form	ate	walked
4.	-*ing* form	eating	walking
5.	-*en* form	eaten	walked

In the language of traditional grammar, a verb is **regular** when both its simple past tense and its past participle (forms 3 and 5) are formed by adding -*ed* (or, in some cases, -*d* or -*t*); this means that the past tense and the past participle of regular verbs are always identical in form. This description applies to most verbs. Only a small number, one hundred or so, are **irregular,** although, like *eat,* they are among the verbs we use most frequently. (Incidentally, regular verbs are sometimes referred to as *weak verbs,* irregular verbs as *strong verbs.*) But because we need to distinguish the past tense and the past participle, we give them different labels. The regular past tense inflection (-*ed*) provides the label for the past tense; the -*en* form of irregular verbs such as *eat* (and *drive, give, break, speak, choose,* etc.) provides the past participle label.

Exercise 6: Fill in the blanks with the four additional forms of the verbs listed on the left. If you have a problem figuring out the -*ed* form, simply use it in a sentence with *yesterday:* "Yesterday I ____." If you have trouble figuring out the -*en* form, use it in a sentence with *have:* "I have ____."

BASE	-s FORM	-ed FORM	-en FORM	-ing FORM
1. go	goes	went	gone	going
2. break	breaks	broke	broken	breaking
3. come	comes	came	come	coming
4. move	moves	moved	moved	moving
5. expect	expects	expected	expected	expecting
6. put	puts	put	put	putting
7. drink	drinks	drank	drunk	drinking
8. think	thinks	thought	thought	thinking
9. like	likes	liked	liked	liking
10. feel	feels	felt	felt	feeling
11. lose	loses	lost	lost	losing
12. pass	passes	passed	passed	passing

13. meet	*meets*	*met*	*met*	*meeting*
14. beat	*beats*	*beat*	*beaten*	*beating*
15. lead	*leads*	*led*	*led*	*leading*
16. read	*reads*	*read*	*read*	*reading*
17. say	*says*	*said*	*said*	*saying*
18. drive	*drives*	*drove*	*driven*	*driving*

EXPANDING THE VERB

The subtle differences in verb meanings we are able to express result not from variations in the verb itself, with its limit of five forms, but rather from the auxiliaries we add. Here again are the versions of *eat* from the list of sentences on page 34:

1. eat	5. eats	9. was eating
2. ate	6. am eating	10. will eat
3. have eaten	7. had eaten	11. might have eaten
4. should eat	8. have been eating	12. may be eating

What is the system underlying these one- and two- and three-word verbs? How many more variations are there? What rules and restrictions of our system will we have to include in that program for the computer in order for it to come up with all of the expanded verbs—to print out all of our possible variations?

To discover the system, we will make some observations about these twelve variations of *eat*, observations that apply to all verbs in English, both regular and irregular:

1. The base form is used both alone [1] and with *should* [4] and *will* [10].
2. The *-ed* and *-s* forms are used alone [2 and 5].
3. The *-en* form is used after a form of *have: had* [7] and *have* [3, 8, and 11].
4. The *-ing* form is used after a form of *be: am* [6], *been* [8], *was* [9], and *be* [12].

We can state these last two observations in terms of a formula:

(have + -en) + (be + -ing)

This formula means that we can use *have* as an auxiliary, but when we do, we follow it with the *-en* form of the verb; it also states that we can use the *-ing* form of the verb, but when we do, we precede it with a form of *be*. The parentheses mean "optional." This simply means that *have* + *-en* and *be* + *-ing* are optional auxiliaries; that is, a grammatical verb string does not require either or both of them.

What further observations can we make about our list of verbs?

5. If both *have* and *be* are used [8], they appear in that order.
6. Besides *have* and *be,* we have another kind of auxiliary: *should, will, may,* and *might.* We call these **modal auxiliaries.**
7. When a modal appears [4, 10, 11, 12], it is the first word in the string.

Now we can add another element to the formula:

(M) + (have + -en) + (be + -ing)

8. A form of *eat,* the main verb, is always the last word in the string.

(M) + (have + -en) + (be + -ing) + V

The **V** does not appear in parentheses in the formula because it is not optional; it is a part of all the verb strings. Now the formula reads as follows: In generating a verb string, we can use a modal auxiliary if we choose; when we do, it comes first. We can also choose *have;* when we do, the *-en* form follows it. We can also choose *be;* when we do, the *-ing* form follows. When we use more than one auxiliary, they appear in the order given: modal, *have, be.*

M [will] + eat = will eat

have + -en + eat = have eaten

be + -ing + eat = am [is, are] eating

will + have + -en + eat = will have eaten

The arrows in the strings above show the -*en* and -*ing* attached to the following word. What happens to the -*en* when we choose both *have* and *be*?

have + -en + be + -ing + eat = have been eating

Because the -*en* (and the -*ing*) get attached to whatever follows, here the -*en* produces *been,* the -*en* form of *be.*

So far we have a simple but powerful formula, capable of generating a great many variations of the verb. But something is missing. How can it generate *had eaten* [7] and *was eating* [9]? What exactly is different about them? *Had* and *was* are past tense (-*ed*) forms of *have* and *be.* This means we have to add one more component to the formula: **tense,** which refers to *time.* Among the five forms of the verb, you will recall, the present and past forms are the only tenses, so T will represent either present or past tense. Here is the complete formula:

T + (M) + (have + -en) + (be + -ing) + V

We can think of T as a tense marker that attaches itself to whatever follows it—that is, to the first word in the verb string, either M, *have, be,* or V. So to generate *had eaten* and *was eating,* we choose *past* as the tense marker:

past + have + -en + eat = had eaten

past + be + -ing + eat = was [were] eating

When there is no auxiliary intervening, the tense will attach itself to the verb, thus producing the simple past tense:

past + eat = ate

We generate the simple present tense by choosing *pres* as the tense marker in the formula:

pres + eat = eat [eats]

If we choose M, the modal auxiliary will carry the tense marker:

past + will + eat = would eat

pres + shall + eat = shall eat

past + can + have + -en + eat = could have eaten

past + can + have + -en + be + -ing + eat = could have been eating

So now the formula is complete. Here is what it says: In generating a verb string, there are only two requirements—tense, either present or past, and the verb; everything else is optional. The tense marker will apply to the first word in the string. We have the option of using three different kinds of auxiliaries: modal, *have,* and *be.* When we use more than one, we use them in that order. The formula also specifies that with *have* we use the *-en* form of the following auxiliary or verb; with *be,* the *-ing* form of the following verb. The last word in the string is the main verb.

Exercise 7: What is the verb that each of the following strings will produce? (Assume in each case that the subject is *Fred.*)

1. pres + have + -en + work   *has worked*
X 2. past + be + -ing + work   *had been working*
3. pres + have + -en + be + -ing + play   *has been playing*
4. past + be + -ing + be   *was being*
5. pres + be + -ing + have   *is having*
6. pres + have + -en + have   *has had*
7. past + have + -en + have   *had had*
8. past + have + -en + be + -ing + be   *had been being*

5 THE MODAL AUXILIARIES

The **modal auxiliaries** are so named because they affect what is called the **mood** of the verb. Mood refers to the manner in which a verb is expressed, such as a fact, a desire, a possibility, or a command. The modals convey conditions of probability, possibility, obligation, or necessity: I *may* eat; I *could* eat; I *should* eat; I *must* eat. These are known as the **conditional mood.** (We should also note that the modals *will* and *shall* produce what we usually think of as the future tense: *will eat* and *shall eat.*)

The modals differ from the auxiliaries *have* and *be,* both of which can fill the role of main verb in addition to their auxiliary role. The modals never fill the main verb slot,[1] nor do they have all five forms that verbs have. They have a maximum of two forms, the base form and the *-ed: can/could, will/would, shall/should, may/might.* Although we call these forms *present* and *past,* they do not necessarily indicate present and past time; these are simply labels indicating the form of the modal. For example, in the sentence "I may eat" (present), the act of eating is not going on; in "I might eat" (past) the act of eating is not over; in fact, in both cases it may never happen. Rather, the present and past forms of *may* indicate degrees of probability regarding present and future events. We should note, too, a difference in the base form of verbs and of modals: The base form of the verb combines with *to* to form the infinitive, which can play a number of roles in the sentence; the base form of the modal does not. We say "to eat," but we do not say "to shall."

In addition to the four modals above, which include past forms, there are two that have only one form: *must* and *ought to.* One other modal-like auxiliary with two forms is *have to/had to.* It differs from the regular auxiliary *have* in that it fills the modal slot in the verb expansion rule. We refer to it as "modal-like" because it does not pattern with *have* + *-en* and *be* + *-ing* as freely as the other modals do. Incidentally, its past form, *had to,* also supplies the past meaning of *must:* "I *must* go today. I *had to* go yesterday."

---

[1] Sometimes modals appear without verbs in elliptical sentences, where the main verb is understood but not expressed:

> Who'll cook the spaghetti?
> I *will.*

> May I join you?
> Yes, you *may.*

The modal auxiliaries enable us to express subtle variations in the meaning of our sentences:

Would you lend me ten dollars? *polite*
Will you lend me ten dollars?
Could you lend me ten dollars?
Can you lend me ten dollars?

These questions express subtle differences—in the degree of politeness, in the extent of the speaker's expectation of getting the money or hesitation in asking, in the perception of the ability of the person addressed to lend the money. In spite of such subtleties, a native speaker has little trouble in choosing the precise modal to fit the social situation. (But we must admit that programming the computer to consider the social nuances would be a challenge.)

Exercise 8: What verb will each of the following strings produce?

1. pres + shall + be + -ing + go *shall be going*
2. past + shall + have + -en + go *should have gone*
3. past + will + come *would come*
4. pres + may + have + -en + be + -ing + play *may have been playing*
5. past + may + play *might play*
6. past + can + have + -en + drink *could have drunk*

Write a complete sentence for each of the verbs. Do your sentences include adverbials of time? Should they?

THE SUBJUNCTIVE MOOD

Before leaving the subject of the verb moods, we should mention another one you may be familiar with: the **subjunctive.** The subjunctive mood is not a matter of adding modal auxiliaries, as the conditional is. Rather, it is simply a variation of the verb that we use in special circumstances. For example, after verbs that convey a strong suggestion or recommendation, we often use a *that* clause:

We suggested that Mary go with us.
Kathy insisted that Bill consult the doctor.
The doctor recommended that Bill stay in the hospital.
I move that the meeting be adjourned.

The use of the base form of the verb in these *that* clauses is an example of the subjunctive mood. Notice that even for a third-person singular subject, which would normally take the -*s* form, we have used the base form: Mary *go;* Bill *consult;* Bill *stay;* the meeting *be.* Other verbs that commonly take clauses in the subjunctive mood are *command, demand, ask, require, order,* and *propose.*

The subjunctive mood also occurs in *if* clauses that express a wish or a condition contrary to fact:

If I were you, I'd be careful.
If Joe weren't so lazy, he'd probably be a millionaire.
If my parents were rich, I wouldn't need a bank loan.

In clauses such as these, *were* is the standard form of *be,* no matter what the subject. However, the use of *was* is also fairly common in sentences like the second example:

If Joe was here, he'd agree with me.

In writing, however, the subjunctive *were* is the standard form.

ASPECT OF THE VERB

The auxiliaries *have* (with -*en*) and *be* (with -*ing*) indicate what we call the **aspect** of the verb, referring to whether the action of the verb is completed or in progress. With our variations in the aspect, we can express both limited and extended actions in the present and the past:

I had eaten dinner. . . .
I have eaten dinner. . . .
I had been eating dinner. . . .
I was eating dinner. . . .
I am eating dinner. . . .

And although we have no future tense among our five forms of the verb, we can express the future with the modals *shall* and *will,* with *be* + *-ing* + *go* ("I'm going to eat soon"), and by using an adverbial in connection with the present tense ("The bus leaves at noon").

The traditional grammarian labels verbs with *have* + *-en* as perfect tenses and those with *be* + *-ing* as progressive. So a verb form labeled "past perfect tense, indicative mood," simply means "past + *have* + *-en* + V." **Indicative** (in contrast to conditional) names the mood that refers to a sentence stated as fact, not probability.

EXCEPTIONS TO THE RULE

The verb-expansion rule is simple, but it is powerful. With it we can expand the verb slot in all of the sentence patterns to express a great many variations in meaning. Given the variety of modals we have, which we can use with or without *have* + *-en* and *be* + *-ing,* the number of possible variations adds up to fifty or more for most verbs. However, we rarely use all of the possibilities for any given verb. Our system restricts the use of some, and others we simply have no occasion for. But we needn't worry about the exceptions, because as native speakers we know intuitively which ones to avoid. Although we may have occasion to say,

He should have been eating.

we would probably never say,

*They should have been remaining friends.

We would probably say, instead,

They should have remained friends. Np₁ V-link N p₁

And when we hear someone say,

*He is seeming happy.
or
*The price of steak is being ridiculous.
or
*I am preferring my coffee black.

we are probably correct in concluding that we are hearing a nonnative speaker of English.

Like the preceding examples, most of the exceptions involve the restriction of *be* + *-ing* with linking verbs, with *be* as main verb, and with a small number of transitive verbs that refer to mental processes, such as *prefer, know,* and *like.* However, in some circumstances *be* + *-ing* may be perfectly acceptable in these patterns:

> He is being silly.
> He is becoming a scholar.
> She is becoming scholarly.
> She is preferring a lot of strange things today.

In Pattern I (NP *be* ADV/TP), on the other hand, the restriction is unequivocal: *be* + *-ing* never appears as an auxiliary:

> The students have been upstairs.
> *The students are being upstairs.
> *The bus is being here soon.

Certainly there are other auxiliary strings we rarely have occasion to use; nevertheless, there remain dozens of ways we can expand all of our verbs. The verb-expansion rule describes the system for doing so.

THE AUXILIARY *DO*

So far we have not discussed sentences in which a form of *do* acts as an auxiliary; *do* is not listed among the modal auxiliaries, nor is it a part of the verb-expansion rule, as *have* and *be* are. Then where in the system does it fit? Here are three sentences that include the auxiliary *did,* the past form of *do:*

> I <u>did</u>n't buy the cat food.
> <u>Did</u> you remember to buy some?
> Yes, I <u>did</u> remember.

All three of these—the negative statement, the question, and the emphatic sentence—are what we call transformations of basic sentences. Our built-in system of grammar requires that before a sentence can be transformed in one of these ways it must have either an auxiliary or a form of *be*. When there is no auxiliary or *be* as part of the main verb in the basic sentence, we add the **"stand-in" auxiliary** *do*.

The use of *do* in these transformations is discussed in more detail in Chapter 3.

THE PASSIVE TRANSFORMATION

In all of the sentences we have examined so far, the subject serves as **agent** or actor, the performer of the action that the verb describes. We call this an active relationship: the **active voice.** In the transitive verb patterns (VII–X), the opposite relationship, the **passive voice,** is also possible. A passive sentence results when the direct object—the original receiver of the action—or, in the case of Pattern VIII, the indirect object becomes the subject.

The traditional diagram of Pattern VII shows the changing roles of the two NPs:

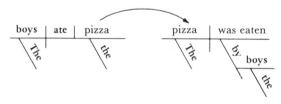

The passive transformation involves three steps:

1. The original direct object, NP$_2$, becomes the subject.
2. *be* + *-en* is added to the active verb.
3. The original subject, NP$_1$, becomes the object of the preposition *by*. This third step is optional; the passive sentence is grammatical without the prepositional phrase.

The first of these steps is obvious; the second might not be, especially in sentences like the following:

> The committee discussed the report. (*Active*)
> The report was discussed by the committee. (*Passive*)

The addition of *be* (in this case, *was*) is obvious, but the addition of *-en* is not. The change shows up clearly, however, when we analyze the components of the active verb:

> past + discuss = discussed

When we add *be* + *-en,* we always insert it just before the main verb:

> past + **be** + -en + discuss = was discussed

In other words, in the active version of the sentence, *discussed* is the *-ed* form (the past); in the passive version, *discussed* is the *-en* form. You will recall that the *-en* and *-ed* forms of all regular verbs (and some irregular ones as well) are identical. In the sentence

> The report was discussed by the committee.

the clue that tells us the verb is passive is the auxiliary *be* without the *-ing* following. Because the verb-expansion rule requires *-ing* following a form of *be,* it is clear that the *be* in this sentence resulted not from the verb-expansion rule but from the passive transformation. (Incidentally, the labels *past* and *passive* are not related: Past refers to *tense;* passive to *voice.* A verb in the passive voice can be either present or past tense.)

Exercise 9: Transform the following active sentences into the passive voice, retaining the same verb tense and aspect.

1. My roommate wrote the lead article in today's *Collegian.*
2. Bach composed some of our most intricate fugues.
3. My brother-in-law builds the most expensive houses in town.
4. He built that expensive apartment complex on Allen Street.
5. The county commissioners try out a new tax collection system every four years.

Now change these passive sentences to the active voice.

1. The football team was led onto the field by the cheerleaders.
2. This year's squad was chosen by a committee last spring.
3. Bill's apartment was burglarized last weekend.

X4. A shipment of fresh lobsters is expected any minute.

5. The elections were held on Tuesday, as usual.

(Note that in Sentences 3, 4, and 5 the agent is missing. In order to change them to the active voice, you will have to supply a subject.)

The other three transitive verb patterns can also undergo the passive transformation. In most Pattern VIII sentences, the indirect object serves as the subject of the passive:

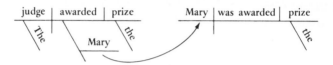

In this pattern, where we have two objects, we retain the direct object in the passive transformation. Traditional grammarians refer to this as the **retained object.** Another possibility in Pattern VIII is to use the direct object as the subject of the passive, as we do in Pattern VII, and then retain the indirect object:

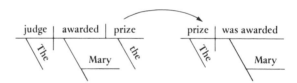

The resulting sentence sounds somewhat formal: "The prize was awarded Mary." Another alternative includes the preposition *to:* "The prize was awarded to Mary."

In the active voice of Patterns IX and X again two complements, the direct object and the objective complement, follow the verb; but in these two patterns only the direct object can serve as the subject of the passive transformation:

PATTERN IX:

PATTERN X:

The diagrams of these passive sentences look like those of the linking verb and *be* patterns, where a subjective complement describes or renames the subject. The relationship of the direct object and the objective complement remains exactly what it was in the active voice, so when the object becomes the subject, it follows that the objective complement becomes the subjective complement. How, then, do we distinguish these passives from Patterns IV and V?

Elizabeth is considered bright.
Their first daughter was named Kristi.

The clue is in the verb: When a form of *be* appears as an auxiliary without *-ing* following, we know the verb is passive. And because only transitive verbs can undergo the passive transformation, *is considered* and *was named* cannot be linking verbs.

Exercise 10: Change the following passive sentences to active. Identify the sentence patterns.

1. Mario Cuomo was elected governor of New York in 1982.
2. The kidnapping victim was found in the woods unharmed.
3. The house next door was painted purple.
4. Marylou was finally given the recognition she deserves.
5. Women are mistakenly called the weaker sex.

The passive verbs used in the examples so far are two-word strings, passive transformations of the simple past or simple present tense verbs: T + *be* + *-en* + V. Expanded verbs, verbs with auxiliaries, can also undergo the passive transformation. We simply add *be* + *-en* before the verb:

$$T + (M) + (have + -en) + (be + -ing) + \mathbf{be} + \textbf{-en} + V$$

The lab assistant was helping us. (past + be + -ing +,help)
We were being helped by the lab assistant. ⬭be + -en⬭

Max has ruined my roller skates. (pres + have + -en +,ruin)
My roller skates have been ruined by Max. ⬭be + -en⬭

You should finish your homework soon. (past + shall +,finish)
Your homework should be finished soon. ⬭be + -en⬭

Longer strings are possible, but rarely called for:

The neighbors have been building their house for five years.
Their house has been being built for five years.

The ties between the transitive verb and the passive voice are so strong—there are so few exceptions—that we can almost define "transitive verb" in terms of this relationship. In other words, a transitive verb is a verb that can undergo the passive transformation. There are a few exceptions, including *have,* one of our most common verbs. In only a few colloquial expressions does *have* appear in the passive voice: "A good time was had by all," "I've been had." Other *have* sentences cannot be transformed:

I had a cold.
*A cold was had by me.

Juan has a new car.
*A new car is had by Juan.

Other verbs that fit Pattern VII but are rarely transformed into passive are *lack* ("He lacks skill in debate") and *resemble* ("Mary resembles her mother"). Linguists sometimes classify these as "midverbs" and assign them to a separate sentence pattern. But on the basis of form (NP_1 V NP_2), we will classify these sentences as Pattern VII and simply look on them as exceptions to the passive rule.

Exercise 11: Change the voice of the following sentences, turning the active ones into passive, the passive into active.

1. We will probably elect a Republican as mayor next year.
2. Gold had been found in Alaska long before the Gold Rush in California.
3. Help in the form of a fuel allowance is now being given to the poor by the federal government.
4. My son and his friends were mixing up a big batch of cookies this morning.
5. The city is raising the subway fare to sixty cents next week.
6. Well-known and knowledgeable critics have called the play witty and warm.
7. According to the weatherman, a snowstorm has been expected since Monday.
8. Six chapters should be studied before the next exam.

USING THE PASSIVE VOICE

The terms *active* and *passive* describe the relationship between the subject and the verb; they mean precisely what they say. In most active sentences, the subject—the actor or agent—is active; the subject is doing something:

The boys ate the pizza.
The judge awarded Mary the prize.

In the passive transformation the relationship between subject and verb is different: It is passive; the subject is doing nothing. In the passive sentence the relationship between the subject and the verb remains what it was between the direct object and verb of the same active sentence: The subject is the receiver of the action or, perhaps to be more accurate, the objective or goal. The former subject of the active verb, if it is still in the sentence, remains the agent or actor:

The pizza was eaten by the boys.
Mary was awarded the prize.

If you're like many students, your first introduction to the passive voice may have appeared in the margin of a freshman theme where your teacher left the cryptic message "pass." This meant either "Why are you using the passive voice?" or, more likely, "Don't use the passive." But is the passive voice always wrong or second best?

Consider the passive sentences above. If pizza is the topic at hand, shouldn't *pizza* serve as the subject of the sentence? In the other example, it's not the judge we're talking about; it's Mary who got the prize, so why not use *Mary* as the subject? In this case it's also possible to make *Mary* the subject without using the passive:

> Mary earned the prize.
> Mary won the prize.

The passive—"Mary was awarded the prize"—removes the emphasis from Mary as active winner to Mary as passive recipient. And how about the pizza?

> The pizza disappeared.

In these examples, instead of insisting on the underlying active sentences, with *the judge* and *the boys* as subjects, we found an active verb that would substitute for the passive one. But certainly the passive voice is sometimes the best choice. For instance, the agent may be obscured in history or simply have no bearing on the discussion:

> In 1905 the streets of Patterson, California, were laid out in the shape of a wheel.

> The Vikings have had a bad press. Their activities are equated with rape and pillage and their reputation for brutality is second only to that of the Huns and the Goths. Curiously, they also have been invested with a strange glamour which contradicts in many ways their fearsome image.
> —JAMES GRAHAM-CAMPBELL and DAFYDD KIDD, *The Vikings*

The authors' purpose in the second passage is not to explain who equates the Vikings with rape and pillage or who invests them with glamour. The use of the passive puts these statements in the category of accepted beliefs.

Sometimes the agent is unknown, as in the first passive verb of the following passage:

> So far as we know, from Einstein's Special Theory of Relativity, the universe is constructed in such a way (at least around here) that no material object and no information can be transmitted faster than the velocity of light.
>
> —CARL SAGAN, *Broca's Brain*

The passive voice is especially common—and deliberate—in technical and scientific writing, in legal documents, and in lab reports, where the researcher is the agent, but to say so would be inappropriate:

> I increased the temperature to 450° for one hour. (*Active*)
> The temperature was increased to 450° for one hour. (*Passive*)

In some instances the passive voice is simply more straightforward:

> Joe was wounded in Vietnam.

And sometimes, in order to add modifiers to the agent, we put it where we can do so more conveniently, at the end of the sentence:

> Early this morning my little poodle was hit by a delivery truck traveling at high speed through the intersection of Beaver and Allen Streets.

MISUSING THE PASSIVE VOICE

The passive voice is a legitimate tool, but like any tool it must be right for the job. Too often the passive produces writing that is lifeless and stilted and wordy. In fact, a common result of the passive voice is prose so stilted that it lacks any resemblance to a human voice:

> It was reported today that the federal funds to be allocated for the power plant would not be forthcoming as early as had been antici-

pated. Some contracts on the preliminary work have been canceled and others renegotiated.

In such "officialese" or "bureaucratese" the nonhuman quality is almost inevitable, as the agent role has completely disappeared from the sentences. In the foregoing example the reader does not know who is reporting, allocating, anticipating, canceling, or renegotiating.

This kind of agentless passive is especially common in official news conferences, where press secretaries and other government officials explain what is happening without revealing who is responsible for making it happen:

> Recommendations are being made to the Israeli government concerning the Middle East problem.
> A tax hike has been proposed, but several other solutions to the federal deficit are also being considered.
> The president has been advised that certain highly placed officials are being investigated.

The faceless passive does an efficient job of obscuring responsibility, but it is neither efficient nor graceful for the writing that most of us do in school and on the job.

Often the inexperienced writer resorts to the passive voice simply to avoid using the first-person point of view. Here is a gardener's active account of spring planting written in the first person (*we*):

> In late April, when the ground dried out enough to be worked, we planted peas and onions and potatoes and prepared the soil for the rest of the vegetables. Then in mid-May we set out the tomato and pepper plants, hoping we had seen the last of frost.

Certainly the first person as used here would seem to be the logical choice for such a passage; nevertheless, some writers take great pains to avoid it (and, unfortunately, some writing texts, for no logical reason, warn against using the first person). The result is a gardener's passive account of spring planting—without the gardener:

> In late April, when the ground dried out enough to be worked, the peas and onions and potatoes were planted and the soil was prepared

for the rest of the vegetables. Then in mid-May the tomato and pepper plants were set out in hopes that the frost was over.

This revision is certainly not as stilted as the earlier examples of agent-less prose, but it does lack the live, human quality that the active version has.

Here's another example of the passive, typical of the student writer who has managed to avoid using *I*, perhaps because the paper has too many of them already or because the teacher has ruled out the first-person point of view:

> The incessant sound of foghorns could be heard along the water-
> front.

But English is a versatile language: First person is not the only alterna-tive. Here's a version of the sentence using *sound* as the verb:

> The foghorn sounded along the waterfront.

And here's one that describes the movement of the sound:

> The incessant sound of foghorns floated across the water.

Many times, of course, the writer simply doesn't realize that the passive voice may be the culprit producing the vagueness or wordiness of that first draft. For example, the writer of the following sentence ended a family Christmas story with no awareness of voice at all:

> That visit from Santa was an occurrence that would never be
> forgotten by the family.

The active version produces a tight, straightforward sentence:

> The family would never forget that visit from Santa.

The writer could also have found an active sentence that retains *visit* as the subject:

> That visit from Santa became part of our family legend.

The passive voice certainly has a place in everyone's writing. It will be effective, however, only when the writer understands it and uses it in a conscious and controlled way.

Exercise 12: Change the following sentences from passive to active, not as you did in Exercise 11, but by substituting a *new verb* that retains the essential meaning of the sentence; use the *same subject*.

> **Example:** The transitive verb patterns can be transformed into the passive voice. (*Passive*)
>
> The transitive verb patterns *can undergo* the passive transformation. (*Active*)

1. The house was being built for five years.
2. Angry demonstrators could be seen crowding the front steps.
3. Rare postage stamps have been received from all over the world.
4. All of my computer cards were lost in the rush of registration.
5. Good family programs are rarely shown on the commercial networks.
6. Wood is now being used extensively for fuel in homes throughout the country.

SUMMARY

Underlying our use of auxiliaries is a simple but powerful rule:

$$T + (M) + (have + \text{-}en) + (be + \text{-}ing) + V$$

This formula describes the system by which we can generate a wealth of variations in every verb we use.

A transformation of the basic formula—the passive voice—is a method of shifting the roles of the noun phrases, of making the direct object or, in the case of Pattern VIII sentences, the indirect object the sentence topic. In the passive transformation we add a form of *be* to the auxiliary and use the *-en* form of the verb. The passive voice can be a valuable resource for the writer who understands it.

SENTENCES FOR PRACTICE

I. Identify the components of the main verb in each of the following sentences. Your answers will be in the form of verb strings, such as those given in Exercise 8.

1. The press has recently labeled our new congressman a radical on domestic issues.
2. During the campaign everyone was calling him reactionary.
3. The teacher should have given the class more information about the exam.
4. According to the students, their teacher was being downright secretive.
5. Rosa invented a new recipe for cheese fondue.
6. Her fondue recipe requires apple wine.
7. The president may soon name three women to top posts in the Justice Department.
8. Our company will try a new vacation schedule in the summer.
9. All the workers are taking their two-week vacations at the same time.
10. Pat has been jogging regularly for six years.
11. Until last week, Mario had never told me his middle name.
12. Many large firms are now hiring liberal arts majors for management positions.
13. Employers value them for their analytical ability.
14. The suspect's alibi may have been a lie.
15. I should have been studying on a regular basis throughout the semester.

II. Decide which of these sentences can be transformed into the passive voice, and then do so. Identifying their sentence patterns will help you in making that decision. Remember that to form a passive verb you must add *be* + *-en* to the active verb string. Remember also that the active and passive versions of the sentence have different subjects.

first six

QUESTIONS FOR DISCUSSION

1. "I've already ate" is a fairly common nonstandard usage in our country. Explain how it deviates from the standard usage described by the verb-

expansion rule. Compare it with "I've already tried"; can you discover a logical reason for the nonstandard usage? Does that particular nonstandard form ever occur with regular verbs?

2. So far you have seen two circumstances in which a single verb string includes more than one form of *be*. What are these two circumstances? In other words, what are the two sources of this phenomenon?

3. The verb *get* shows up quite regularly with other verbs. Identify the patterns of these sentences, all of which include a form of *get:*

> They got married in July.
> The window got broken.
> The dog got lost.
> I get tired at basketball games.
> The cookies always get eaten before they get cold.
> I got there too late.

Should we alter the passive rule to account for any of these sentences? How does "The window was broken" differ from "The window got broken"?

4. Use the following verbs in sentences:

past + have + -en + work *had worked*

past + have + -en + receive *had received*

past + have + -en + play *had played*

Make sure that your verb is the most accurate form you can use in the context of your sentence. What does this tell you about our use of "past perfect" verbs in relation to time? *not necessarily anything*

5. The difference between the tricky verbs *lie* and *lay* is that one is transitive and one is intransitive. With these six correct sentences as data, figure out the *-ed* and *-en* forms of each. Then identify whether the verb is transitive or intransitive.

intr. lie lay lain
tr. lay laid laid

1. Please lay the fire for me.
2. The cat has never lain quite so still before.
3. I worried yesterday when he lay so still.
4. I like to lie in the sun.
5. The baby started to cry when I laid him on the bed.
6. Our new carpet was laid yesterday.

Quiz

BASE FORM	LIE	LAY
-*ed* form	————	————
-*en* form	————	————
Transitive or intransitive?	————	————

6.) English teachers and parents often correct children when they say *ain't,* as in "Ain't I nice?" Is it ungrammatical? One alternative is "Aren't I nice?" Is that O.K.? Do you consider "I ain't going" more acceptable than "He ain't going"? Should you?

7. The difference between two such sentences as

He is tall   *and*   He is silly   *be + ing can occur in some contexts*

is obviously in the adjective that fills the subjective complement slot. We cannot say

*He is being tall.

but we can say

He is being silly.

so there must be a fundamental difference between the two adjectives.

The contrast is between **stative** and **dynamic** qualities—the one describing a state, usually permanent, and the other a changing quality. What is there about *be* + *-ing* that makes this restriction seem logical? Can you think of other stative adjectives (other than *tall*) that are restricted from the subjective complement slot with *be* + *-ing*?

Perhaps a better way of describing the contrast between *silly* and *tall*—between silliness and height—concerns the presence or absence of volition, the power of choice. Which of the following adjectives describe characteristics that are willed: *young, tough, nice, red, absorbent, reckless, round*? Can these adjectives serve as subjective complements with *be* + *-ing*?

8. Consider further restrictions on *be* + *-ing:*   *see 7*

*Mary is resembling her mother.
*The blue dress is fitting you.

Can we speak of dynamic and stative or willed and nonwilled qualities of verbs as well as of adjectives? Consider the following verbs: *assume, suit,*

equal, enjoy, desire, agree with, mean, know, contain, lack, like. Do any of these
have restrictions? Why?

9. Do nouns carry such distinctions, too? Try the following nouns in the
subjective complement slot of Pattern III: *a doctor, a nuisance, a hero, a nice
boy, a gentleman, a hard worker, a construction worker.* Here is the slot: "He is
being ____." Can all of them be used with *be* + *-ing*? What conclusions can
you draw about NPs? Does volition, or the power of choice, make a difference?

10. Consider the following sentences:

> I have studied since January.
> *I have studied in January.
> I have worked on this project for six months.
> *I have worked on the project six months ago.
> I worked on this project six months ago.

What do these ungrammatical structures tell you about our use of *have* +
-en? What kinds of time adverbials does this auxiliary require or reject?
Why?

11. Examine the use of the passive voice in the following familiar passage. Try your hand at transforming it into the active voice or supplying
new, active verbs. Have you improved it?

> We hold these truths to be self evident, that all men are created equal,
> that they are endowed by their creator with certain unalienable rights,
> that among these are life, liberty, and the pursuit of happiness. That to
> insure these rights governments are instituted among men, deriving
> their just powers from the consent of the governed.

12. In the discussion of the verb-expansion rule, we observed that with
the auxiliary *have* we must use the *-en* form of the verb, and with the *-ing*
form of the verb we always use *be.* But we cannot make the opposite statement: We cannot say, "With the *-en* form we always use *have* and with *be* we
always use *-ing.*" Why can't we say this?

13. In the following sentences, what does *'s* stand for?

> He's had enough.
> Mary's not here.
> She's already gone.
> She's already left.
> He's finished.

Now consider the following sentences:

> Are you done?
> Mike is already gone.

In what way do they appear to violate the rules?

14. Consider the following sentences from Shakespeare and the King James *Bible*. In what way is the Modern English verb system different from that of the early seventeenth century?

> Laertes is come.   *we would say*
> His lordship is walked forth.   *has come*
> When they were come to Bethlehem.   *has walked forth*
>   *had come*

15. All of the following sentences include the auxiliary *must*, which, as you recall, usually has a meaning of necessity or obligation. Demonstrate its meaning in these sentences by paraphrasing each of them—that is, by coming up with a sentence that means the same thing.

> You must have seen Lisa; she walked right by you.
> You must be exhausted.
> It's such a lovely day for a picnic; you must have had a wonderful time.
> You mustn't bother with the dishes; I'll do them later.
>   *shouldn't*

16. Using your understanding of verbs—phrasal verbs, transitive and intransitive verbs, active and passive verbs—explain how these sentences differ. Be sure to think about their sentence patterns, too.

> Pablo slept in this morning.   *phrasal verb*
> George slept in his clothes.
> Max slept in spite of the noise.

17. The traditional rule prescribing the use of *shall* and *will* assigns *shall* to the first person (*We shall go soon.*) and *will* to the second and third (*You will go with us; they will follow later.*)—except for emphatic statements, where the opposite rule applies (*I will go; you shall go if I tell you to.*)

Compare those rules with actual speech, using yourself as a typical speaker. Check your own usage against the following sentences and see if the rules apply. Is either *will* or *shall* required in any of these?

> Will you have another helping?
> I will try to join you later.

Shall we share a ride?

Will we get there on time?

You will clean your room right now, young man!

Mary and Jim shall be there shortly.

Joe will join us later.

I shall expect you for dinner this evening.

3

Transforming
the Basic Patterns

The ten sentence-pattern formulas described in Chapter 1 represent the underlying framework of almost all of the sentences we speak and write. For example, underlying the sentence you just read, the first one in this paragraph, is a basic Pattern VII sentence:

The formulas	represent	the framework.
NP_1	V-tr	NP_2

The two NP slots have been expanded with a variety of phrases and clauses, but the underlying subject and verb and direct object are there, in order, just as the formula describes them; you can pick out the basic skeleton with little trouble.

But it's not always so easy. We don't always use straightforward statements (**declarative sentences**) like that one; sometimes we alter the word order to ask questions (**interrogative sentences**); sometimes we suppress the subject and give commands (**imperative sentences**); sometimes we shift the object or complement before the subject for special emphasis (**exclamatory sentences**):

Interrogative:	Have you ever found those books you lost?
	Where do you think you lost them?
Imperative:	Find those books.
✗*Exclamatory:*	What an unreasonable librarian we have!

The ten sentence-pattern formulas describe basic declarative sentences; all ten patterns can undergo the transformations that turn them into these other three sentence types. In this chapter we will look briefly at the three alternatives; we will also take up two other transformations that, like the passive voice, alter the word order and emphasis of certain basic sentences: the *there* transformation and the cleft sentence.

INTERROGATIVE SENTENCES

One of the first lessons in the study of a foreign language is how to turn statements into questions. In our native language, of course, we begin asking questions automatically, without lessons, at an early age. A child's questions develop along with statements in stages, beginning with one- and two-word strings—"Why? Where go?"—progressing in a short time to more complicated constructions—"Can I go with Daddy? Where is Daddy going?"

The two questions about Daddy, although they look similar, represent two basic kinds of questions we have in English: the "yes/no question" and the "*wh*-question," or interrogative-word question. Both kinds of questions are transformations of basic sentences in which one or more elements are shifted from their usual sentence positions.

In the yes/no question, we shift the auxiliary—or the first auxiliary, if there is more than one—to the beginning of the sentence:

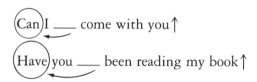

For most speakers of English, the yes/no question is also signaled by rising intonation at the end, as indicated by the arrow (and indicated in writing by the question mark).[1] The yes/no question, as its label suggests, permits "yes" and "no" as appropriate answers, although other answers are also possible:

> *Q:* Can I come with you?   *A:* We'll see.
> *Q:* Have you been reading my book?   *A:* Do you mind?

---

[1] One of the dialect distinctions in parts of Central Pennsylvania (and perhaps in other parts of the country as well) is the absence of this rising intonation. For many speakers who are natives of the area, yes/no questions have the same intonation pattern as statements and *wh*-questions:

$$\text{Can I come }^{\text{with}}_{\text{you.}}$$

We diagram the question as we would the statement underlying it. And because the diagram includes no marks of punctuation, our only clue to its original question form is the capitalized auxiliary:

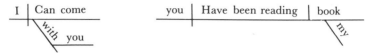

The *wh*-question is somewhat more complicated than the yes/no question, in that it involves two movement operations. It begins with a question word, or interrogative, that elicits specific information, such as *why, where, when, who, what,* and *how.* In our example, the information asked for fills the optional adverbial slot in a Pattern VI sentence:

Daddy	is going	where?
NP	V-intr	ADV

The interrogative can also fill an NP slot: <u>What</u> have you been reading?

You	have been reading	what?
NP$_1$	V-tr	NP$_2$

Some interrogatives act as determiners: <u>Whose</u> car are you taking?

As with yes/no questions, to diagram *wh*-questions, we transform them into their underlying patterns:

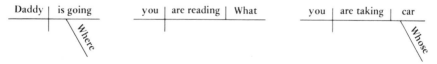

As the preceding examples show, the slots of the basic sentence pattern of questions will be out of order because the interrogative word always comes first, no matter what grammatical function it has. However, when the information being elicited is a *who* or *what* that fills the subject slot, then normal word order is maintained:

Who	broke	the window?
What	is making	that noise?
NP$_1$	V-tr	NP$_2$

The other difference between the *wh*-question and the statement is the shifted first auxiliary:

Where (is) Daddy ____ going? (Daddy is going where?)

What (have) you ____ been reading? (You have been reading what?)

Again, this shift will not occur when the interrogative fills the subject slot:

What is happening in there?
Who has been eating my porridge?

Exercise 13: Identify the underlying sentence patterns of the following questions; diagram them. *try tree*

1. Where have you been hiding?
2. Can the neighbor kids come with us on the picnic?
3. Has the committee raised enough money for the party?
4. What have you been doing with all your time?
5. Was Marie feeling better after her nap?
6. Who cuts your hair?
7. What class are you going to now?
8. Should all of us be there at noon?

THE "STAND-IN" AUXILIARY

So far the system of transforming statements into questions seems fairly simple; certainly we should be able to program a computer to replace a sentence slot with the appropriate interrogative word and to shift the first auxiliary. But a complication arises in certain sentences that have no auxiliary. Consider the possible questions contained in the following statement:

Steve polishes his car every week.

There are no complications with a *who* question, where the word order remains the same:

Who polishes his car every week?

But a yes/no question or one that asks *what* or *how often* introduces another step into the process:

What does Steve polish every week?
How often does Steve polish his car?
Does Steve polish his car every week?

Turning these questions back into statements, we end up with a new element:

Steve <u>does</u> polish his car every week.

Does polish is not one of the verb strings we can generate from the verb-expansion rule. The choice of auxiliaries under that rule is limited to the modals and to forms of *have* and *be; do* is not among them. But in the original sentence—"Steve polishes his car every week"—there is no auxiliary. And because we need an auxiliary for the auxiliary shift in the question transformation, we add a form of the **"stand-in" auxiliary,** *do.* In this case we have used *does;* if the underlying sentence had been in the past tense instead of the present, we would have used *did:*

Steve <u>polished</u> his car last night.
<u>Did</u> Steve polish his car last night?

Like the other auxiliaries, *do* carries the tense, so the past tense has shifted from the verb *polish* to the auxiliary *do.* The addition of *do* as a stand-in auxiliary is known as the ***do* transformation.**

Incidentally, the *do* transformation does not apply to sentence Patterns I, II, and III, even when there is no auxiliary. When a form of *be* is the main verb, the *be* itself does the shifting:

The teacher is at her desk ⟶ Is the teacher at her desk?

The *do* transformation also applies in two circumstances other than questions: in both negative statements and emphatic statements.

Negative Statements. Negative statements are similar to questions in their need for an auxiliary or for *be* as the main verb to carry the negative marker and the tense:

> Steve is polishing his car ⟶ Steve is not polishing his car.

Without the auxiliary or *be,* a form of *do* carries the negative and the tense:

> Steve polished his car ⟶ Steve didn't polish his car.

Emphatic Statements. In statements spoken with normal intonation, the loudest stress generally occurs after the verb, on the complement or modifier:

> Steve is polishing his CAR.
> I'm going HOME tomorrow.
> He's reading your BOOK.

One way to make the statement more emphatic is to shift stress to the auxiliary:

> Steve IS polishing his car.
> I AM going home tomorrow.
> He IS reading your book.

But in the absence of an auxiliary, a form of *do* can be added to carry the stress:

> Steve polishes his car ⟶ Steve DOES polish his car
>   every week   every week.
>
> Steve polished his car ⟶ Steve DID polish his car
>   yesterday   yesterday.

When the *do* transformation is applied to a verb in the past tense, such as *polished,* the *do* will carry the past marker, as it does in negative statements and questions. Note that the resulting emphatic verb is *did polish;* the main verb is the base form, *polish,* not the past tense.

In its role as a stand-in auxiliary, *do* has no effect on meaning. It merely acts as an operator that enables us to add emphasis to sentences not containing auxiliaries or *be* and to transform them into negatives and questions.

Exercise 14: Transform the following statements into yes/no questions.

Do 1. Most of the children on the block own roller skates.
Does 2. The girl next door skates all evening long.
Did 3. Helen's children wanted skates for Christmas.

Now make the same three statements negative.
Now make the same three statements emphatic.

IMPERATIVE SENTENCES

Imperative sentences, or **commands,** take the base form of the verb without auxiliaries:

> Help yourself.
> Kiss me again.
> Tell me a story.

The subject of the imperative sentence is the understood *you,* the personal pronoun that refers to the person or persons being addressed. Although commands can be made from all of the sentence patterns, there are certain verbs that rarely produce imperative sentences: *resemble, lack, seem.* These are among the stative verbs generally—verbs that refer to a state rather than an action; and many are the same verbs that are not expanded with *be* + *-ing,* which we saw in Chapter 2 as exceptions to the verb-expansion rule. We should also note certain negative commands, some of which are rarely spoken as positive:

> Don't be silly.

Don't do anything I wouldn't do.
Don't forget to write.

Negative commands require the stand-in auxiliary *do* (*don't*) to carry the negative marker. And in the following imperative sentence, *do* has been added for emphasis:

Do be careful.

EXCLAMATORY SENTENCES

We usually think of an **exclamation** as any sentence spoken with heightened emotion, written with an exclamation point:

I hate purple!
Take that cat out of here this minute!

But in terms of form, the first sentence immediately preceding is *declarative,* a straightforward statement, and the second is *imperative,* a command. In contrast, the exclamatory sentence includes a shift in word order that focuses special attention on a complement:

What an unreasonable librarian we have!
How very peaceful the countryside is.
What a hard-working president we elected!

The *what* or *how* that usually introduces the emphasized element is added to the underlying sentence pattern:

We have an unreasonable librarian. (*Pattern VII*)
The countryside is very peaceful. (*Pattern II*)
We elected a hard-working president. (*Pattern VII*)

OTHER SENTENCE TRANSFORMATIONS

The sentence types we have just seen—interrogative, imperative, and exclamatory—are variations of the basic declarative sentence that apply with few exceptions to all ten sentence patterns. In Chapter 2 we studied the passive voice, the result of a transformation that applies to the transitive verb patterns. We will now look briefly at two other fairly common transformations that alter word order for purposes of emphasis in certain kinds of sentences.

The There *Transformation.* Like the exclamatory sentence, the *there* transformation includes an introductory word that plays no grammatical role in the basic sentence pattern. It also includes a shift in word order: The unstressed *there,* known as an **expletive,** introduces the sentence; the subject of the sentence follows *be:*

> There's a fly in my soup.
> There are some error messages showing up in my program.

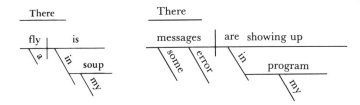

To diagram a *there* transformation, we must recognize the underlying pattern. As the diagram shows, *there* has no grammatical function in the basic sentence. It is an operator that enables us to delay the subject, giving it greater emphasis by shifting it to the point of main stress, which generally occurs after the verb:

> There's a flý in my soup.
> There are some erŕor messages showing up in my program.

The *there* transformation not only adds stress (loudness) and length to the subject, it diminishes the stress normally given to other slots in the predicate.

The unstressed *there* is not the same word as the adverb *there:*

> We're going <u>there</u> this afternoon.
> <u>There</u> he goes.

In these two sentences, *there* is providing information of place. The unstressed *there,* on the other hand, plays a structural role only, not a semantic one.

The *there* transformation applies in fairly limited circumstances. Generally the subject of the sentence is indefinite: "*a* fly" or "*some* error messages" rather than "*the* fly" or "*those* error messages." We might have occasion to say,

> Thére's that fly that knows good soup.

if a particular fly under discussion lands in the soup. But this is not the unstressed *there*. The stress it carries marks it as an adverb providing information of place. The same is true of

> Thére are those error messages I told you about.

In these sentences with definite subjects, we have simply shifted the order of the basic sentence pattern, as we sometimes do to emphasize adverbials:

> Here's your book.
> Right off the end of the pier plunged the getaway car.

In addition to the indefinite subject, the *there* transformation usually has a form of *be* either as the main verb or, in the case of the transitive and intransitive patterns, as an auxiliary. Pattern I (NP *be* ADV/TP) is the most common pattern we transform with *there;* neither Patterns II and III, in which *be* acts as a linking verb, nor Patterns IV and V, the linking verbs, will accept the *there* transformation.

The form of *be* will, of course, depend on the tense and on the number of the subject, whether singular or plural:

> There *were* some problems with the heat in our new apartment.
> There *has* been a problem with the plumbing, too.

But an exception to the general rule of subject–verb agreement occurs with the *there* transformation. A compound subject, which we usually treat as plural, may take the *-s* form of *be* under some circumstances:

> There was some great blocking and some fine running and passing in Saturday's game.

In this sentence "there were" would be awkward, even though the subject is compound.

The *there* transformation without a form of *be* is also possible, but such sentences are not very common:

> There came from the alley a low moaning sound.
> There followed a series of unexplained phenomena.
> There remains an unanswered question.

Listen to the difference between these sentences and those with *be*. These have a tight, controlled quality about them. Notice also that when a verb other than *be* follows *there* it shares the stress with the subject.

Exercise 15: Identify the sentence patterns of the following sentences; ~~diagram them~~. Underline any instances of the adverbial *there*.

1. There are hundreds of blackbirds feasting in our cornfield. *NP V int*
2. They do a great deal of damage there in the late summer. *NP₁ V-tr NP₂*
3. There was a serious bird problem there at the end of August. *NP be ADV*
4. There's always a flock of them lining the telephone wire. *?*
5. There they are now. *NP be ADV*

The Cleft Sentence. Another sentence variation that provides a way to shift the focus of attention is the cleft transformation, so called because it divides a clause into two parts: It cleaves it. The cleft sentence allows a writer to accomplish by means of word order what a speaker can do by varying the point of main stress or loudness. For example, in the following sentence a speaker can change the focus or meaning simply by putting stress on different words:

> MARY wrecked her motorcycle in Phoenix during the Christmas break. (It wasn't Diane who did it.)

> Mary wrecked her MOTORCYCLE in Phoenix during the Christmas break. (Not her car.)

Mary wrecked her motorcycle in PHOENIX during the Christmas break. (Not in Albuquerque.)

Mary wrecked her motorcycle in Phoenix during the CHRISTMAS break. (Not Thanksgiving.)

Because the conventions of writing do not include capital letters for words that should get main stress, as shown in the preceding sentences, the writer's intended emphasis may not always be clear. The cleft transformation solves the problem. In one kind of cleft sentence the main subject is *it* with a form of *be* as the main verb. In reading the following sentences aloud, you'll notice that you automatically stress the word or phrase following *was:*

It was <u>Mary</u> who wrecked her motorcycle in Phoenix during the Christmas break.

It was <u>her motorcycle</u> that Mary wrecked in Phoenix during the Christmas break.

It was <u>in Phoenix</u> that Mary wrecked her motorcycle during the Christmas break.

It was <u>during the Christmas break</u> that Mary wrecked her motorcycle.

Another kind of cleft sentence uses a *what* clause in subject position. Note that the added *was* separates the original sentence into two parts:

Mary wrecked her motorcycle.
What Mary wrecked <u>was</u> her motorcycle.

Sometimes *what* shifts the original verb phrase into subject position. Again, a form of *be* is added as the main verb:

A branch lying across the road <u>caused the accident</u>.
<u>What caused the accident</u> was a branch lying across the road.

Thick fog <u>reduced the visibility to zero</u>.
<u>What reduced the visibility to zero</u> was the thick fog.

Because the cleft transformation produces fairly complicated structures, with clauses filling certain slots in the sentence, we will not be concerned here with their diagrams. We'll take them up again in Part IV.

Exercise 16: Transform each of the following sentences into as many cleft variations as you can.

1. Bill's grandmother nicknamed him Buzz when he was in third grade.
2. Glenda loves break dancing.
3. Sir Humphrey Davy invented the carbon arc light seventy years before Edison's first incandescent lamp.
4. In 1983 Sally Ride became the first American woman to travel in space.
5. The San Diego Padres won the National League pennant in 1984.
6. Tom's casual remark about cat lovers made Brenda furious.

SUMMARY

In this chapter we have looked at the transformations that turn the basic sentence patterns into questions, commands, and exclamations. In some cases the sentences require the stand-in auxiliary *do* to complete the transformation. Certain negative and emphatic sentences also require *do*. Two other sentence transformations change the sentence by redirecting its emphasis and changing its point of stress: the *there* transformation and the cleft sentence. Underlying all of these variations are the basic sentence patterns. It's true that the pattern will not always be apparent at first glance; but with practice you will come to recognize the sentence as a particular transformation—a question or an exclamation or a *there* transformation. Isolating the elements that have been shifted or added will then help you discover the underlying pattern.

SENTENCES FOR PRACTICE

Using the transformations you have studied in this chapter (interrogative, imperative, exclamatory, "there," and cleft), write as many variations of the following sentences as you can.

1. Hundreds of angry women were protesting the senator's position on day care at yesterday's political rally in the student union.

2. Myrtle's special marinated mushrooms added a festive touch to the salad.

3. A big family is moving into the apartment upstairs next week.

4. A strange man was lurking suspiciously on the neighbor's front porch last night.

5. The encroachment of civilization on wilderness areas bothers a great many environmentalists.

6. Women athletes from all over the world made an impressive showing at the 1984 Olympic Games.

7. A month of unseasonably warm weather almost ruined the ski season last winter.

8. An old stone bridge near our home is a popular subject for local photographers.

9. Several gangs of kids in the neighborhood are cleaning up the empty lot on the corner.

10. The new word-processing program works very efficiently.

O Denotes DO

QUESTIONS FOR DISCUSSION

1. The stand-in auxiliary *do* never appears in a passive sentence. Why not?

2. Why do the following sentences from Shakespeare and the King James *Bible* sound strange to our twentieth-century ears? What particular change that has taken place in the language do these sentences illustrate?

Let not your heart be troubled.
Know you where you are?
Whereof the ewe not bites.
Revolt our subjects?

paper

3. In this chapter we looked briefly at our system for turning sentences into questions, a process that sometimes requires *do*. The tag question is another method for turning statements into questions:

> John is washing his car, <u>isn't he?</u>
>
> Perry should wash his too, <u>shouldn't he?</u>

Add the tags that turn the following statements into questions:

> Harold has finally stopped smoking,   _____?
> The students are not studying Latin,   _____?
> Bev finished her book on schedule,   _____?
> Tim and Joe are good carpenters,   _____?
> Kris is a good carpenter, too,   _____?
> She builds beautiful cabinets,   _____?

Now look at the system you followed for adding these questions. How many steps are involved? What will our computer program require so that it, too, can generate tag questions?

Here are three more tags to supply:

> Harold should stop smoking,   _____?
> Harold ought to stop smoking,   _____?
> Harold may stop smoking soon,   _____?

Take a poll among your friends to get their responses to these three. Do all the respondents agree? Do they follow the procedure you described in the first set? What do these tags tell you about the changing nature of the language?

4. We usually think of contractions (*doesn't, shouldn't, I'll, he'd,* etc.) as optional, informal variations of verbs. And we generally think of them as forms that are best avoided in formal writing. Consider the following sentences in this light. Are the foregoing assumptions true?

> Can't you come with me?
> Doesn't the sunset look beautiful this evening?
> Hasn't everyone tried to conserve energy?
> Are you sure he'll try hard enough to win?
> I'm very hungry.

5. In what way do the following sentences differ from the imperative sentences we looked at on page 69?

> Buy one and you'll get the second one free.
> Lose any more weight and we won't know you.

6. In some *there* transformations, the verb *be* means "exist":

> There are honest politicians.
> There are more than 3,000 languages in the world.

What happens when you change these sentences to their underlying patterns? Try substituting *exist* for *be*. Does it make a difference?

7. The imperative sentence is usually easy to identify because its subject (*you*) is understood—that is, the subject is missing from the sentence. The following sentences have an imperative quality about them, but they also have subjects. How should we classify them? Notice that the first two are punctuated with exclamation marks.

> You get out of here!
> Don't you tell me what to do!
> You'll do exactly what I tell you to do.
> You made your own bed; now you lie in it.

8. In Chapter 1 we looked briefly at sentence variations that help us distinguish verb–particle combinations (phrasal verbs) from verb–adverb combinations:

> We jumped up. ⟶ Up we jumped.
> We made up. ⟶ *Up we made.

The cleft transformation, introduced in this chapter, can also be useful in identifying properties of verbs:

> He came by the office in a big hurry. *object of prep.*
> He came by his fortune in an unusual manner. *phrasal verb*
> NP_2

> Where he came was by his office.
> *Where he came was by his fortune.

> Joe turned on the bridge and looked around.
> Joe turned on the light and looked around.

It was on the bridge that Joe turned and looked around.
*It was on the light that Joe turned and looked around.

Here are some other pairs that look alike. Use transformations to demonstrate their differences:

The student looked up the word.
The teacher looked up the hall.

Sharon called up the stairs.   *Where Sharon called was up the stairs*
Karen called up the club members.
        Who Sharon called up were the club members.

An old jalopy turned into the driveway.
Cinderella's coach turned into a pumpkin.

II

THE
PARTS OF SPEECH

W E began our study of grammar in Part I by focusing on complete sentences, concentrating on the differences in the predicate that determine sentence categories, or patterns, and on the transformations that produce variations of basic sentences. Our goal in Part I was to see the sentences as patterns and to recognize the various slots, the parts, that make up those patterns. But because the sentence slots are filled with words and groups of words, it's obvious that we can't study sentences without also studying words.

In Part II the words themselves will be our focus. In the next four chapters we will concentrate on differences in the form of words, in their function in the sentence, and in their meaning. These are the differences that determine the classification of words into categories known as the parts of speech.

If you heard a man say, "Boy wants drink water," your first response would probably be to label the speaker as foreign. Your second would be to share your water supply, because in spite of the ungrammatical sentence you understood the message. Under the same circumstances, a native speaker would have said, "My boy wants a drink of water," or "This boy wants to drink that water," or "The boy wants a drink of your water." The message is more explicit, but the result would be the same: You'd share your water. The extra words haven't changed the effect of the message, but they have provided a certain kind of meaning, a precision that the nonnative speaker's sentence lacks. Clearly, then, different kinds of words function in different ways to contribute different kinds of meaning.

First consider the differences between the words the nonnative

81

speaker used and those he left out. The ones he included gave the sentence the lexical meaning necessary to communicate effectively: *Boy wants drink water.* What he omitted were certain grammatical signals. We don't know, for example, if *drink* is a noun or a verb; nor do we know the relationship of the speaker or the listener to the nouns *boy* and *water.* Nevertheless, the circumstances of the conversation, its setting or context, made the message clear.

This distinction between lexical and grammatical meaning determines our first division of the parts of speech: form-class words and structure-class words. In general, the **form classes** provide the primary lexical content; the **structure classes** explain the grammatical or structural relationships. We can think of the form-class words as the bricks of the language and the structure words as the mortar that binds them together.

FORM CLASSES	STRUCTURE CLASSES
Noun	Determiner
Verb	Auxiliary
Adjective	Qualifier
Adverb	Preposition
	Conjunction
	Interrogative
	Expletive

The clearest difference between the two classes is characterized by their numbers. Nouns, verbs, adjectives, and adverbs are large, open classes; new form-class words regularly enter the language, as new technology and new ideas require them. They are sometimes abandoned, too, as the dictionary's "obsolete" label testifies. But with few exceptions, the structure classes remain constant—and limited. We have managed with the very same small store of prepositions and conjunctions for generations, with few changes. It's true that we don't see "whilst" and "betwixt" in contemporary prose and poetry, but most of our structure words are identical to those that Shakespeare and his contemporaries used.

Another difference has to do with form. As their label suggests, the form classes are those that can undergo changes in form—that are, in fact, distinguishable by their form—whereas the structure classes are not. But, as with almost every "rule" of the language, we will encounter exceptions. For example, auxiliaries are among the structure classes, although some of them, because they are verbs, show form variations; some of the qualifiers are also distinguishable by their form. On the other hand, there are many words in the form classes that have no distinctions in form and do not undergo change—nouns like *chaos,* adjectives like *main,* and adverbs like *there.* We should note, too, that the structure classes are sometimes called "function" words, a label that underscores another difference between the two large classes. Such labels as "determiner" and "qualifier" and "conjunction" clearly name functions in the sentence, whereas a label such as "noun" specifies a form. The functions served by nouns, which we refer to as nominal functions, are subject, direct object, indirect object, and so on.

There is also one important class that doesn't appear on either of the preceding lists: the pronoun. Like the structure words, pronouns are a small, closed class, admitting no new members, so they are generally classified with the structure words; further, the possessive and demonstrative pronouns constitute important subclasses of determiners, one of the structure classes. But like the form-class words, most pronouns can undergo changes in form, depending on their antecedent and their grammatical role in the sentence, which is generally the role of a noun or noun phrase, so they do have some characteristics of the form classes. We will describe the pronouns, with all of their subclasses and roles, in a separate chapter, not only to acknowledge that dual nature but also to keep this "parts of speech" inventory as clear as possible.

Before looking at the classes individually, we need to take up the basic unit of word formation, the morpheme; an understanding of the morpheme is central to the conscious understanding of words. Then we will take up the form classes, the structure classes, and pronouns.

4

Morphemes — *smallest meaningful unit*

Syntax refers to the arrangement of sentence elements into meaningful patterns. When we study sentence patterns and their transformations and expansions, we are studying syntax. But the structural linguist begins the study of grammar not with syntax but with **phonology,** the study of individual sounds. At the next level comes **morphology,** the study of **morphemes,** combinations of sounds with meaning. Then comes the study of **syntax,** the third level in the grammar hierarchy.

In this book we are concerned primarily with syntax, the systematic arrangement of words and phrases and clauses into sentences. But a thorough understanding of syntax depends on the understanding of the words that combine to form those larger units. So in this chapter, before taking up the word classes—the parts of speech—we will look briefly at morphemes, the units that make up words. (For an overview of phonemes, the individual sounds, see Appendix A.)

The definition of *morpheme,* a combination of sounds that has meaning, may sound to you like the definition of *word.* That's not surprising because many morphemes are, in fact, complete words; *head* and *act* and *kind* and *walk* (as well as *and*) are words consisting of a single morpheme, a single meaningful combination of sounds. But others, such as *heads* and *actively* and *unkindly* and *walking,* consist of two or more morphemes, each of which has meaning itself. The success you had years ago in learning to read and spell was in part dependent on your awareness of the parts of words. For instance, in spelling a word like *actively,* you probably break it into its three morphemes automatically: Its stem, or **base,** is the verb *act;* the suffix *-ive* turns it into an adjective; and the suffix *-ly* turns the adjective into an adverb. Each of these three morphemes, the base and the two suffixes, has meaning itself; and each appears in other environments (other words) with the same meaning. These are the features that identify morphemes.

The individual morphemes in a word are not always quite as obvious as they are in words like *actively*. In the word *reflections,* for example, we can recognize the verb *reflect,* the *-ion* ending that turns it into a noun, and the *-s* that makes it plural: *reflect* + *ion* + *s*. But how about the word *reflect?* Is that a single morpheme, or is it two? Are *re* and *flect* separate morphemes? Do they both have meaning? Do they appear in other environments with the same meaning? Certainly there are many words that begin with the prefix *re-: reverse, rebound, refer*. In all of these, *re-* means "back," so *re* passes the morpheme test. How about *flect?* There's *inflect* and *deflect*. The dictionary reveals that all three words with *flect* are based on the Latin verb *flectere,* meaning "to bend." So in the word *reflections* we can identify four morphemes: *re* + *flect* + *ion* + *s*.

Incidentally, it's not unusual to need the dictionary to understand the morpheme structure of a word. The meanings of words often change, and their origins become obscure. Take the word *obscure,* for example. How many morphemes does it have, one or two? What does *scure* mean? Does it appear in other words with the same meaning? And is *ob* the same morpheme we find in *observe?* What does it mean? And how about *observe?* Is that the verb *serve?* Such meanderings into the dictionary in search of clues about morphemes can heighten our awareness of words and appreciation of language. And certainly an awareness of morphemes can enhance the understanding of language essential to both reader and writer. When we study etymology or historical linguistics, we begin to understand the intricacies of morphemes, their changes, and their variations. But in our limited examination of morphemes here, we will look mainly at those that signal the form classes, that contribute to our understanding of the parts of speech.

BASES AND AFFIXES

All words, as we have seen, are combinations of morphemes, or, in the case of a word like *act* (as well as the eight words preceding it in this sentence), single morphemes. All morphemes are either **bases** (*act*), which we define as the morpheme that gives the word its primary lexical meaning, or **affixes** (*-ive*, *-ly*); and all affixes are either **prefixes,** those that precede the base (*re-*), or **suffixes,** those that follow it (*-ion*):

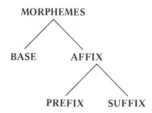

MORPHEMES

BASE   AFFIX

PREFIX   SUFFIX

Exercise 17: The following four sets of words illustrate some of the relationships of morphemes. In each set find the common base. What does the base mean? Draw vertical lines in the words to show the separate morphemes.

aud = hear   *dur = hard*

nova	auditor	durable	conceive
renovation	audience	endure	capable
innovate	inaudible	duration	susceptible
novice	auditorium	during	capture
novelist	audio	endurance	intercept

BOUND AND FREE MORPHEMES

One other feature of morphemes concerns their ability to stand alone. Many cannot. For example, the affixes are **bound,** or attached, to another morpheme rather than **free** to stand alone; that's what *affix* means. In the word *actively,* only the first morpheme is free: *-ive* and *-ly* are bound. In *reflections,* even the base is bound; *flect* is not a word that can stand by itself. We call this a bound base. Other examples of words without free morphemes are *concur, conceive, depict, expel,* and many others with these common prefixes. There are also a few affixes that are free, such as *full* (spelled "ful" when used as an affix), *like,* and *less.* The solid arrows in the following diagram represent the most common circumstance, the broken ones the less common:

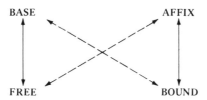

Exercise 18: Find a word to fit each of the following formulas. Include only the morphemes called for.

Examples: free + bound = *birds*
bound + free = *rerun*

1. free + bound
2. bound + free
3. free + bound + bound
4. bound + free + bound
5. free + free
6. bound + free + bound + bound
7. bound + bound
8. bound + bound + bound

ALLOMORPHS

In Exercise 17 the base morphemes *aud* and *dur* are pronounced and spelled the same in all five words in their lists. However, the morpheme *nov* in that same exercise has two pronunciations; in *nova* and *novelist* the vowels are different, comparable to the difference between *node* and *nod*. In the last group in the exercise, the difference from one word to the next is greater still, with variations in spelling as well as pronunciation. In fact, without the help of a dictionary we would be tempted to label *ceive* and *cap* and *cept* as different morphemes altogether, rather than variations of the same one. Such variations of morphemes, which are extremely common in English, are known as **allomorphs**.

Sometimes the base morphemes have allomorphic variations as the result of suffixes. For example, a word ending in *f* often takes a *v* in the plural:

leaf → leaves   wife → wives   elf → elves

We would call *leav* and *wiv* and *elv* allomorphs of *leaf* and *wife* and *elf*. Here are some other examples in which the pronunciation of the base morpheme changes with the addition of a suffix: *type/typify; please/ pleasant; press/pressure; able/ability; oblige/obligation; child/children.* And because these allomorphs of the base are not used without the suffix, we would include them in the category of bound bases.

Prefixes and suffixes, too, undergo such variation; that is, they also have allomorphs. For example, notice the negative prefix we add to these adjectives: *unkind, improper, illegal, irrelevant, ineligible.* All of these prefixes mean *not,* so it is probably accurate to consider *im, il, ir,* and *in* as allomorphs of the prefix *un,* the most common among them. At any rate, their sounds are determined by their environment.

Suffixes also have allomorphic variation. Consider, for example, the sound you add to make nouns plural:

cat → cats   dog → dogs   kiss → kisses

Even though the first two are spelled the same, the sounds are different: in *cats* the sound is an *s;* in *dogs,* it's a *z.* And in *kisses,* the *es* represents an unstressed vowel sound followed by *z.* These variations are discussed in further detail in Appendix A, "Phonology."

HOMOPHONES

You're probably familiar with the meaning of the word *homonyms:* words with different meanings that sound alike, such as *sail* and *sale, there* and *their,* or *to, two,* and *too.* These are also known as **homophones,** a label that refers not only to words but also to morphemes, to parts of words that sound the same but have different meanings. Prefixes and suffixes, for example, can be homophones. The *ex* in *exchange* and the *ex* in *ex-wife* have two different meanings: "from" and "former." So do the *er* in *singer* and the *er* in *brighter:* "one who" and "more." And the *s* endings we add to verbs and nouns are different. All of these are examples of homophones.

DERIVATIONAL AND INFLECTIONAL MORPHEMES

There is one more feature of morphemes we want to recognize—the classification of affixes as either derivational or inflectional:

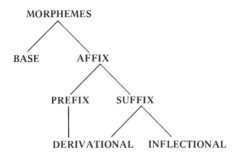

As the branching diagram shows, all prefixes are derivational, whereas suffixes are either derivational or inflectional. Although we have several hundred suffixes, distinguishing between the derivational and inflectional ones is easy to do. Only eight are **inflectional.** You'll recognize four of them from the discussion of verbs in Chapter 2.

1. *-s* (plural)   ⎫ Noun inflections
2. *-s* (possessive)   ⎭

3. *-s* (3rd-person singular) ⎫
4. *-ed* (past tense)   ⎬ Verb inflections
5. *-en* (past participle)   ⎪
6. *-ing* (present participle) ⎭

7. *-er* (comparative) ⎫ Adjective and Adverb inflections
8. *-est* (superlative) ⎭

All of the other suffixes, as well as all the prefixes, are **derivational.**

The term *derivational* refers to the change that a word undergoes when a derivational morpheme is added: Either the meaning of the word changes or the class, the part of speech, changes—or both. Take the word *inactivity,* for example. With the derivational morpheme *-ive,* the verb *act* becomes the adjective *active*—that is, we derive one class of word from another. When we add *in-,* the class remains the same— *active* and *inactive* are both adjectives—but the prefix does affect the meaning, as prefixes generally do; in other words, we derive a new meaning. Finally, with the addition of *-ity* the adjective becomes the noun *inactivity.*

The significance, then, of derivational morphemes is this ability they give us to derive new words: *Active* and *inactive* are two different words; so are *active* and *actively;* so are *act* and *action.*

The inflectional affixes also change words, of course, but the changes do not represent new words in the same sense that the changes with derivational morphemes do. It is probably accurate to consider the verb *acting* as simply a variation of *act;* likewise, the inflections we add to nouns—the plural and possessive—produce variations of the singular noun; we think of *dogs* and *dog's* simply as variations of *dog,* rather than as different words.

There are two other attributes of derivational morphemes that distinguish them from the inflectional morphemes:

1. Derivational morphemes are arbitrary. Unlike the inflectional morphemes, which apply in a systematic way to all, or at least to a significant number of, the words in a class, the derivational morphemes are quite unsystematic. For example, every verb—without exception—takes the inflectional *-s* and *-ing* endings (this may, in fact, be the only rule in our grammar without an exception); and almost all verbs have an *-ed* and *-en* inflection as well. However, there's nothing systematic about the derivational endings that we add to other word classes to form verbs: The adjective *able* becomes a verb with the addition of the prefix *en-* (*enable*); *sweet* takes the suffix *-en* (*sweeten*); *legal* takes *-ize* to become a verb (*legalize*); *active* takes *-ate* (*activate*). For many adjectives, however, we have no derivational morpheme at all for producing verbs; we have no way to turn such adjectives as *big, good, happy,* and *vicious* into verbs. On the other hand, we can derive nouns from these particular adjectives by adding *-ness.* As you might expect, however, *-ness* is not our only noun-forming suffix: The adjective *generous* takes *-ity* to become a noun; *supreme* takes *-acy;* *brave* takes *-ery.* We have no rules to explain what goes with what, no system to account for these differences; that lack of system is what "arbitrary" means.

2. Derivational morphemes often change the class of the word. Most of the time, in fact, that change in class is their very purpose; they produce new words. Inflectional morphemes, on the other hand, never change the class. And, as mentioned earlier, we generally don't even consider the inflected form of a word as a different word.

If all of these derivational and inflectional morphemes seem complicated to you, it's probably because you haven't thought about them before. If you're a native speaker, they're really not complicated at all;

you use them without even thinking. In fact, there is probably no feature of English that illustrates more clearly the innate ability that native speakers have than this inventory of prefixes and suffixes that gives the language such versatility.

Exercise 19: Draw vertical lines in the following words to indicate their morpheme boundaries. Identify each morpheme as follows: *bound* or *free; base* or *affix*. Identify each affix as *derivational* or *inflectional*. You will probably need to consult your dictionary.

1. precision	5. unaware	9. illegal
2. candidate	6. money	10. wealthy
3. detoured	7. sidewalks	11. television
4. excessively	8. promotion	12. revises

SUMMARY

In this chapter we have looked briefly at morphemes—sounds or combinations of sounds that have meaning. Words are made up of morphemes. All words have at least one base, the morpheme that contributes the primary lexical meaning. In addition, our language has several hundred affixes, both prefixes and suffixes, that add meaning to the base morphemes. In the next chapter we will look at the four form classes and the derivational and inflectional affixes that identify them.

QUESTIONS FOR DISCUSSION

1. Most morphemes are made up of combinations of sounds. Give some examples of morphemes that are single sounds.

2. Consider how the meaning of a word comes about. Explain the origin of the following words:

ambulance	calculate	cigar	easel
budget	candidate	dial	escape

| fancy | lunatic | meal | prevaricate |
| hussy | magazine | sabotage | vaccine |

3. In Exercise 18 you came up with words containing various combinations of bound and free morphemes. Which of those sequences do you suppose is a compound word? Define *compound word* on the basis of its morpheme content.

4. Consider the difference between derivational and inflectional suffixes. What can you say about their positions when both appear on the same word? Is the rule fairly constant? Is it possible for more than one derivational and/or inflectional suffix to appear on a single word?

5. Which of the following words appears to violate the system that you described in Question 4?

inflectional   microscopy   teaspoonsful

6. How can the awareness of morphemes be of help in spelling problem words, such as the following?

| entirely | professor | inaudible | disappoint |
| safety | innovate | misspell | roommate |

7. In his "On Language" column in *The New York Times* for October 14, 1984, William Safire cites four different meanings for the suffix *-ful,* as reported to him by the editorial director of Merriam-Webster, the dictionary publisher: (1) "full of"; (2) "characterized by"; (3) "resembling or having the qualities of"; and (4) "tending to or given to." Here are the four words he used as examples:

| masterful | mournful |
| painful | eventful |

Which word goes with which meaning?

8. Still on the subject of the suffix *-ful,* explain the difference between the words "painful" and "pained." Under what circumstances would the following sentences be accurate?

He had a pained expression on his face.
He had a painful expression on his face.

Now think about the difference between "healthy" and "healthful." Would you say that carrots are a healthy food to eat?

9. The athletic contests that take place between different groups in school are called "intramurals." Why *intra-* instead of *inter-*? And what's the difference in meaning between *interpersonal* and *intrapersonal*?

5

The
Form Classes

Know what a form word is

The contrast in the sentences of the native and nonnative speakers in the introduction to this section illustrates the difference in the kind of meaning that form-class words and structure-class words contribute to the sentence. The nonnative speaker communicated with nouns and verbs, the form-class words that provide the semantic content of the language: *Boy wants drink water.* The native speaker's version of that sentence includes such word classes as determiners and prepositions, the structure words that signal grammatical meaning: "*My* boy wants *a* drink *of your* water." One difference between the two kinds of words, then, is meaning.

The characteristic of form, introduced in the chapter on morphemes, is another difference between them. In general, the four form classes are distinguishable by their inflectional suffixes and by certain characteristic derivational suffixes and prefixes. In this chapter we will look at these features of nouns, verbs, adjectives, and adverbs.

NOUNS

We traditionally define *noun* on the basis of meaning, as the *name* of a person, place, thing, idea, event, or the like, and that definition works fairly well. After all, we've been learning names since we spoke our first words: *mama, daddy, cookie, baby.* The word *noun,* in fact, comes from *nomen,* the Latin word for "name."

But in distinguishing nouns from other parts of speech, meaning is only one clue. We also recognize nouns by the words that signal them. When we see a determiner—a word such as *the, my,* or *an*—we know what part of speech will follow, although not necessarily as the next word: *the* books, *my* sister, *an* honest opinion. Determiners are simply not used without nouns. Our third criterion, form, is somewhat more objective than the others; we can often differentiate the form classes from each other without reference to either meaning or context, simply on the basis of their derivational and inflectional suffixes.

Noun Derivational Suffixes. Each of the four form classes has its own inventory of derivational suffixes. The *-ion,* for example, converts the verb *reflect* into a noun, so we call it—or its variations *-tion, -sion, -cion,* and *-ation*—a noun-forming suffix. A quick check of the dictionary reveals that all of the *-ion* words listed on the first few pages are also nouns formed from verbs:

abbreviation	abstraction	accusation
abolition	acclamation	acquisition
abomination	accommodation	action
abortion	accreditation	activation
abrasion	accumulation	adaptation

Two examples of *-ion* words that function as both nouns and verbs are *partition* and *mention;* you may be able to think of others. But chances are you will find few, if any, *-ion* words that are not nouns; *-ion* is a reliable signal. Many other derivational suffixes do the same job, that of converting verbs into nouns:

accomplish	+	-ment	⟶	accomplishment
accept	+	-ance	⟶	acceptance
arrive	+	-al	⟶	arrival
assist	+	-ant	⟶	assistant
deliver	+	-y	⟶	delivery
depart	+	-ure	⟶	departure
teach	+	-er	⟶	teacher

This variety of noun-forming suffixes that we add to verbs—and, incidentally, there are many more than these—illustrates not only our versatility in changing one part of speech to another but also the sometimes arbitrary way in which we do so. Why, for example, do we say "delivery" and "deliverance" but not "deliverment"? Why "departure" rather than "departation"? Why "deportation" rather than "deporture"? There is no good answer to such questions.

The same arbitrariness runs through all the word classes. For example, many adjectives become nouns with the addition of *-ness:* prettiness, laziness, strangeness, happiness, helplessness. But there is a long list of other suffixes that do the same job: tru*th*, wis*dom*, just*ice*, partial*ity*. We also have a number of suffixes that simply alter the meaning of the word in one way or another without changing the class: boy*hood*, king*dom*, friend*ship*, Spani*ard*, garden*er*, terror*ism*.

Finally, the nouns *partiality* and *activation* illustrate another feature of derivational suffixes, where a noun-forming suffix is added to a word that already has one or more derivational suffixes:

part   +   -ial   =   partial   +   -ity   =   partiality
(*noun*)   (*adj.*)   (*noun*)

act + -ive = active + -ate = activate + -ion = activation
(*verb*)   (*adj.*)   (*verb*)   (*noun*)

The best-known example of this adding on is that legendary "longest word in English," *antidisestablishmentarianism.* This feature also illustrates another difference between derivational and inflectional suffixes. The inflectional suffixes do not add on in this way. With the exception of the plural and possessive morphemes of nouns, which may appear in combination, the form-class words will have only one inflectional suffix, and it will always come at the end of the word, after any derivational suffixes.

Exercise 20: Transform the following verbs into nouns by adding a derivational suffix. Are there any that have more than one noun form?

1. please   + ___ = _____

2. regulate   + ___ = _____

3. steal   + ___ = _____

4. heal   + ___ = _____

5. derive   + ___ = _____

6. inflect   + ___ = _____

7. form   + ___ = _____

8. revive   + ___ = _____

9. seize   + ___ = _____

10. retire   + ___ = _____

Noun Inflectional Suffixes. The other aspect of form that differentiates the four form classes both from the structure classes and from each other is the set of inflectional morphemes that each form class has. In contrasting English and French verbs in Chapter 2, we saw how relatively free from inflections our verbs are; nouns, too, lack most of the case and gender inflections they once had, variations that make other languages seem so complicated when we study them. Our nouns have only two grammatical inflections, one indicating **number (plural)** and one indicating **case (possessive)**:

		SINGULAR	PLURAL
SINGULAR	PLURAL	POSSESSIVE	POSSESSIVE
cat	cats	cat's	cats'
dog	dogs	dog's	dogs'
horse	horses	horse's	horses'
mouse	mice	mouse's	mice's

The nouns *cat* and *dog* and *horse* illustrate that in speech we can't always distinguish among inflected forms of nouns: *Cats, cat's,* and *cats'* are all pronounced exactly the same. Only in writing can we differentiate the plural from the possessive and from the plural possessive. In the case of *mouse,* with its irregular plural, we of course make the distinction in speech as well as in writing.

The preceding examples illustrate another point about noun inflections: Sometimes the plural inflection is not a single /s/ or /z/ sound, as in *cats* and *dogs.* It may be two sounds, an entire syllable, complete with vowel, as in *horses.* The sound we add is determined by the final sound of the noun. With words ending in what is called a sibilant sound—usually spelled with *s, z, sh,* or *ch*—we must add a syllable to form the -*s* plural (as well as the possessive): kiss*es,* maz*es,* sash*es,* church*es.* (This system is discussed further in Appendix A.)

Exercise 21: The possessive marks are missing from the following noun phrases. Read each one aloud; then punctuate each phrase in two ways to show its two possible meanings.

1. all my teachers assignments
   all my teachers assignments

2. the horses sore legs
   the horses sore legs

3. my sisters husbands business
   my sisters husbands business

4. the Americans great showing in the competition
   the Americans great showing in the competition

5. my sons problems
   my sons problems

Recognizing whether or not the added sound is a complete syllable can be a useful clue in spelling. Spelling the plural and possessive of words that end in an /s/ or /z/ sound is sometimes confusing; they not only sound strange, they tend to look strange when they're written:

Mr. and Mrs. Jones are the Joneses. (*Plural*)
Their cat is the Joneses' cat. (*Possessive*)

To turn *Joneses,* the plural of *Jones,* into the possessive case, we add only the apostrophe because we add no new sound, the usual procedure for possessive plurals: *cats', horses', leaders'.* The possessive of singular nouns ending in *s* can also look strange:

The cats of Ross and Kris are Ross's and Kris's cats.
The nephew of Sis is Sis's nephew.

Here we add the extra syllable when we pronounce the possessive of these words, so we add *'s* when we spell them, the usual procedure for the singular possessive. (We should note that some writers prefer to add only the possessive mark, the apostrophe, even though they add a syllable in speech—*Ross'* and *Kris'* and *Sis';* both spellings are acceptable.) But when the singular has more than one syllable and more than one /s/ or /z/ sound in the last syllable, we generally do not add a sound, so we do not add an *s* when we write the possessive:

> The followers of Jesus are Jesus' followers.
> The laws of Texas are Texas' laws.

A good rule of thumb is this: If the pronunciation does not change when you make a noun possessive, then do not add the -*s* inflection when you spell it; add only the apostrophe.

The plural and possessive inflections provide a test of sorts for "nounness." Can the word be made plural and/or possessive? If so, it's a noun. If not? Well, the possibility for nounness is still there. In applying the inflection test to the nouns in the preceding section, we find that all of the words on the -*ion* list can take the plural inflection, but most of them will not take the possessive *'s*. With many nouns the *of* prepositional phrase is more common than the possessive *'s* inflection: In general, the more specific or concrete the sense of the noun, the more likely it is that the inflections will be acceptable. *Action* and *acquisition* and *delivery* can refer to specific events; when they do, the possessive inflection is possible. We could discuss either the consequences of an action or the "action's consequences." Or when the museum's acquisition of a forgery caused an uproar, we could refer to the aftermath as the "acquisition's aftermath." Likewise, we might be troubled by a particular "delivery's delay." But even in such cases of specific events, the *of* construction is probably more common.

Exercise 22: Transform the *of* possessive phrase into the inflected noun.

1. The son of Mr. Price is Mr. _____ son.

2. The daughter of Ms. Hedges is Ms. _____ daughter.

3. The computer belonging to James is _____ computer.

4. The governor of Massachusetts is _____ governor.

5. The blanket belonging to Linus is _____ blanket.

6. The garden of the neighbor is the _____ garden.

7. The garden of the neighbors is the _____ garden.

8. The curls on the head and tail of Miss Piggy are _____ curls.

9. The club the women belong to is the _____ club.

10. The wisdom of Confucius is _____ wisdom.

The Meaning of the Possessive. In the examples we have seen so far, the relationship between the possessive noun and the headword is actually one of possession, or ownership, but such a relationship is not always the case. As the following examples show, the possessive noun can be simply a description:

an evening's entertainment
a bachelor's degree
today's news

It can also be a measure of value or time:

a day's wages
a moment's notice
a dollar's worth

It can denote origin:

the teacher's suggestion
Lincoln's Gettysburg Address

And sometimes the actual relationship is unclear, even in context:

We admired Van Gogh's portrait.

This possessive could refer either to a portrait *of* the artist or to a portrait *by* the artist.

Irregular Plural Inflections. Before leaving the noun inflections, we should note the many instances of irregular plurals, such as *mice,* in our lexicon. Some are old forms of English that have resisted becoming regularized: *foot–feet, tooth–teeth, man–men, child–children, ox–oxen.* A number of animal and fish names are irregular in that they have no inflection for the plural: *sheep, deer, bass, salmon, trout.* And a large number of borrowed words have retained their foreign plural inflections: *larva–larvae, criterion–criteria, alumnus–alumni, appendix–appendices.* Incidentally, some of these borrowings are now in the process of acquiring regular plurals. *Appendixes* appears along with *appendices; indexes* and *formulas* are even more common than *indices* and *formulae; stadiums* has all but replaced *stadia. Memorandum* is giving way to the shortened *memo,* along with its regular plural, *memos;* and the added complication of gender in *alumnus–alumni* (masculine) and *alumna–alumnae* (feminine) no doubt encourages the use of the simpler, gender-free—and informal—*alum* and *alums.* The borrowed words ending in -*s*—*analysis–analyses, nucleus–nuclei, hypothesis–hypotheses, stimulus–stimuli*—are less likely to lose their foreign inflections; the addition of -*es* to the singular would be cumbersome.

The irregularity of noun inflections, incidentally, applies only to the plural; the possessive follows the regular rule:

SINGULAR	SINGULAR POSSESSIVE	PLURAL	PLURAL POSSESSIVE
man	man's	men	men's
child	child's	children	children's
deer	deer's	deer	deer's
mouse	mouse's	mice	mice's
larva	larva's	larvae	larvae's

Note that these plural possessives look different from regular plural possessives (*dogs'*), only because for regular plural nouns we don't add an -*s* to make the word possessive; the regular plural already has one.

Plural-Only Forms. Some nouns, even when singular in meaning, are plural in form. One such group refers to things that are in two parts—that are bifurcated, or branching: *scissors, shears, pliers, pants, trousers, slacks, shorts, glasses, spectacles.* As subjects of sentences, these nouns present no problems with subject–verb agreement: They take the same verb form as other plural subjects do. Interestingly, even though a pair of shorts is a single garment and a pair of pliers is a single tool, we use the plural pronoun in reference to them:

> I bought a new pair of shorts today; they're navy blue.
> I've lost my pliers; have you seen them?

A different situation arises with certain plural-in-form nouns that are sometimes singular in meaning. A noun such as *physics, mathematics,* and *linguistics,* when referring to an academic discipline or course, is treated as singular:

> Physics is my favorite subject.
> Linguistics is the scientific study of language.

But sometimes such nouns as *mathematics* and *statistics* are used with plural meanings:

> The mathematics involved in the experiment are very theoretical.
> The statistics on poverty levels are quite depressing.

These uses also call for plural pronouns.

Collective Nouns. Nouns such as *family, choir, team, majority, minority*—any noun that names a group of individual members—can be treated as either singular or plural, depending on context and meaning:

> The family have all gone their separate ways.
> The whole family is celebrating the holidays at home this year.
> The majority of our city council members are Republicans.
> The majority always *rules.*

Other singular-in-form nouns, such as *remainder, rest,* and *number,* also have a plural meaning in certain contexts; their number depends on their modifiers:

> The remainder of the job applicants *are* waiting outside.
> The rest of the books *are* being donated to the library.
> A number of customers *have* come early.

This system also applies to certain indefinite pronouns, such as *some, all,* and *enough:*

> Some of the books *were* missing.
> All of the cookies *were* eaten.

Notice what happens to the verb in such sentences when the modifier of the subject headword is singular:

> The rest of the map *was* found.
> Some of the water *is* polluted.
> All of the cake *was* eaten.
> The remainder of this chapter *is* especially important.

The pronoun to use in reference to these noun phrases will depend on the meaning, and it will usually be obvious:

> They (some of the books) were missing.
> It (some of the water) is polluted.

One special problem occurs with the word *none,* which has its origin in the phrase *not one.* Because of that original meaning, many writers insist that *none* always be singular, as *not one* clearly is. However, a more accurate way to assess its meaning is to recognize *none* as the negative, or opposite, of *all* and to treat it in the same way, with its number (whether singular or plural) determined by the number of the modifier or of the referent:

> None of the guests *want* to leave.
> None of the cookies *were* left.
> None of the cake *was* eaten.
> All of the guests *are* staying; none of them *are* leaving.

Semantic Features of Nouns. Nouns can be classified according to certain built-in semantic features that affect their distribution. At an early age children begin this process of classification, recognizing, for example, whether a noun can be counted. We can say "one cookie" or "two cookies"; but a noun like *milk* is not countable. This understanding is evident in the child's selection of determiners:

I want milk.
I want a cookie.
I want some milk.

Within a few short years our linguistic computers have been programmed to make distinctions like this among noun classes that we are hardly aware of. The nonnative speaker, on the other hand, must work conscientiously to make such distinctions. The person who says "I need a new luggage" or "I have a lot of homeworks" or "I am looking forward to a peace and quiet this weekend" has not distinguished between countable and noncountable nouns. Linguists have described these features of our nouns in a hierarchy, each level of which has consequences for selecting determiners and other parts of the sentence:

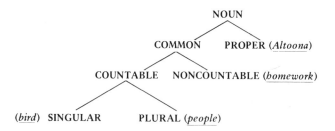

The restrictions built into the word determine its place in the hierarchy; each word carries with it only those features in the higher intersections (or *nodes*) that it is connected with: *Homework* is a noncountable, common noun; *bird* is a singular, countable, common noun. Determiners have related built-in features or restrictions; the determiner *a* (or *an*) includes the features "singular" and "countable," so we are restricted from using it with *homework*. It will signal only those nouns that fit in the lowest, left-hand branch, like *bird*.

As native speakers we also recognize that some nouns appear in both branches of a node, depending on their meaning. For example, some nouns can be both countable and noncountable:

I had a strange experience yesterday.
I've had experience working with animals.

I baked a cake today.
I'll have some cake.

I drink a lot of soda.
I've had three sodas today already.

All nouns have features other than those shown here, features that affect more than just the selection of determiners. The nouns *cake* and *soda,* for instance, carry the feature "solid" and "liquid," respectively. Such features would restrict their use with certain verbs, such as *pour* or *splash* or *cut:* We don't pour or splash cake, nor do we cut soda. The branching system below shows some other features of countable nouns.

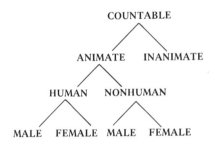

All of the branches at the bottom of the tree can be further branched into "singular" and "plural" and into "child" and "adult."

All of these features affect our use and understanding of words. The animate/inanimate distinction may affect the selection of the verb. A verb such as *notice* or *think,* for example, requires a subject with the feature "animate"; it would not have an inanimate noun such as *rock* or *chair* as its subject. Further, a verb such as *quibble* or *explain* requires still another feature, a "human" as well as "animate" subject; only human animals quibble and explain. The male/female distinction, which is built into many nouns (*woman, man, waiter, waitress, stallion, mare*) will affect the choice of pronouns; and it may also affect other selections, such as adjectives: a *ruddy* complexion, a *lovely* figure.

Our store of words, or **lexicon,** is like a dictionary marked with restrictions and features that define each entry. The definitions not only carry information about the meaning of words, they carry information about the other parts of the sentence with which the word may be combined.

Exercise 23: List all of the nouns in the following passage. Identify any inflectional and derivational morphemes that helped you identify their class.

We hold these truths to be self-evident, that all men are created equal, that they are endowed by their creator with certain unalienable rights, that among these are life, liberty, and the pursuit of happiness.

NOUN	DERIVATIONAL MORPHEMES	INFLECTIONAL MORPHEMES
_____	_____	_____
_____	_____	_____
_____	_____	_____
_____	_____	_____
_____	_____	_____
_____	_____	_____
_____	_____	_____
_____	_____	_____

Do any of the nouns in the passage have no clues of form? How did you recognize them as nouns?

VERBS

The traditional definition of *verb,* like that of *noun,* is based on meaning: a word denoting action, being, or state of being. When we look for the verb in a sentence, we look for the word that tells *what is happening,* and most of the time this method works. But a much more reliable criterion for defining *verb* is that of form. Some verbs have derivational endings that signal that they are verbs; and all verbs, without exception, fit into the verb-expansion rule, the system of adding auxiliaries and inflections described in Chapter 2.

Verb Derivational Affixes. Many of the root words, or bases, that take noun-forming suffixes are verbs to begin with; for example, most of our nouns with *-ion* are formed from verbs. The opposite operation—deriving verbs from other form classes—is less common. We are more likely to turn a noun into a verb without changing its form at all: We *chair* meetings and *table* motions; the carpenter *roofs* the house; the cook *dishes* up the food; the painter *coats* the wall with paint; the gardener *seeds* the lawn and *weeds* the garden; the winemaker *bottles* the wine.

But there are a few verb-forming affixes that combine with certain nouns and adjectives:

type	+	-ify	⟶ typify
dark	+	-en	⟶ darken
active	+	-ate	⟶ activate
legal	+	-ize	⟶ legalize

In addition to these suffixes, the prefixes *en-* and *be-* can turn nouns and adjectives into verbs and can alter the meaning of other verbs: *enable, enact, enchant, encounter, encourage, encrust, endear, enforce, enlighten, enthrone, bedevil, bewitch, besmirch.* But compared with the large number of derivational morphemes that signal nouns, the inventory of verb-forming affixes is fairly small.

Verb Inflectional Suffixes. The verb-expansion rule describes the system of adding auxiliaries and inflectional suffixes to all verbs, without exception. So as a clue in identifying the part of speech we call *verb,* the inflectional system is completely reliable. All verbs, without exception—even those with irregular *-en* and *-ed* forms—have both *-s* and *-ing* forms. This is one of the few rules in English without an exception. This means we can identify a word as a verb simply by noting its *-s* and *-ing* forms. Every verb has the other three forms as well—the base, the *-ed,* and the *-en*—but they may not be as recognizable: Verbs such as *hit* and *put,* for instance, show no changes in form from the base (*hit, put*) to the *-ed* form (*hit, put*) to the *-en* form (*hit, put*). Yet the *-s* and the *-ing* forms are exactly like those of every other verb: *hits, puts, hitting, putting.* The verb inflectional system is so regular, in fact, that we can define *verb* on that basis alone. A word that doesn't have an *-s* or an *-ing* form is simply not a verb.

Exercise 24: Add inflectional endings to demonstrate the "verb-ness" of the following words; then write a sentence using the form of the verb called for.

	BASE	*-s* FORM	*-ed* FORM	*-ing* FORM	*-en* FORM
	TREE	_____	_____	_____	_____
(*-ed*)	_____				
	WATER	_____	_____	_____	_____
(*-s*)	_____				
	ROCK	_____	_____	_____	_____
(*-en*)	_____				
	AIR	_____	_____	_____	_____
(*-ing*)	_____				
	FIRE	_____	_____	_____	_____
(*-en*)	_____				

ADJECTIVES

In terms of form, adjectives are not as easily identifiable in isolation as are nouns and verbs. Often we need either meaning or context for clues. In Chapter 1 we made use of a fairly reliable "adjective test" frame, a way to use the context of a sentence to discover if a word is an adjective:

The ____ NOUN is very ____ .

Only an adjective will fit into both slots. But in some cases the form of the word also provides clues. A number of derivational suffixes signal adjectives.

Adjective Derivational Suffixes. The most reliable derivational suffix identifying a word as an adjective is *-ous:* We know that *gorgeous, porous, courageous,* and *contagious* are adjectives simply on the basis of form. Here are some other adjective-forming suffixes:

-y	merry, funny
-ful	beautiful, wonderful
-ic	terrific, ascetic
-ate	fortunate, temperate
-ish	childish, reddish
-ary	fragmentary, complimentary
-ive	punitive, active
-able	variable, amenable

As clues to adjectives, these suffixes are not as reliable as *-ous,* as they show up occasionally on other form classes too: hand*ful* (noun), pan*ic* (noun, verb), pun*ish* (verb). But it is safe to say that most words with these endings are adjectives.

Adjective Inflectional Suffixes. The inflectional suffixes that pattern with adjectives are *-er,* the sign of the comparative degree, and *-est,* the superlative:

Positive:	young	smart
Comparative:	younger	smarter
Superlative:	youngest	smartest

The *-er* form is used in the comparison of two nouns—that's why this form is called the **comparative** degree:

Mary is <u>younger</u> than Phyllis.
Phyllis is the <u>smarter</u> of the two.

The comparative degree with *than* can also be followed by a clause rather than a noun phrase:

Mary is younger <u>than I suspected.</u>

The -*est* form, the **superlative** degree, is used when singling out one of more than two nouns:

Tom was the <u>oldest</u> person in the room.
Of the three candidates, Sarah is the <u>smartest</u>.

A small group of words that take these inflections can serve as either adjectives or adverbs, so the inflectional test is not completely reliable in identifying a word as an adjective:

early	fast	late	high
earlier	faster	later	higher
earliest	fastest	latest	highest
hard	long	low	deep
harder	longer	lower	deeper
hardest	longest	lowest	deepest

Another word we could add to this list is *near* (*nearer, nearest*), which can serve not only as an adjective and an adverb, but also as a preposition ("Our seats were *near* the fifty-yard line")—the only preposition that takes inflections. In short, the possibility of making a word comparative or superlative is not exclusive to adjectives.

For many adjectives the comparative and superlative degrees are not formed with -*er* and -*est* but with *more* and *most,* which we can think of as alternative forms, or allomorphs, of the morphemes -*er* and -*est*. In fact, adjectives of more than one syllable generally pattern with *more* and *most,* with certain exceptions: two-syllable adjectives ending in -*y* or -*ly* (*prettiest, friendlier, lovelier*); some ending in -*le* (*nobler, noblest*), -*ow* (*narrower, narrowest*), and -*er* (*tenderest*).

But *more* and *most* are not exclusive to adjectives either. The -*ly* adverbs, those derived from adjectives, also have comparative and superlative versions: *more quickly, most frequently.* And there are some adjectives, such as *former, main,* and *principal,* that have no comparative and superlative forms.

In spite of all of these limitations, we have no difficulty distinguishing adjectives in sentences. First of all, we know the positions they fill in the sentence patterns—as subjective and objective complements and in noun phrases as prenoun modifiers. And although nouns can also fill all of these slots, the differences in the form of nouns and adjectives make it easy to distinguish between them.

On the subject of the comparative and superlative degrees, we should also note that adjectives can be compared in a negative sense with *as, less,* and *least:*

> This picnic is not <u>as exciting as</u> I thought it would be.
> This picnic is <u>less exciting than</u> I thought it would be.
> This is the <u>least exciting</u> picnic I've ever attended.

(A different version of the first sentence would be "The picnic is *about as exciting* as I expected" or, simply, "The picnic is *as exciting as* I expected," both of which may convey a somewhat negative meaning.)

We should also note some exceptions to the regular comparative and superlative forms:

good	bad	far	far
better	worse	farther	further
best	worst	farthest	furthest

Exercise 25: Fill in the blanks with the comparative and superlative degrees of the adjectives listed. Do any of them require *more* and *most?*

POSITIVE	COMPARATIVE	SUPERLATIVE
friendly	_____	_____
helpful	_____	_____
staunch	_____	_____
wise	_____	_____
awful	_____	_____
rich	_____	_____
mellow	_____	_____
expensive	_____	_____
valid	_____	_____
pure	_____	_____

able _____ _____

cheap _____ _____

Subclasses of Adjectives. The adjective test frame (The ___
NOUN is very ___), which is useful in identifying adjectives, is also
useful in helping distinguish subclasses of adjectives: those that are
limited to the prenoun slot and those that are limited to the complement slots.

There are actually three slots that adjectives fill in the sentence patterns: as subjective and objective complements (where they are called
predicative adjectives) and as modifiers in the noun phrase (where
they are called **attributive** adjectives). Most adjectives can fill all three
slots; the test frame uses two of them: attributive and subjective complement.

But a small number will not fill the complement slots. The following adjectives are attributive only: *main, principal, former, atomic, late*
(meaning "dead"), and such technical adjectives as *sulfuric* and *hydro-
chloric.* These do not serve as either subjective or objective complements in the verb phrase, nor do they take qualifiers, such as *very:*

He is the former president.
*The president is former.
*My reason is main.
*My main reason is very main.

Many of the so-called A-adjectives—*ablaze, afraid, aghast, alone,
awake, aware*—are predicative only:

The house was <u>ablaze</u>.
*The <u>ablaze</u> house burned down in an hour.

The children were <u>awake</u>.
*The <u>awake</u> children were noisy.

There are a few others—*fond, ready, ill, well*—that rarely appear in
attributive position in reference to animate nouns. We may refer to a
"ready wit" but rarely to a "ready person." We may talk about an "ill

omen" but rarely an "ill person"; we are more likely to say a "sick person."

Incidentally, not all predicative adjectives take *very,* the sample qualifier in the test frame. We probably wouldn't say "very afraid" or "very awake"; we would be more likely to say "very much afraid" or "very much awake." But these adjectives do combine with other qualifiers: *quite* afraid, *extremely* afraid, *completely* awake, *wide* awake.

A number of adjectives in predicative position appear frequently with complements in the form of phrases or clauses; some adjectives, such as *fond* and *aware,* are rarely used without them:

> The children were afraid that the dog would bite.
> The children were aware that the dog would bite.
> The dog was fond of biting children.
> We were conscious of the problem.
> *The dog was fond.

Another subclassification of adjectives relates to their ability to combine with qualifiers. Certain adjectives denote meanings that are absolute in nature: *unique, round, square, perfect, single, double.* These can fill both the attributive and predicate slots, but they generally cannot be qualified or compared:

> The plan is unique.
> *The plan is very unique.
> The plan is very unusual.
> *My plan is more unique than yours.
> My plan is more unorthodox than yours.

Unique means "one of a kind"; there are no degrees of uniqueness, just as there are no degrees of roundness: Something is either round or it's not. Because of this absolute meaning, many writers avoid such phrases as "more perfect" or "very round."

ADVERBS

Of all the form classes, adverbs are the hardest to pin down in terms of both form and position. Many of them have no distinguishing affixes, and except in Pattern I they fill no required slots in the sentence patterns. (Certain verbs in Patterns VI and VII, however—among them, *put, set,* and *lay*—do require adverbials.) The fact that adverbs are often movable is perhaps their most distinguishing characteristic.

Adverb Derivational Suffixes. One common indicator of form we do have is the derivational suffix -*ly*, which we use to derive adverbs of manner from adjectives—adverbs that tell *how* or *in what way* about the verb:

> He walked slowly.
> She answered correctly.

But -*ly* is not completely reliable as a signaler of adverbs; it also occurs on nouns (*folly, bully*) and on adjectives (*friendly, homely, godly, lovely, ugly*). But we are safe in saying that most -*ly* words are adverbs, simply because there are so many adjectives that we can turn into adverbs with this addition.

There are some restrictions on this derivational process, however: Not all adjectives can become manner adverbs. These restrictions are related to meaning. Some adjectives describe a state, such as *tall* and *old,* or a fixed or inherent characteristic, such as *Norwegian;* others describe characteristics that change, such as *weak, active,* and *industrious.* Another distinction can be drawn between objective characteristics, such as *tall* and *old,* and subjective ones, such as *nice* and *splendid.* The adjectives that refer to objective or stative or inherent qualities rarely become manner adverbs: *tall, old, fat, young, short, thick, large, flat, round, red.* When they do, they are likely to have a specialized, often metaphorical, meaning: *shortly, hardly, flatly, squarely, widely.* These usages cause problems for nonnative speakers who fail to distinguish them from the majority of manner adverbs that mean simply "in the manner of":

> *helpfully* = in a helpful manner
> *actively* = in an active manner
> *firmly* = in a firm manner

However, *squarely* usually means "exactly" (He hit the nail squarely on the head); *flatly* usually means "unequivocally" (He flatly refused).

Besides -*ly*, three other derivational suffixes produce adverbs: -*ward,*

-like, and *-wise*. Words ending in *-ward* signal direction: *homeward, forward, backward, upward, downward*. The others generally indicate manner: *-like* is a cognate of *-ly*—*birdlike, wavelike; -wise* words include both old usages, such as *otherwise, lengthwise*, and *crosswise*, and new ones that are considered by some writers as unnecessary jargon, such as *budgetwise, weatherwise, moneywise*, and *profitwise*.

Adverb Inflectional Suffixes. The comparative and superlative inflections, *-er* and *-est* (or their alternate forms *more* and *most*), combine with adverbs as well as with adjectives, although in a much more limited way. In the discussion of adjectives, we listed a few words that serve as both adjectives and adverbs: *early, late, hard, fast, long, high, low, deep*, and *near*. These are simply adverbs made from adjectives without the addition of *-ly;* they are referred to as **flat adverbs.** Except for a few others such as *soon* and *often*, they are the only adverbs that take *-er* and *-est;* most of the *-ly* adverbs take *more* and, occasionally, *most* in forming the comparative and superlative degrees.

A great many adverbs have neither derivational nor inflectional affixes that distinguish them as adverbs. Instead, we recognize them by the information they provide, by their position in the sentence, and often by their movability:

Time: now, today, nowadays, yesterday, then, already
Duration: always, still
Frequency: often, seldom, never, sometimes, always
Place: there, here, everywhere, somewhere, upstairs
Direction: away, thence
Concession: still, yet

There are also a number of words without form distinctions that can serve as either prepositions or adverbs: *above, around, behind, below, down, in, inside, out, outside, up.*

Exercise 26: Demonstrate the class of the following words by adding the inflectional endings that will combine with them.

launch _____

staunch _____

paunch _____

deep _____

keep _____

jeep _____

nice _____

rice _____

splice _____

SUMMARY

In this chapter we have looked at the four form classes—nouns, verbs, adjectives, and adverbs—called "form classes" because, for the most part, these words are distinguishable by their form. These are the open classes; they regularly get new membership as the language has need of new words. They are the classes that provide the semantic content of the language, the bricks; in the next chapter we will look at the structure classes, the mortar that binds the form-class words together.

Exercise 27: Fill in the blanks with variations of the words shown on the chart, changing or adding derivational morphemes to change the word class.

	NOUN	VERB	ADJECTIVE	ADVERB
1.	grief	_____	_____	_____
2.	_____	vary	_____	_____
3.	_____	_____	_____	ably
4.	_____	defend	_____	_____
5.	economy	_____	_____	_____
6.	_____	_____	pleasant	_____
7.	type	_____	_____	_____

8. _____	prohibit _____	_____	_____
9. _____	_____	_____	long _____
10. _____	_____	valid _____	_____
11. _____	appreciate _____	_____	_____
12. beauty _____	_____	_____	_____
13. _____	accept _____	_____	_____
14. _____	_____	pure _____	_____
15. _____	continue _____	_____	_____

QUESTIONS FOR DISCUSSION

1. A government spokesman recently used the following clauses in a discussion of the economy:

> When we were approaching crunch. . . .
> When push comes to shove. . . . —> *semantic shift*

What part of speech are *crunch, push,* and *shove?*

2. In response to a question about Egypt's agreement with Israel, President Sadat made the following statement:

> Some parts we're not very glad with, and some we'd like to see with different languages.

What particular "rules" was he having trouble with? In what way do those problems illustrate the arbitrariness of English?

3. In what sentence patterns would you classify the following sentences?

> Tell me your problem.
> Explain your problem to me.

Can you switch the two verbs?

> Explain me your problem.
> Tell your problem to me.

Can you substitute *it* for *your problem* in all of the sentences?

4. One possible branch in the noun hierarchy on page 105 is that of animate/inanimate. How would you classify the nouns *breeze* and *wind*? What happens to their classification when we say "The breeze sang a lullaby" and "The wind whistled a tune"? In discussing poetry, we use the word *personification*. In terms of the noun hierarchy, what does it mean?

5. Consider what you know about sentence patterns and the subject–verb relationship. Then explain the label *double-sided verb* in connection with the following:

> She photographs well.
> The book is selling well.

Write a sentence in which *read* is double-sided. Can linking verbs also be classed as double-sided?

> The fur feels soft.
> The soup tastes good.

6. The traditional Latin term for possessive case is *genitive*. Consider the relationship between the possessive noun and its headword in the following noun phrases:

> the teacher's explanation
> the car's overhaul

Explain what is meant by *subjective genitive* and *objective genitive*.
Now consider the following ambiguous sentence:

> I was disturbed about Tom's punishment.

What is the source of the ambiguity?

7. We looked briefly at adjectives that pattern with complements:

> We were <u>conscious</u> of the problem.
> The kids were <u>afraid</u> that they would miss the party.
> Joe is <u>determined</u> to win the race.
> The dog was <u>fond</u> of biting children.

What do these adjectives have in common? Tell which of the following adjectives will pattern with complements: *young, big, pretty, green, slow, nice, splendid, British, disgusting, tired, cylindrical*. What generalization can you make about the system?

8. The following sets of sentences illustrate further restrictions on adjectives:

The trees are high.	The grass is high.
The trees are tall.	The grass is tall.
*The trees are long.	The grass is long.

Consider the way we use these same adjectives for describing mountains, buildings, tree trunks, weeds, fence posts, and flagpoles. Could the restrictions be related to semantic features of the nouns?

9. We often use verbs adjectivally, as noun modifiers, as we will see in Chapter 9. But many words that look like verbs—that were, in fact, originally verbs—now have the characteristics of adjectives. We have said that we can identify a word as an adjective if it can fit into the adjective test frame (The ____ NOUN is very ____). We also have an inflectional test for adjectives: Can the word be made comparative and superlative? Using those two tests, identify the underlined words in the following sentences: Are they adjectives or verbs?

Joe took the <u>broken</u> chair to the dump.
That <u>disgusting</u> movie wasn't worth five dollars.
The football rally was <u>exciting</u>.
I feel <u>tired</u>.
Joe was <u>drunk</u> last night.
Many <u>working</u> mothers have problems with day-care.
The <u>decorated</u> tree looks beautiful.

10. Sometimes verbs are used as nouns (gerunds), as we shall see in Chapter 10. What test can you apply to the following words to test their part of speech? Are they verbs or nouns?

The <u>meeting</u> was boring.
Julie looked lovely at her <u>wedding</u>.
The committee's <u>finding</u> surprised everyone.
<u>Jogging</u> is good exercise.

11. If words have only one inflectional suffix (except in the case of plural possessive nouns), how do we account for words like *meetings, leavings,* and *betters?*

12. Explain the ambiguity of the following sentence in terms of its possible sentence patterns and its parts of speech:

My mother is always entertaining.

13. Certain adjectives are restricted from the prenoun position and others from the complement positions. How shall we classify *occasional, criminal,* and *medical?*

14. In the discussion questions following Chapter 2, we applied the terms *volition* and *nonvolition*—i.e., the power of choice—to adjectives. The adjective *careless* describes a condition under control of the will; such conditions as *short* and *tall,* on the other hand, cannot be willed. Can this distinction also be useful in describing the restrictions on deriving adverbs from adjectives? Which adjectives can or cannot take *-ly?*

15. Careful writers avoid writing sentences like the following:

There have been less traffic accidents in the county this year.
I have also noticed an increase in the amount of bicyclists on the roads.

Where in the noun hierarchy on p. 104 would you find *accidents* and *bicyclists?* How does *fewer* differ from *less* and *number* from *amount?* How can these sentences be improved?

16. The dictionary labels *today* as both an adverb and a noun. Are those labels based on form or function? How should we define *yesterday* and *tomorrow?* Are they also members of both classes? Examine the following passage from *Macbeth* to see how Shakespeare used the words:

Tomorrow, and tomorrow, and tomorrow
Creeps in this petty pace from day to day
To the last syllable of recorded time,
And all our yesterdays have lighted fools
The way to dusty death.

17. In this chapter we have seen how easy it is to turn verbs into nouns by adding derivational morphemes. In his book *Style: Ten Lessons in Clarity and Grace*, Joseph M. Williams shows how easily such nominalizations can detract from clear writing. The following sentences violate what Williams calls the first principle of clear writing: "Try to state who's doing what in the subject of your sentence, and try to state what that who is doing in your verb."

Determination of foreign policy takes place at the presidential level.
A need for a reevaluation of his condition by a doctor exists.
We had a discussion of the matter.
We conducted an investigation of it.

There will be a suspension of these programs by the dean until his evaluation of their progress has occurred.

Identify the nominalized verbs in the sentences. Then rewrite them following Williams' principle of clear writing.

6

The
Structure Classes

In contrast to the large, open form classes, the categories of words known as structure classes are small, comprising only a few hundred members in all. These classes are also closed. Although new words regularly enter the language as nouns and verbs as the need arises for new vocabulary, the structure classes—determiners, prepositions, auxiliaries, and the like—remain constant from one generation to the next. As native speakers we pay little attention to the structure words, and until we hear a nonnative speaker struggling with them, we probably don't appreciate the importance of the grammatical sense that they contribute.

Part of that grammatical sense comes from the stress–unstress pattern of speech, the rhythm of the language. Most structure words are unstressed: They have the lowest volume, providing valleys between the peaks of loudness that fall on the stressed syllables of the form-class words. One reason we must listen so carefully in order to understand the inexperienced foreign speaker—and often the experienced one as well—is the breakdown of that signaling system. When structure words are given equal stress, their role as signaler tends to be lost.

The first three structure classes we will look at are those that signal specific form classes: determiners, the signalers of nouns; auxiliaries, the signalers of verbs; and qualifiers, the signalers of adjectives and adverbs. Then we will look at prepositions and conjunctions, both of which have connective roles; interrogatives, the signalers of questions; and expletives, which serve as structural operators of various kinds.

DETERMINERS

Chapter 5 on "The Form Classes" opened with a sentence lacking all of the structure words: *Boy wants drink water.* Most noticeably missing are the determiners, the signalers of nouns. **Determiners** signal nouns in a variety of ways: They may define the *relationship* of the noun to the speaker or listener (or reader); they may identify the noun as *specific* or *general;* they may *quantify* it specifically or refer to quantity in general. Following are the most common classes of determiners, many of which have appeared in our sample sentences:

ARTICLES	POSSESSIVE NOUNS	DEMONSTRATIVE PRONOUNS	NUMBERS
the	John's	this/these	one
a(n)	my son's	that/those	two
	etc.		etc.

POSSESSIVE PRONOUNS		INDEFINITE PRONOUNS			
my	its	several	few	each	all
your	our	little	fewer	every	both
his	their	many	more	either	some
her	whose	much	most	neither	any
		enough	less	no	

We should note that possessive nouns as determiners retain their own determiners: *my son's* teacher; *the week's* groceries; *our cat's* fur.

Many of the features of nouns in the hierarchy shown on page 104 affect our selection of determiners. A noun appearing in the lowest, left-hand branch of the diagram, for example—a singular, countable noun—rarely appears without a determiner:

This cookie tastes good.
*Cookie tastes good.

John is my friend.
*John is friend.

There are certain exceptions to this rule. For example, the nouns *town, school,* and *car* are singular, countable nouns; nevertheless, in some prepositional phrases they appear without determiners:

> the other side of town
> going to school
> the best kind of car

These exceptions present no problems for native speakers, of course. We're used to the sometimes arbitrary nature of the determiner:

> We say, "I walked to town," but not "I walked to city."
> We say, "I have a cold," but not "I have a flu."
> We say, "I attend college," but not "I attend university."
> We say, "I'm going into town," but not "I'm going into hospital."

(The British, incidentally, do "go into hospital," "attend university," and "look out of window.")

The difficulty for the nonnative speaker comes with learning which nouns are countable nouns and which are not. Other complications arise in selecting the determiners because, like all of the words in our lexicon, determiners have built-in restrictions. Some will signal only plural nouns (*these, those, many, few, several*), some only singular nouns (*a, one, each, either, neither, every*), some only noncountables (*much, less*), and others only countables (*few, many, a, one*).

Another fairly regular rule concerns the limitation of determiners with certain noncountable nouns, sometimes called **mass nouns,** such as *luggage, furniture, beer, cake, sugar, rice, coal, steel, water.* When mass nouns are used as noncountable, they cannot be plural, so they do not combine with determiners that have either the "plural" or "countable" feature: *a, one, two, these, several, many.*

> *These furnitures are sturdy.
> *Many furnitures are expensive.
> *Each furniture has its own charm.

Some determiners have both countable and noncountable features built into them (*this, some, most, all*), so they can combine with both kinds of nouns:

This furniture is lovely.
This chair is comfortable.
Some furniture is expensive.
Some chairs are expensive.
Most chocolate cake is high in calories.
Most coconut macaroons are delicious.
All polluted water is undrinkable.
All rules are not necessarily good rules.

The nonnative speaker must consciously learn these features of both nouns and determiners. But a further complication arises when these mass nouns take on countable meanings:

These whole-grain flours are popular now.
The light beers are getting better all the time.

Abstract nouns also present problems for the nonnative speaker because they may appear either with or without determiners:

I have finally regained peace of mind.
I have finally regained my peace of mind.

In some cases the determiner is tied to the presence of a modifier, such as a *that* clause:

*The peace of mind is hard to acquire in these insecure times.
The peace of mind that comes with financial security is my goal.

Even a proper noun may require a determiner when it has certain kinds of modifiers:

The Altoona of my childhood was a railroad town.

Finally, some determiners are extremely versatile. The **definite article,** *the,* can signal all classes of nouns that can take determiners when the definite meaning is called for—unlike the **indefinite** *a,* which is restricted to countables. The possessives, too—both nouns and pronouns—are wide-ranging, without built-in distribution restrictions.

Exercise 28: Underline the determiners in the following sentences.

1. My sister doesn't have enough money for her ticket.
2. John's roommate went home for the weekend.
3. Every course I'm taking this term has a midterm exam.
4. Bill spent more money on the week's groceries than he expected to.
5. I spend less time studying now than I did last term.
6. I haven't seen either movie, so I have no preference.

The Expanded Determiner. A determiner is not always a single word. In fact, we can think of the determiner slot itself as a series of slots with optional pre- and postdeterminers. The following formula will account for some fairly common **expanded determiners,** although a description that accounted for all of the possibilities would be far more complex. This simplified scheme, however, should help you appreciate the intricacies of the grammar rules built into your linguistic computer.

(predeterminer) **+ DETERMINER +** (postdeterminer)

		ORDINAL NUMBERS	CARDINAL NUMBERS
all (of)	the	first	one
both (of)	a	second	two
half (of)	my	etc.	etc.
only	these	next	
especially	etc.	last	
just			
double			

The pre- and postdeterminers are, of course, optional, so they are shown in parentheses in the formula.

In the following sentences, the pre- and postdeterminers are underlined; the determiner is capitalized:

All of THE cookies disappeared.
Only MY pretzels disappeared.

THE first ten students in line were chosen.
Only THE next two students complained.
Both (of) THESE students wrote A papers.
Half (of) THE class took part in the demonstration.
I have just ENOUGH gas for the trip.

Another type of expanded determiner is the phrasal quantifier; it can occur with either countable or noncountable nouns:

a lot of classes
a lot of homework
a great many friends
a large number of people

In terms of **subject–verb agreement,** it is the number of the noun—whether singular or plural—that determines the verb: homework *is;* classes (friends, people) *are.*

We also have a large open class of quantifying noun phrases that we use with noncountable nouns; they enable us to count those noncountables:

a quart of milk
a pound of butter
a piece of furniture
a spoonful of sugar

When these noun phrases are subjects, their number is determined by the number of the quantifier: *two quarts* of milk *are; a quart* of milk *is.* We might, in fact, be tempted to call the quantifiers the headwords of these noun phrases, just as we would call *end* and *back* the headwords in the following:

the end of the alley
the back of my hand

The traditional diagram would, in fact, treat these noun phrases and those with the quantifiers in the same way, with the *of* phrase as a modifier of the noun, even though the quantifiers are much more clearly functioning as determiners.

Despite such questions of analysis, however, as native speakers we know intuitively how to follow our determiner "rules," as complicated and arbitrary as they sometimes are.

Exercise 29: In the following sentences, circle the pre- and postdeterminers; identify the subclass of the main determiner.

1. Professor Brown assigned only one term paper.
2. I spent all of my money on books.
3. The first two chapters of the book were fascinating.
4. The next three chapters were even better.
5. Only that last chapter was difficult to read.

AUXILIARIES

Like the determiners and the other structure classes, the **auxiliary** class is limited in membership and closed to new members. Counting the forms of *have* and *be,* the modals, and the forms of *do,* the list of regular auxiliaries numbers around two dozen:

have	be	can	do
has	is	could	does
had	are	will	did
having	am	would	
	was	shall	
	were	should	
	been	may	
	being	might	
		must	
		ought to	

The following modal-like verbs also sometimes act as auxiliaries:

have to	get	keep
has to	gets	keeps
had to	got	kept

He <u>has to</u> go.
She <u>got</u> going.
She <u>got</u> to go.
They <u>kept</u> going.

Two other modal-like verbs, *dare* and *need,* commonly appear in negative sentences and in questions:

She <u>need</u> not go.
I <u>don't dare</u> go.
<u>Dare</u> we go?
<u>Need</u> you go?

The auxiliaries differ somewhat from the other classes of structure words in both form and function. With only two exceptions, *must* and *ought to,* the auxiliaries have inflectional variations that signal changes in meaning. Because *have* and *be,* our most frequently used auxiliaries, can also fill the verb slot, they of course have all of the usual verb inflections. *Be* has even more than usual, with its eight forms. Even the stand-in auxiliary *do* and the other marginal modals undergo inflectional variations in their auxiliary roles. So in terms of their form, auxiliaries are very much like the form-class words.

In function, the auxiliaries are perhaps more intimately connected to verbs than are determiners to nouns, because they alter the verb's meaning in important ways and often determine the form that it takes. Forms of *have* require the *-en* form of the main verb and forms of *be* the *-ing* form—or, in the case of the passive transformation (see Chapter 2), the *-en* form.

Another important difference between the auxiliaries and the other structure classes lies in their systematic distribution. Determiners and qualifiers are somewhat arbitrary in distribution; but with few exceptions every verb can be signaled (preceded) by every auxiliary. The modals and *have* and *do* combine with every verb; only *be* is restricted in any way, as we saw in Chapter 2, where we noted a few verbs, such as *seem,* that rarely appear with *be* + *-ing.* This regularity accounts for the relative ease with which nonnative speakers are able to learn the compound verb forms of English.

Exercise 30: Underline the auxiliaries in the following sentences. Circle the main verb.

1. I have been having problems with my car.
2. Many women don't dare walk alone in this neighborhood after dark.
3. I should never eat tomatoes.
4. Apparently some people can't even look at them.
5. Sally will be helping us with the party.
6. Margie has to leave early.
7. The kids are really frustrating me today.
8. The teens can be frustrating years for some adolescents.
9. Bill didn't register his car before the deadline.
10. Mine has been registered for months.

QUALIFIERS

As the following lists demonstrate, there are many words that can act as **qualifiers** or **intensifiers** to alter the meaning of adjectives and adverbs. (In the adjective test frame the word *very* is used to represent all the possible qualifiers.)

In the traditional classification of parts of speech, these modifiers of adjectives and adverbs are classed with the adverbs. However, we are limiting our use of the label *adverb* to modifiers of verbs, that is, to those words that add to the verb information of time, place, frequency, cause, manner, and the like. We separate the two classes, adverbs and qualifiers, because, except for a few words such as *really* that serve both functions ("I really tried," "I tried really hard"), they tend to be mutually exclusive classes. In American English we rarely use *very* or *quite* or *extremely* to modify verbs; they generally qualify or intensify adjectives and adverbs:

> We walked very slowly.
> *We walked very.
> He tried quite hard.
> *He quite tried.

The following list of qualifiers can be used with the positive form of most adjectives, such as *good* and *soft,* and with adverbs of manner, such as *rapidly:*

very	really	fairly
quite	pretty	mighty
rather	awfully	too

A second group of qualifiers can be used with the comparative degree of adjectives, such as *better* and *nicer,* and with comparative adverbs, such as *sooner, later, nearer,* and *farther:*

still	some	no
even	much	

And there are a number of others that have a limited distribution:

right now	just about there
wide awake	almost there
just so	

Many others are used in colloquial expressions:

right nice	darn right
damn sure	real pretty

Some of the adverbs of manner, the *-ly* adverbs, are themselves used as qualifiers with certain adjectives:

dangerously close	politically expedient
particularly harmful	technically possible
absolutely true	especially difficult

Because of the *-ly* adverbs in their ranks, the qualifier class is not as closed as the other structure classes.

In their relationship to the form classes, the qualifiers are different from the determiners and auxiliaries in that they are optional; all of the *present participle* (handwritten annotation)

past participle (handwritten annotation)

adjectives and adverbs they modify can appear without them. This is not true of the relationship of nouns and verbs to their signal words: Many nouns cannot appear without a determiner; and two of our verb forms—the *-en* and the *-ing* forms—require auxiliaries to function as the main verb. But like the other structure words, the qualifiers signal the form classes; they provide a useful test to differentiate adjectives and adverbs from other parts of speech.

Exercise 31: Add *quite, rather,* or *very* to each of the following sentences. Is the word that you qualified an adjective or an adverb?

	ADJ OR ADV?
1. I felt tired after work.	_____
2. We worked fast cleaning the house.	_____
3. The assignment we got today was ridiculous.	_____
4. Frankly, I know nothing about gardening.	_____
5. Our dog is intelligent.	_____
6. The students worked well together on their class project.	_____

PREPOSITIONS

The **preposition** (meaning "placed before") is a structure word found in pre-position to—preceding—a noun phrase. Prepositions are among our most common words in English; in fact, of our twenty most frequently used words, eight are prepositions: *of, to, in, for, with, on, at,* and *by.* [1] Prepositions can be classified according to form as simple (one-word) or phrasal (multiple-word):

---

[1] This frequency count, based on a collection of 1,014,232 words, is published in Henry Kučera and W. Nelson Francis, *Computational Analysis of Present-Day English* (Providence, R.I.: Brown University Press, 1967).

Simple Prepositions. The following list includes the most common simple prepositions:

about	beneath	into	through
above	beside	like	throughout
across	between	near	till
after	beyond	of	to
against	but (except)	off	toward
along	by	on	under
among	concerning	onto	underneath
around	down	out	until
as	during	over	up
at	except	past	upon
before	for	per	with
behind	from	regarding	within
below	in	since	without

in front of
in back of

Note that we label these words as prepositions only when they are followed by a noun phrase—that is, only when they are part of prepositional phrases. In the following sentence, for example, *up* functions as an adverb, not a preposition:

The price of sugar went <u>up</u> again.

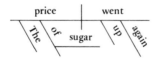

Words like *up* also function as particles in two-word, or phrasal, verbs, such as *hold up:*

A masked gunman <u>held up</u> the liquor store.

But in the following sentence, *up* is a preposition, part of a prepositional phrase:

We hiked <u>up the steep trail</u>.

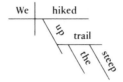

Phrasal Prepositions. Some phrasal prepositions are simply two prepositions combined to produce a third meaning:

along with	but for	out of
up to	off of	

Many of the phrasal prepositions are combinations of other parts of speech with prepositions:

according to	in place of
because of	in spite of
in accordance with	instead of
in connection with	in regard to
in front of	on account of
in lieu of	on top of

In a traditional diagram, we usually treat these phrases as we do the simple prepositions:

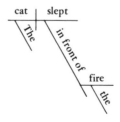

Because *in front of the fire* can also be analyzed as one prepositional phrase embedded in another, we can diagram it another way:

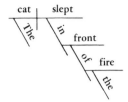

The above lists include the most common, although certainly not all, of the prepositions. We use prepositions automatically, as we do the other structure words, in spite of the sometimes subtle differences in meaning they can express: *below* the stairs, *beneath* the stairs, *under* the stairs, *underneath* the stairs; *in* the room, *inside* the room, *within* the room. As native speakers we understand these distinctions, and, except for a few idioms that sometimes cause problems of usage, we rarely hesitate in selecting the right preposition for the occasion.

Exercise 32: Underline the prepositions in the following sentences.

1. The Browns have lived in Memphis since 1977.
2. They like it there because of the hot weather.
3. I like Memphis in spite of the heat.
4. According to the latest government figures, the cost of rearing a child rose to $85,000 during the 1970s.
5. I look on such statistics with skepticism.

CONJUNCTIONS

We use **conjunctions** to connect words and phrases and clauses within the sentence and to connect the sentences themselves. Within the sentence our most common connectors are the simple **coordinating** conjunctions and the **correlative** conjunctions. For joining sentences we use, in addition, the **subordinating** conjunctions, also called subordinators, and **conjunctive adverbs**. **Relative pronouns** also function as connectors, joining relative, or adjectival, clauses to nouns; **relative adverbs** introduce both adjectival and adverbial clauses.

Coordinating conjunctions: *and, or, but, yet, for, nor*
Correlative conjunctions: *both–and, either–or, neither–nor, not only–but also*
Conjunctive adverbs: *however, therefore, moreover, nevertheless, so, then, likewise, yet,* etc.
Simple subordinators: *after, although, as, because, before, if, like, since, when, while,* etc.
Phrasal subordinators: *as if, as long as, as soon as, even though, in order that, provided that,* etc.
Relative pronouns: *who, whose, whom, which, that*
Relative adverbs: *where, when, why*

Coordinating Conjunctions. We can use a coordinate structure for any slot in the sentence by using a coordinating conjunction:

> John and Tim worked out on Saturday.
> I'll meet you at the ticket window or in the grandstand.
> The dessert was simple yet elegant.
> Eager to start the new job but sad at the thought of leaving home, Jason packed the car and drove away from the familiar row of houses on Ruskin Lane.

The coordinating conjunctions also join complete sentences:

> I disapproved of his betting on the horses, and I told him so.
> He claims to have won fifty dollars, but I suspect he's exaggerating.
> She won't come to the party, nor will she explain why.

Notice that the clause introduced by *nor* requires a subject–auxiliary shift.

Correlative Conjunctions. Like the coordinating conjunctions, the correlatives connect both complete sentences and elements within the sentence. Within the sentence *either–or* and *neither–nor* are used alike:

$$ I \; will \left\{ \begin{array}{c} either \\ neither \end{array} \right\} meet \; you \; in \; the \; lobby \left\{ \begin{array}{c} or \\ nor \end{array} \right\} come \; to \; your $$

room.

As a connector of sentences, *neither–nor* requires the subject–auxiliary shift; *either–or* does not:

> Neither <u>will I</u> meet you in the lobby, nor <u>will I</u> come to your room.
> Either I <u>will</u> meet you in the lobby, or <u>I will</u> come to your room.

Structures connected by the correlatives should be parallel, with both members of the conjunction introducing structures of the same form, such as verb phrases or noun phrases:

> He <u>both</u> tried <u>and</u> succeeded.
> <u>Either</u> run slowly <u>or</u> walk fast.
> I want <u>neither</u> the pudding <u>nor</u> the shortcake.

But in the case of complete sentences, the following are also common, especially in speech, where the *either* and *neither* come after the subject in one clause, even though the *or* and *nor* come before it in the next:

> I <u>will</u> neither meet you in the lobby, <u>nor will I</u> come to your
> room.
> I <u>will</u> either meet you in the lobby, <u>or I will</u> come to your room.

Not only–but also can be used both within and between sentences.

> <u>Not only</u> the coaches and players but <u>also</u> the fans had high hopes of defeating the Crimson Tide.
> <u>Not only</u> did the government's economists underestimate the level of inflation that the 1980s would bring, <u>but</u> they <u>also</u> delayed in taking action to bring it under control.

This sentence would be equally grammatical with either *but* or *also,* rather than both.

Both–and does not connect complete sentences; it connects elements within the sentence only:

> Franco is a good sport, <u>both</u> on <u>and</u> off the playing field.
> <u>Both</u> Jeanne <u>and</u> Marie worked hard to get their manuscript finished on schedule.

Conjunctive Adverbs (Adverbial Conjunctions). As their name suggests, the conjunctive adverbs join sentences to form coordinate structures as other conjunctions do, but they do so with an adverbial emphasis. The following list includes not only the conjunctive adverbs listed earlier but also certain simple adverbs (*also, instead*) and adverbial prepositional phrases (*in the meantime, on the contrary*) that function as sentence connectors:

Result: *therefore, so, consequently, as a result*
Concession: *however, nevertheless, yet, at any rate*
Apposition: *for example, that is*
Addition: *moreover, furthermore, also, in addition*
Time: *meanwhile, in the meantime*
Contrast: *instead, on the contrary, on the other hand*

Conjunctive adverbs differ from other conjunctions in that, like many other adverbials, they tend to be movable; they need not introduce the clause:

> My tax accountant is not cheap; <u>however,</u> the amount of tax she saves me is far greater than her fee.
> My tax accountant is not cheap; the amount of tax she saves me, <u>however,</u> is far greater than her fee.

Subordinating Conjunctions. The subordinators are conjunctions, too, although their function is not to connect independent ideas as equals but rather to show a relationship between two ideas in which one of them is a **dependent** or **subordinate clause.** As the list on page 136 shows, the subordinators are both single words and phrases. This list is by no means complete; we have many more such words and phrases that introduce subordinate clauses.

Subordinate clauses can come either before or after the main clause. This movability feature provides a test to differentiate between subordinators and coordinators. The coordinators—the conjunctive adverbs as well as the coordinating conjunctions—introduce only the second clause:

> Because we had missed the last bus, we decided to walk.
> We decided to walk, for we had missed the last bus.

*For we had missed the last bus, we decided to walk.

We missed the bus, so we decided to walk.

*So we decided to walk, we missed the bus.

Relatives. Relative pronouns—*who, whose, whom, which,* and *that* —and relative adverbs—*where, when, why*—perform a dual function in the noun phrase: They introduce the relative, or adjectival, clause, connecting the clause to the noun it modifies; and they play a part in the clause, the pronouns as nominals and the adverbs as adverbials.

The price *that* we pay for sneakers keeps going up.

The man *who* lives next door rides a bicycle to work.

Nothing exciting ever happens in the small town *where* I was born.

Adjectival clauses are also introduced by the **indefinite relative pronouns,** such as *whoever, whomever, whosever, whichever, whatever,* and *what* (meaning "that which"). These pronouns are called "indefinite" because they have no specific referent; instead, they have a general, indefinite reference. See pages 154–155.

All of the adjectival clauses are discussed in detail in Chapter 9. The relative adverbs *when* and *where,* which introduce adverbial as well as adjectival clauses, are discussed in Chapter 8 as well.

INTERROGATIVES

As their name implies, the **interrogatives**—*who, whose, whom, which, what, how, why, when, where*—introduce questions:

What are you doing here?

How did you get here?

When are you leaving?

The function of such questions, of course, is to elicit particular information.

The interrogatives also introduce clauses that fill NP slots in the sentence patterns. Such clauses are sometimes referred to as *indirect questions:*

Tell me why he came.

I wonder <u>who came with him.</u>
<u>Whose car he drove</u> is a mystery to me.

These clauses, which act as noun phrase substitutes, are discussed in Chapter 11. (We should note that the interrogatives are the same words that in other contexts are classified as relative pronouns or relative adverbs.)

EXPLETIVES

Rather than providing grammatical or structural meaning as the other structure-word classes do, the **expletives**—sometimes defined as "empty words"—generally act simply as operators that allow us to manipulate sentences in a variety of ways.

There. The *there* transformation, as we saw in Chapter 3, enables us to delay the subject in certain kinds of sentences, thus putting it in the position of main stress, which generally falls in the predicate half of the sentence:

An airplane is landing on → There's an aírplane landing
    the fréeway.   on the freeway.

As the following diagram shows, the expletive *there* plays no grammatical role in the sentence. To analyze the sentence pattern, you have to transform the sentence back into its original form, eliminating the expletive and shifting the subject in front of the *be:*

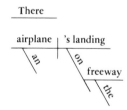

It. In the following sentences, the *it* acts much like *there,* in that it delays the actual subject:

<u>It</u>'s nice to be here with you. (<u>To be here with you</u> is nice.)
<u>It</u>'s nice seeing you again. (<u>Seeing you again</u> is nice.)

This use of *it*, sometimes referred to as the anticipatory or preparatory *it*, is different from other expletives in that it fills a grammatical slot—subject or object. The actual subject or object, the anticipated construction, can also be a clause:

> It was nice that you could come.
> Some people don't like it that grocery stores are open on Sunday.

It can also be a noun phrase:

> It was really beautiful, that display of blooms at the orchid show.

This use of *it* can also be construed as the pronoun *it* acting as the subject (or object), with the verb phrase or clause or noun phrase (the actual subject or object in terms of meaning) as an appositive:

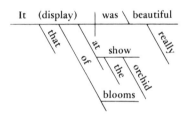

It also serves as the grammatical subject in certain fixed expressions concerning weather and time:

> It's a nice day.
> It's raining.
> It's going to be windy today.
> It's nearly seven.
> It's dinner time.
> It's Friday.

That. One of our most common expletives, *that*, introduces a nominal clause:

> I hope that our exam is easy.

Unlike the relative pronoun *that,* which introduces adjectival clauses, the expletive *that* plays no part in the clause:

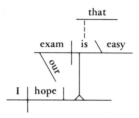

That can be left out when the clause is in object position:

I hope our exam is easy.

However, when the clause is in subject position, *that* cannot be omitted:

That we will have an exam is fairly certain.

We also use the expletive *that* to turn a direct quotation into indirect discourse:

He said, "I will come." ⟶ He said that he would come.

"Expletive" is not the only label given to this use of the word *that;* it is sometimes called a "nominalizer," because its function is to turn a clause into a nominal, that is, a noun phrase substitute. And sometimes it is called a "subordinator." The label "expletive" is used by traditional grammarians to emphasize the "empty word" quality of *that,* in that it serves strictly as an operator; it plays no role in the clause itself. The use of *that* in nominal clauses is taken up in detail in Chapter 11.

Or. The expletive *or* introduces an explanatory appositive:

The study of sentences, or syntax, helps us appreciate how much we know when we know language.
The African wildebeest, or gnu, resembles an ox.

This *or* should not be confused with the conjunction or. The diagram shows its expletive role:

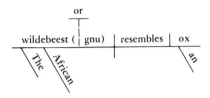

These appositives are taken up in Chapter 9.

As. Another fairly common expletive introduces certain objective complements in Patterns IX and X:

We elected him as president.

Again, the diagram shows its role outside of the grammatical structure of the sentence:[2]

Leaving out the *as* does not change the meaning of this sentence; whether to choose it or not is usually a matter of emphasis or rhythm.

---

[2] An alternative analysis for these phrases with *as* is to consider them prepositional phrases:

(This is the analysis of Randolph Quirk and Sidney Greenbaum in *A Concise Grammar of Contemporary English* [New York: Harcourt Brace Jovanovich, 1973].)

Admittedly, the word *as* presents something of a problem; however, to call it an expletive, or operator, does help alleviate the problem somewhat. First, it makes clear the membership of these sentences in Patterns IX and X, pointing out the optional nature of *as* with some of the verbs. It also avoids the introduction of what would be a deviant prepositional phrase: a preposition followed by an adjective (I consider him *as exceptionally clever*). Other prepositions do not take adjectives as objects. Finally, it acknowledges the resemblance between the role of *as* in these sentences and the expletive role of *or* and *that* in the previous sections, where the *or* and *that* have no grammatical role in the sentence itself.

With verbs like *refer to, think of,* and *know,* however, *as* is required with the objective complement:

> I refer to Professor Buck <u>as</u> a man of character.
> I think of him <u>as</u> a man of many talents.
> I think of him <u>as</u> exceptionally clever.
> I know him <u>as</u> a friend.

Exercise 33: Label the part of speech of each underlined word.

1. I found some rare stamps <u>and</u> postmarks <u>on</u> <u>an</u> old envelope <u>in</u> the attic.
2. <u>Four</u> friends of mine <u>from</u> the dorm waited in line <u>for</u> sixteen hours, <u>for</u> they were determined to get tickets for the World Series.
3. <u>As</u> the experts predicted, the Republicans chose <u>an</u> ultraconservative <u>as</u> their party's candidate <u>at</u> the convention.
4. We should <u>be</u> arriving <u>by</u> six, <u>but</u> don't wait for us.
5. Our group <u>of</u> tourists will take <u>off</u> at dawn <u>if</u> the weather permits.
6. We <u>are</u> now studying the structure <u>of</u> sentences, <u>or</u> syntax, in <u>our</u> English class.
7. We <u>will</u> warm up <u>with</u> a game of one-on-one <u>while</u> we wait for the rest of the players.
8. We had <u>too</u> many problems with our <u>two</u> new puppies, so we gave them both <u>to</u> the neighbors.

SUMMARY

In general the structure classes provide structural and grammatical meaning rather than lexical content, as the nouns and verbs and adjectives and adverbs do. The structure words are important signals: They are as important to meaning in sentences as the mortar is to the bricks in a building. They provide the unstressed syllables between the peaks of stress that fall on the form classes, giving the language its rhythm. And although they are small, closed classes, they are our most common words. In fact, on the frequency list cited earlier in this chapter, only three of the first sixty-five words (in order of frequency) are from the form classes; all the rest are structure words and pronouns.

QUESTIONS FOR DISCUSSION

1. Prepositions are among the most difficult words in the language for foreign speakers to master. Why do you suppose this is so? Look at the following sentences. How would you explain the selection of prepositions to a learner of English?

> Be sure to fill out the form carefully.
> Be sure to fill in the form carefully.

> I like to jog in the early morning.
> I like to jog on a sunny morning.

> Our house burned down last week.
> All of my books burned up.

> I'm working on my math.
> I'm really working at it.

2. Do the sentences in Question 1 say anything about the arbitrariness of English? Consider the following in light of the examples in Question 1.

> "We hope to reach the solution that we are dreaming for."
> "That is the solution we are hoping of."

Are these quotations from native speakers?

3. In what sense are *keep, dare, get,* and *have to* modal-like? In thinking about this question, consider their place in the verb expansion rule.

In what sense are these verbs *not* like the other modals? Consider the following examples:

> He kept playing all afternoon.
> Did he keep playing?

> Do I dare walk alone?
> You dare not walk alone around here at night.

> He got fired.
> He was fired.
> He wasn't fired.
> He didn't get fired.

4. In answering an interviewer's question, an economist recently said, "I do not foresee any improvement in the economy, absent any change in the elements that are driving it." What part of speech is *absent*?

5. Some observers of English usage object to the inclusion of *like* in the list of subordinating conjunctions; they maintain that *like* is a preposition and that *as* must be used when a clause is introduced. For example, we should say,

> He takes to it as a duck [takes] to water.

and not

> He takes to it like a duck [takes] to water.

In explaining their definition of *like* as a conjunction, *Webster's Ninth Collegiate Dictionary* says

> There is no doubt that after 450 years of use, *like* is firmly established as a conjunction. It has been used by many prestigious literary figures of the past, though perhaps not in their most elevated works; in modern use it may be found in literature, journalism, and scholarly writing. While the present objection to it is perhaps more heated than rational, someone writing formal prose may want to use *as* instead.

The *Dictionary* includes the following quotation from Norman Mailer in the citation: "middle-aged men who looked like they might be out for their one night of the year." Would *as* (with *if* or *though*) be a better choice in that context?

Check your own use of *like* and *as*. Under what circumstances do you use them? Check also current textbooks and newspapers. Can you think of any reason why language experts should find controversy in this issue?

Stop

CHAPTER

7

Pronouns

As their name suggests, pronouns are words that stand for nouns. *phrases*
Perhaps a more accurate label would be *pronominal,* because they actually stand for any construction that functions as a nominal in the sentence. We refer to the noun or nominal that the pronoun stands for as its **antecedent.**

Most pronouns replace an entire noun phrase:

The pistachio nut ice cream at Meyer's Dairy is delicious.
It   is delicious.

My friend Jan, who lives in Houston, was in her forties when
                                   she finished college.
         She   was in her forties when
                                   she finished college.

Pronouns also substitute for other nominals, such as verb phrases and clauses:

The judge warned my brother to stay out of trouble.
He told me   that,   too.

Where you spend your time is none of my business.
$\left\{\dfrac{\text{That}}{\text{It}}\right\}$ is none of my business.

All pronouns are not alike. The label *pronoun* actually covers a wide variety of words, many of which function in quite different ways. What follows is a brief description of the main classes of pronouns.

147

PERSONAL PRONOUNS

The **personal pronouns** are the ones we usually think of when the word *pronoun* comes to mind. We generally label them on the basis of person and number:

PERSON	NUMBER	
	Singular	*Plural*
1st	I	we
2nd	you	you
3rd	he / she / it	they

[handwritten marginalia: me us, him her, them]

For example, we refer to *I* as the "first-person singular" pronoun and *they* as the "third-person plural." In addition, the third-person singular pronouns include the feature of **gender**: masculine (*he*), feminine (*she*), and neuter (*it*).

The term **pronoun-antecedent agreement** describes our selection of the pronoun in reference to the noun or noun phrase (or nominal) it replaces: The personal pronoun "agrees with" its antecedent in both number and, for third-person singular, gender. Note that the second person (*you*) has neither gender nor number distinctions.

The forms given in the preceding set are in the **subjective** (also called "nominative") case; this is the form used when the pronoun serves as the subject or subjective complement. The personal pronouns also inflect for the **possessive** ("genitive") case, as nouns do, and the **objective** ("accusative") case, an inflection that nouns do not have. The possessive case forms of pronouns function as determiners, as we saw in Chapter 6. The objective case is used for pronouns in all of the other NP slots: direct object, indirect object, objective complement, and object of the preposition.

Subjective:	I	we	you	he	she	it	they
Possessive:	my	our	your	his	her	its	their
	(mine)	(ours)	(yours)	(his)	(hers)		(theirs)
Objective:	me	us	you	him	her	it	them

Alternative forms of the possessive case, shown here in parentheses, are used when the headword of the noun phrase is deleted:

This is <u>my book</u>.   This is <u>mine</u>.
This is <u>her book</u>.   This is <u>hers</u>.

The same is true of possessive nouns:

This is <u>John's book</u>.   This is <u>John's</u>.
<u>Mary's book</u> is missing.   <u>Mary's</u> is missing.

We should note that the source of a great deal of the sexism in our language is the absence of a singular third-person pronoun that could refer to either gender. Our plural pronoun (*they*) includes both male and female; but when we need a pronoun to refer to an unidentified person, such as "the writer" or "a student" or "the doctor," the long-standing tradition has been to use the masculine (*he/his/him*):

The writer of this news story should have kept his personal opinions out of it.

Attempts to promote *s/he* in recent years have been unsuccessful. Perhaps someday the plural pronoun will be accepted for both singular and plural, a usage that has become quite common in speech:

Someone broke into our car last night; they stole our tape deck and all our tapes.

(This issue is discussed further on pages 333–336.)

Exercise 34: Substitute personal pronouns for the underlined nouns and noun phrases in the following sentences.

1. <u>John and Betty</u> have bought a new house.
2. <u>Bev and I</u> will be going to the game with <u>Otis</u>.
3. Betsy bought <u>that beautiful new car of hers</u> in Chicago.
4. Both of <u>her cars</u> are gas guzzlers.
5. There have always been uneasy feelings between <u>the neighbors and my husband</u>.

6. I want Tony to approve of the project.
7. The kids gave their father and me a bad time.
8. My brother, who works for the Navy in California, spends his weekends in Las Vegas.

REFLEXIVE PRONOUNS

Reflexive pronouns are those formed by adding *-self* or *-selves* to a form of the personal pronoun:

PERSON	SINGULAR	PLURAL
1st	myself	ourselves
2nd	yourself	yourselves
3rd	himself herself itself	themselves

The reflexive pronoun is used as the direct object, indirect object, and object of the preposition when its antecedent is the subject of the sentence:

John cut himself.

I glanced at myself in the mirror.

I cooked dinner for Tim and myself.

Joe cooked dinner for Mary and himself.

The reflexive pronoun *myself* is also fairly common in certain spoken sentences where the standard written version would call for the objective case, *me:*

Joe cooked dinner for Mary and myself.

In Standard Written English the object of the preposition *for* would be

Mary and me because the antecedent of *myself* does not appear in the sentence:

Joe cooked dinner for <u>Mary and me</u>.

Both versions are unambiguous; both forms of the first-person pronoun, *me* and *myself,* can refer only to the speaker. However, with third-person pronouns different forms produce different meanings:

Joe cooked dinner for Mary and <u>himself</u> (Joe).
Joe cooked dinner for Mary and <u>him</u> (someone else).

Exercise 35: Fill the blanks with the appropriate reflexive pronouns.

1. Mary gave _____ a black eye when she fell. *herself*

2. Joe and Henry cooked _____ a steak. *themselves*

3. The ceramic figurine sat by _____ on the shelf. *itself*

4. We sat by _____ in the front row. *ourselves*

5. Kris cooked a delicious Mexican feast for Ross and <u>*herself*</u>.

6. Wearing our new designer jeans, Sheila and I admired <u>*ourselves*</u> in the mirror.

---

appositive

INTENSIVE PRONOUNS
Also known as the *emphatic reflexive pronouns,* the **intensive pronouns** have the same form as the reflexives. The intensive pronoun serves as an appositive to emphasize a noun, but it need not directly follow the noun:

I <u>myself</u> prefer chocolate.
I prefer chocolate <u>myself</u>.
<u>Myself</u>, I prefer chocolate.

Because *myself* is in apposition to *I* in all three versions, the diagram will not distinguish among them.

I (myself) | prefer | chocolate

Appositives are discussed in Chapter 9.

Exercise 36: Add an intensive pronoun to each of the following sentences.

1. Claudia composed the music for the show. *herself*
2. I never read the comic page. *myself*
3. Gil and Kim wrote their wedding ceremony. *themselves*
4. I will pay for the cost of the trip *myself* but not extras.
5. Harold gave the tip to the waitress. *himself*

Are variations possible in any of the sentences, either in the choice of the pronoun or its position?

RECIPROCAL PRONOUNS

Each other and *one another* are known as the **reciprocal pronouns.** They serve either as determiners (in the possessive case) or as objects, referring to previously named nouns: *Each other* generally refers to two nouns; *one another* to three or more:

> John and Claudia help <u>each other.</u>
> They even do <u>each other's</u> chores.
> All the students in my study group help <u>one another</u> with their
>   homework.

DEMONSTRATIVE PRONOUNS

In our discussion of determiners we noted that the selection of a determiner is based on certain inherent features, such as definite or indefinite, countable or noncountable. **The demonstrative pronouns,** one of the subclasses of determiners, include the features of "number" and "proximity":

PROXIMITY	NUMBER	
	Singular	*Plural*
Near	this	these
Distant	that	those

That documentary we saw last night really made me think, but this one is simply stupid.

Those trees on the ridge were almost destroyed by gypsy moths, but these seem perfectly healthy.

Like other determiner classes, the demonstrative pronoun can be a substitute for a nominal as well as a signal for one:

These old shoes and hats will be perfect for the costumes.
These will be perfect for the costumes.

To be effective as a nominal, the demonstrative pronoun must replace or stand for a clearly stated antecedent. In the following example, *that* does not refer to "solar energy"; it has no clear antecedent:

Our contractor is obviously skeptical about solar energy. That really surprises me.

Such sentences are not uncommon in speech, nor are they ungrammatical. But when a *this* or *that* has no specific antecedent, the writer can usually improve the sentence by providing a noun headword for the demonstrative pronoun—by turning the pronoun into a determiner:

Our contractor is obviously skeptical about solar energy. That attitude (or His attitude) really surprises me.

A combination of the two sentences would also be an improvement over the vague use of *that:*

Our contractor's skepticism about solar energy really surprises me.

RELATIVE PRONOUNS

The **relative pronouns** are *who, which,* and *that;* they introduce clauses that modify the nouns that are the antecedents of these pronouns. *Who* inflects for both possessive and objective cases: *whose* (possessive) and *whom* (objective).

The man who lives across the street sold me his car.

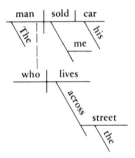

In this sentence *who* renames *man,* its antecedent, and plays the part of subject in the relative (adjectival) clause. In the next sentence the relative pronoun is in the possessive case form, *whose:*

The man whose car I bought was not very honest about the gas mileage.

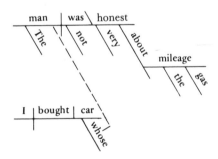

Here *whose,* the possessive relative pronoun, again stands for *man;* in its own clause it acts as the determiner for *car,* the role that possessives normally play.

Whose also acts as the possessive form of *which:*

The wooded ridge across the valley, whose trees were infested by gypsy moths, turned brown in mid-June.

The relative pronoun *that* is generally subjective or objective, never possessive:

I lost the backpack that I bought yesterday.

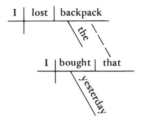

That renames *backpack* and acts as the object within its own clause. In object position, *that* can be omitted:

I lost the backpack I bought yesterday.

When *that* is the subject of the clause, however, it cannot be omitted:

The route that will get us there fastest is straight across the mountain.

The *wh-* relative pronouns also have an expanded form with the addition of *-ever,* known as **indefinite relative pronouns:** *whoever, whosever, whomever,* and *whatever.* The expanded relatives have indefinite referents rather than specific ones as the simple relatives do:

I will give a bonus to whoever works the hardest.
I will pay you whatever you deserve.

What is also considered an indefinite relative pronoun when it introduces adjectival clauses and means "that which."

I will pay you what you deserve.

The relative (adjectival) clauses are discussed more fully in Chapter 9.

INTERROGATIVE PRONOUNS

The list of **interrogative pronouns** is similar to that of the relatives: *who (whose, whom), which,* and *what.* The interrogatives, as their name suggests, are among the question words that produce information questions (in contrast to yes/no questions):

> <u>What</u> do you want for lunch?
> <u>Whose</u> car is that?
> <u>Which</u> section of history did you get?

As we saw in Chapter 3, the interrogative word plays a part in the sentence. For example, in the first preceding sample sentence, *what* fills the direct object slot: "You do want *what* for lunch?" In a sentence such as "What flavor do you prefer?" the interrogative *what* acts as a determiner for the noun *flavor.* In the other two examples listed, *whose* and *which* also act as determiners: *whose car, which section.* Because of this modifying function, *which, what,* and *whose* are sometimes classified as **interrogative adjectives.**

The interrogative pronouns also introduce nominal clauses and, like the relative pronouns, play a part in the clause. There is an indirect question involved in such clauses—either implied or stated, asked or answered:

> Tell me <u>what you want for lunch.</u>
> I know <u>who gave you that black eye.</u>

We shall take up nominal clauses in Chapter 11.

INDEFINITE PRONOUNS

The **indefinite pronouns** include a number of words listed earlier as determiners:

Quantifiers: *enough, few, fewer, less, little, many, much, several, more, most*
Universals: *all, both, every, each*
Partitives: *any, either, neither, no, some*

One is also commonly used as a pronoun (as are the other cardinal numbers—*two, three,* etc.) along with its negative, *none.* As a pronoun, *one* often replaces only the headword, rather than the entire noun phrase:

>*The blue shoes that I bought yesterday* will be perfect for the trip.
>*The blue ones that I bought yesterday* will be perfect for the trip.

The personal pronoun, on the other hand, would replace the entire noun phrase:

>They will be perfect for the trip.

The universal pronoun *every* and the partitives *any, no,* and *some* can be expanded with *-body, -thing,* and *-one:*

$$
\text{some} \begin{cases} \text{body} \\ \text{thing} \\ \text{one} \end{cases} \qquad \text{every} \begin{cases} \text{body} \\ \text{thing} \\ \text{one} \end{cases}
$$

$$
\text{any} \begin{cases} \text{body} \\ \text{thing} \\ \text{one} \end{cases} \qquad \text{no} \begin{cases} \text{body} \\ \text{thing} \\ \text{one (two words)} \end{cases}
$$

These pronouns can take modifiers in the form of clauses:

>Anyone *who wants extra credit in psych class* can volunteer for to-night's experiment.

They can also be modified by verb phrases:

>Everyone *reporting late for practice* will take fifteen laps.

And by prepositional phrases:

>Nothing *on the front page* interests me anymore.

And unlike most nouns, they can be modified by adjectives in post-headword position:

>I don't care for anything *sweet.*
>I think that something *strange* is going on here.

SUMMARY

Like the structure words, pronouns constitute a small, closed class; some substitute for nouns and noun phrases; others signal nouns as determiners. They come in a variety of forms, some of which take modifiers and some of which do not. We use pronouns automatically as we do the structure words, with little conscious thought. They are among our most commonly used words.

Exercise 37: Underline the pronouns in the following sentences. Identify the subclass to which each pronoun belongs.

1. When Bob ordered a pizza with everything, I ordered one too.
2. Millie and Bev shopped for new shoes but couldn't find any they liked.
3. Someone was standing in the shadows, but we couldn't see who it was.
4. All that I had for lunch was an apple.
5. Jim and Ralph didn't eat much either, but they both ate more than I.
6. I will go along with whatever you decide.
7. One hour of studying was enough for me.
8. Quarreling among themselves, the committee members completely disregarded one another's suggestions.
9. Tell me what color I should paint your sign.
10. The employment office will find a job for whoever wants one.

QUESTIONS FOR DISCUSSION

1. The relative pronoun agrees with its antecedent in person and number but not necessarily in case. How do the following sentences illustrate that statement?

I don't know the women who live next door.
It is I who am the culprit.

2. Comment on the choice of pronouns in the following sentence. Are they correct?

I didn't know who felt worse: him or me.

3. In Chapter 1, Discussion Question 12, we looked at the following ambiguous sentence:

Sandy called her mother.

What is the source of the ambiguity? Would a sentence about Sam and father instead of Sandy and mother be equally ambiguous? What's the difference?

4. What is the difference in the meaning of *one* in the following sentences?

<u>One</u> farmer told me there hadn't been rain in eight weeks.
<u>One</u> can only hope that the weather changes soon.

5. The telephone rings and you answer it. When you hang up, your roommate asks, "What did they want?" Does your roommate really believe you were talking to more than one person? If not, what is there about our language that would produce such a strange question?

6. In the discussion of the expanded or indefinite relative pronouns, the following three sample sentences appear:

I will give a bonus to whoever works hardest.
I will pay you what you deserve.
I will pay you whatever you deserve.

Explain why a traditional diagram of such sentences would look like this:

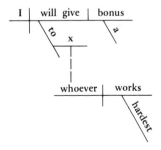

Is there another way to diagram them that would be equally plausible?

7. The case of the pronoun is determined by the part that it plays in its own clause. Notice the case of the relative pronouns in the following sentences. Are they correct?

> We will give the prize to whomever the committee chooses.
> We will give the prize to whomever the committee believes deserves it.
> Whom shall I say is calling?

8. How do you explain the use of *we* and *us* in the following sentences?

> We graduates lined up to go into the gym.
> The speaker told us graduates that we were the hope of the future.

Is *we* used correctly in the following sentence?

> It wasn't a good idea for we dishwashers to go on strike.

9. Explain the source of the ambiguity in the following sentence:

> You know yourself better than anyone.

How would a spoken version clear up the ambiguity?

10. Notice the difference that an apostrophe makes in the following phrases:

> for all its worth
> for all it's worth

Provide a context for each to demonstrate that both versions are possible.

11. Here's a statement with a single, straightforward meaning:

> I invited everyone in the class to my party.

The follow-up sentence is not quite as clear; in fact, it's ambiguous:

> Everyone didn't come.

Here's another ambiguous sentence:

> Everything doesn't cause cancer.

Paraphrase the two negative sentences in two ways to demonstrate their meanings. Then consider the meaning of *everyone* and *everything* and explain why their use with the negative should produce ambiguity.

12. Examine the following sentences; then explain the "rule" that a non-native speaker learning English must understand in connection with *some* and *any*.

> Mario wants some dessert. Rosa doesn't want any.
> I lent someone my book. I didn't lend anyone my class notes.
> Are you going somewhere special for lunch? I'm not going anywhere.

Why would that student of English find the following sentences ungrammatical?

> Anyone can have seconds on dessert.
> I haven't given some of the volunteers their assignments yet.

What would happen to the meaning of those two sentences if that English student were to follow the "some/any rule"?

13. The word *as*—listed in the previous chapter as a preposition, a subordinating conjunction, and an expletive—is given two more identities in *Webster's Ninth New Collegiate Dictionary*: pronoun and adverb. The following sentences demonstrate those added roles:

> ***Pronoun:*** He must be a nonnative speaker, as is evident from his accent.
> ***Adverb:*** My opinion, as distinguished from Tom's, favors the defendant.

Now determine which of the five labels applies to *as* in each of the following sentences. Do we need any more labels?

> I have a new job, <u>as of</u> this morning.
> He acted <u>as</u> my lawyer.
> Improbable <u>as</u> it seems, it's true.
> We lingered in the garden <u>as</u> the sun set.
> Possessive nouns <u>as</u> determiners retain their own determiners.
> He works <u>as</u> an accountant.
> Do <u>as</u> I say, not <u>as</u> I do.
> He's <u>as</u> cool <u>as</u> a cucumber.
> The group selected Pam <u>as</u> treasurer.

PART
III

EXPANDING
THE BASIC PATTERNS

Most of the sentences used so far to illustrate the sentence patterns are short and spare, with unadorned noun phrases and verb phrases filling the required slots. In contrast, the sentences you have been reading in paragraphs such as this one, which explain the sentence patterns and the parts of speech, include structures with names like *relative clause, participial phrase, appositive, gerund,* and *absolute phrase.* Now you may not recognize these labels—in fact, you probably aren't able to pick out the two passive participles in the first sentence on this page; yet you have no problem understanding the language in these paragraphs. In fact, every day you process sentences that include these structures when you listen and when you read; and you actively use gerunds and participles and relative clauses when you speak and when you write. Your linguistic computer has had many years of experience in handling all of these structures with their formidable-sounding names.

In the chapters that follow we will take up these and other structures that modify nouns and verbs and sentences and that substitute for noun phrases; we will also look at ways of compounding sentences and their parts. You will discover that we use these methods of sentence expansion in highly systematic ways—that, in fact, many of the structures that we add to sentences are themselves based on the sentence patterns you learned in Chapter 1. You will also find that a conscious understanding of these structures can help you make more effective use of them in your own writing.

FORM AND FUNCTION

Before looking at the structures we use in expanding the basic sentence patterns, we need to recognize the two sides of sentence analysis: form and function. In analyzing a sentence, it is not enough to look at the words simply as "parts of speech." We must also consider the functions represented by the slots in the sentence patterns into which the words fall in actual sentences, that is, the roles that those words fill.

For example, many of the slots in the sentence patterns are filled by nouns or noun phrases: A noun or noun phrase can function as subject, direct object, indirect object, subjective complement, objective complement, or object of the preposition. Because these are jobs that nouns normally do, we call these functions **nominal**. In the sentence pattern formulas these slots are indicated by the symbol *NP,* which stands for "noun phrase." But structures other than nouns or noun phrases can also fill these slots:

> <u>Jogging</u> is good exercise.
> I enjoy <u>jogging</u>.

Here is where the two-sided analysis becomes important. In *form, jogging* is a *verb;* that is, in terms of its part of speech it is a verb. But in the two sentences above, the *function* of *jogging* is *nominal:* It fills the subject slot in the first one, the direct object slot in the second. Even complete clauses can fill an NP slot:

> I wonder <u>who will win the marathon.</u>

Here the direct object of *wonder* is a complete Pattern VII clause, a structure with its own subject (*who*) and predicate (*will win the marathon*). In terms of form, then, *who will win the marathon* is a clause; its function in this sentence is nominal. In Chapter 11 we shall examine both verb phrases and clauses in their roles as nominals.

Chapter 10 is concerned with **adjectivals:** structures that play the part of adjectives. What are those adjectival roles in the sentence? You may recall, from the discussion of adjectives in Chapter 5, that we have two subclasses of adjectives: predicative and attributive. The predicative adjectives are the two ADJ slots in the sentence patterns—the subjective complements in Patterns II and IV and the objective complement in Pattern IX; the attributive adjectives are modifiers in the prenoun slot—my *new* coat, the *little* house. But as you have probably guessed, words other than adjectives can fill those same slots:

> my <u>winter</u> coat
> the <u>brick</u> house

So in terms of the two-sided analysis, we would label *winter* and *brick* as *nouns* in *form* and as *adjectivals* in *function*.

We can also modify nouns with phrases and clauses:

> my coat <u>with the fur lining</u> (prepositional phrase)
> the house <u>designed by Frank Lloyd Wright</u> (verb phrase)
> the house <u>that Jack built</u> (clause)

In Chapter 9 we will examine these and other forms that fill the role of adjectival.

The adverbial slot, too, can be filled by structures other than adverbs. The term **adverbial** refers to the function of any structure that modifies the verb, providing information relating to time, place, manner, cause, means, and the like—what we think of as "adverbial information":

> The movie starts <u>immediately</u>.
> The movie starts <u>in ten minutes</u>.

In the first sentence the adverbial slot contains an adverb; in the second, however, the adverbial information is provided by a different structure, a prepositional phrase. Again, the two-sided analysis would describe *in ten minutes* as a *prepositional phrase* in *form* and an *adverbial* in *function*.

Before you begin your study of adverbials, you might find it useful to turn to the Contents and read the headings for Chapter 8. Notice that the chapter title names the function: "Modifiers of the Verb: Adverbials." The subheadings name the forms that carry out that function, beginning with "adverbs."

In this section of the book we will again use the sentence diagram. Its purpose is to illustrate the various ways of expanding sentences, first with adverbials, then with adjectivals, nominals, sentence modifiers, and coordinated structures. The sentences are beginning to get long and complex, it's true; however, if you remember to consider the two-sided analysis of form and function, the diagrams will enhance your understanding. Each of the various forms we have discussed—noun phrase, prepositional phrase, verb phrase, clause—has a particular diagram, no matter what its function in the sentence. For example, a prepositional phrase is always diagrammed as a two-part structure, with the preposition on the diagonal line and the object of the preposition on the attached horizontal line; a noun phrase is always diagrammed with the headword on the horizontal line and its modifiers attached below it.

Always begin your analysis of a sentence by identifying the underlying pattern, one of the ten basic sentences you diagrammed in Chapter 1. Then analyze each of the slots to see how it has been expanded; adverbials will slope from the verb; adjectivals will slope from the noun headword, and so on. If you take these expansions one step at a time in the chapters that follow, asking yourself questions about form and function, you'll come to understand the system that produces the sentences of your language.

8

Modifiers
of the Verb: Adverbials

Read (handwritten, left margin)

Quiz through Nine (handwritten, left margin)

Although only one of the sentence patterns has an adverbial in a required slot—Pattern I: NP *be* ADV/TP—the symbol for an optional adverbial, (ADV), could be added to all ten formulas. Adverbial information—structures telling where, when, why, how, and so on—is common in every sentence pattern. And no sentence is limited to a single adverbial. In the following sentence, each of the underlined structures adds adverbial information to the verb *gasped:*

The audience gasped nervously throughout the theater when the magician thrust his sword into the box.

The audience gasped (How?) nervously.
The audience gasped (Where?) throughout the theater.
The audience gasped (When?) when the magician thrust his sword into the box.

Even though all of the adverbials follow the verb in the preceding sentence, there is really no fixed slot for most adverbials; in fact, movability is one of their most telling characteristics. In the preceding sentence, for example, there are several possibilities for ordering the three adverbials:

When the magician thrust his sword into the box, the audience nervously gasped throughout the theater.

Throughout the theater the audience gasped nervously when the magician thrust his sword into the box.

167

The position may depend on the writer's emphasis, on the rhythm of the sentence, or simply on the desire for sentence variety.

In Pattern I sentences the adverbial of time or place nearly always follows the verb, although even with this pattern there are certain exceptions:

> The committee members are <u>here</u>.
> <u>Here</u> they are.

We should note that other adverbials can be added to Pattern I sentences with the same versatility with which they are added to the other patterns:

> The committee members are <u>finally</u> here.
> <u>At noon</u> the teacher was in the library <u>to do some research</u>.

But no matter what positions the adverbials occupy—whether at the beginning, middle, or end of the sentence—a diagram will show them as modifiers of the verb:

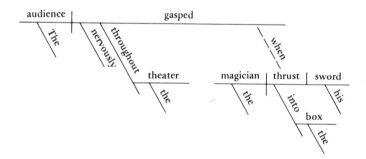

Even though the diagram shows the modifiers in the order that they appear in the sentence, an exact reading of the diagram may still not be possible. For instance, this one does not show whether *nervously* comes before or after *gasped*. But because the purpose of diagramming is to illustrate visually the relationship of the various parts of the sentence, an exact left-to-right reading of the diagram is not necessarily important.

The preceding sample sentence includes structures of three different forms functioning adverbially: an adverb, a prepositional phrase, and a clause. Other structures that provide adverbial information are noun phrases and verb phrases. In this chapter we shall take up each of these forms in its role as adverbial.

ADVERBS

The words we recognize as adverbs most readily are the adverbs of manner—the *-ly* words, such as *nervously, quietly,* and *suddenly*. These adverbs, derived from adjectives, usually tell "how" or "in what manner" about verbs:

> They gasped nervously = in a nervous manner
> They talked quietly = in a quiet manner
> It stopped suddenly = in a sudden manner

The manner adverbs are probably the most movable of all the adverbials; they can appear before or after the verb, as well as at the beginning or end of the sentence:

> Suddenly the crowd grew restless.
> The crowd suddenly grew restless.
> The crowd grew restless suddenly.

Notice that all three versions of the sentence are diagrammed the same; the only clue to word order is capitalization:

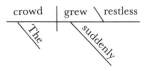

A single-word adverb can even come within the verb phrase, between the auxiliary and the main verb:

> The roof was suddenly blown off by a strong gust of wind.

Or between two auxiliaries:

> Carmen has regularly been helping the neighbors with their shopping and other errands.

In all positions the manner adverbs can be marked by qualifiers, words such as *very, quite, so,* and *rather:*

> Quite suddenly the crowd grew restless.
> The old woman crooned very softly.
> The airline employees handled our luggage rather carelessly.

And like the adjectives they are derived from, these adverbs can be compared by combining with *more:*

> More suddenly than the police expected, the crowd grew restless.
> The sails flapped more and more furiously as the wind grew stronger.

(The superlative degree, *most,* is much more common with adjectives than with adverbs.)

Besides the *-ly* adverbs, many other single-word adverbs provide information of time, place, frequency, and the like: *now, then, nowadays, today, often, always, sometimes, seldom, never, here, there, everywhere,* and many others.

> I still jog here sometimes.
> Nowadays I seldom swim.

Some of these, like the manner adverbs, can be qualified and compared:

> I should jog more often.
> Nowadays Judd and Betty jog quite often.

Although movability is a characteristic of all single-word adverbs, the various subclasses are bound by certain restrictions as to order. For example, in the following sentence, the adverbials of place and time cannot be reversed:

I am going <u>there</u> <u>now</u>.
*I am going <u>now</u> <u>there</u>.

And although we would say

<u>Often</u> I jog <u>here</u>.
I <u>often</u> jog <u>here</u>.
<u>Now</u> I am going <u>there</u>.
I am <u>now</u> going <u>there</u>.

a native speaker of English would rarely say

<u>Here</u> I jog <u>often</u>.
or
<u>There</u> I am going <u>now</u>.

and would never say

*I <u>here</u> jog <u>often</u>
or
*I <u>there</u> am going <u>now</u>.

The rules governing the order and movement of adverbs are quite complex, but as native speakers we are unaware of that complexity; our linguistic computers are programmed to follow the rules automatically.

Exercise 38: Underline the adverbs in the following sentences. How many ways can you vary each sentence by shifting the positions of the adverbs?

1. The leaves are falling <u>steadily</u> <u>now</u>.
2. <u>Very</u> <u>soon</u> the snow will be <u>everywhere</u>.
3. Winter <u>often</u> arrives <u>here</u> <u>suddenly</u>.
4. <u>Sometimes</u> winter sneaks in <u>quietly</u>.

PREPOSITIONAL PHRASES

The **prepositional phrase** is our most common structure of modification, appearing regularly in both noun phrases and verb phrases.

Prepositional Phrase

Preposition	Noun Phrase
throughout	the theater
during	the Christmas break
along	the shore
in	our backyard
for	my sake
according to	the weatherman
by	yourself

As the branching diagram illustrates, the prepositional phrase is a binary structure, consisting of a preposition and a noun phrase or other nominal structure, known as the object of the preposition.

The term "prepositional phrase" is a label referring to *form*. Even out of context we can identify a structure such as *during the Christmas break* as a prepositional phrase in form; but only when it appears in a sentence can we label its *function*—either as adjectival, a modifier of a noun ("The weather *during the Christmas break* was unseasonably mild"), or as adverbial, a modifier of a verb ("I worked for the Post Office *during the Christmas break*").[1]

Adverbial prepositional phrases provide the same kind of information as adverbs do:

Direction

We hiked ⎰ toward the pond.
⎱ beyond the ridge.
⎩ across the field.

---

[1] On rare occasions the prepositional phrase appears in an NP slot, usually as the name of a time or place:

After lunch will be too late.
Beyond the baseline is foul territory.

Place

We fished
{
on the bank.
along the shore.
near the island.
in the pond.
under the pier.

Specific Time

We arrived
{
at noon.
on Wednesday.

Duration

We hiked
{
until three o'clock.
for several days.
during the term break.
throughout the winter.

Manner

She walked with dignity.
I sunbathe in the nude.
I went by myself.

Measure

She won by a mile.
He came within an inch.

Means

She does her best work with a palette knife.
They cleared the land through sheer determination.

Cause or Reason

We went out for a pizza.
We were late because of the storm.

In the diagram the adverbial prepositional phrase is always attached to the verb:

Sentences often have more than one adverbial prepositional phrase:

We hiked in the woods for several hours on Saturday.

And like adverbs, adverbial prepositional phrases can occupy several positions, with those referring to time often more movable than those referring to place, especially when both appear in the same sentence:

On Saturday we hiked in the woods for several hours.

We are less likely to say

In the woods we hiked on Saturday for several hours.

But no matter where in the sentence they appear—whether at the beginning, the middle, or end—in the diagram the adverbial prepositional phrases will be attached to the verb:

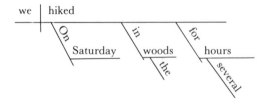

Exercise 39: Underline the adverbial prepositional phrases in the following sentences.

1. In winter we burn wood for our heat.
2. Wood is now being used in homes throughout the country for fuel.
3. Tim chopped down the oak tree on Saturday.
4. He stacked the oak wood on the back porch under the eaves.

5. According to the latest reports, the price of oil will go up <u>before January</u>.

Are all of these prepositional phrases movable? Are some more movable than others?

Because prepositional phrases can modify both verbs and nouns, ambiguity is fairly common. The prepositional phrase in the following sentence, for example, could be interpreted as meaning either "with whom" or "which problems":

They discussed their problems <u>with the teacher</u>.

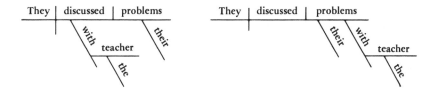

Sometimes the difference between the two possible interpretations is simply a matter of emphasis:

I'll see you at the game <u>on Saturday</u>.

Here the question is whether *on Saturday* modifies the noun *game* or the verb *see*. If we can move the prepositional phrase without distorting the meaning, then it must be adverbial—it must modify *see*—because only adverbial prepositional phrases are movable. So if it's possible to reverse the order of the two prepositional phrases and say

I'll see you <u>on Saturday</u> at the game.

or to make *on Saturday* the sentence opener,

<u>On Saturday</u> I'll see you at the game.

then *on Saturday* is clearly adverbial. If, however, the phrase specifies Saturday's game as opposed to Friday's game, then the function is to modify the noun *game,* and shifting its position would distort the meaning. In a conversation the speaker's intonation would make the meaning clear. But even in context the intention of the writer may not be clear. There is often no way of knowing which interpretation is more accurate:

> I'll see you at [the game on Saturday]
>
> *or*
>
> I'll see you [at the game] [on Saturday]

In a sentence such as this, where the two interpretations mean essentially the same thing, the ambiguity is not really a problem for the reader or listener. But in the earlier example—"They discussed their problems with the teacher"—a genuine question of meaning does exist. In speech, meaning is rarely a problem, and when it is, the listener can ask for clarification. But the writer is not present to be asked "What do you mean?" or "How's that again?" So the writer has an obligation to make such questions unnecessary. Understanding when modifiers are ambiguous is important for writers; avoiding ambiguity is a requirement of clear writing.

Exercise 40: Rewrite each of the following sentences in two ways to show its two possible meanings.

1. I'm going to wax the car in the garage.
2. Tim chopped the wood on the porch.
3. I hid from the neighbors upstairs.
4. Fred tripped his teammate with the bat.
5. Susan washed the stones she found in the river.

NOUN PHRASES

Noun phrases that function adverbially consist of a fairly short list of words and phrases designating time, place, manner, and quantity. Here are some of them:

> We walked <u>home</u>.

NP, V-int

I'm leaving <u>Monday morning</u>.
I'm going <u>your way</u>.
The book cost <u>ten dollars</u>.
<u>Every day</u> he studied <u>two hours</u>.
I travel <u>a great deal</u>.
We are flying <u>tourist class</u>.
I sent the package <u>airmail</u>.
The Boy Scouts hiked <u>single file</u> down the trail.
He arrived <u>this evening</u>.

These noun phrases work like prepositional phrases—like prepositional phrases with missing prepositions. The traditional grammarian labels them **adverbial objectives** and diagrams them as though they were the objects in prepositional phrases:

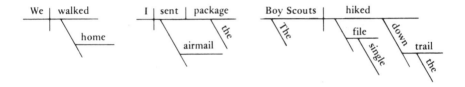

In some of these sentences the preposition is optional: (*on*) Monday morning, (*for*) two hours, (*by*) airmail, (*in*) single file.

This method of diagramming the adverbial noun phrase acknowledges both its *form*—a noun headword on a horizontal line with or without modifiers—and its *function*—a modifier of the verb.

Because these adverbial modifiers are, in form, noun phrases, you might be tempted to analyze a sentence such as

We walked home.
    or
He arrived this evening.

as NP₁ V-tr NP₂—in other words, as Pattern VII. The clues that tell you otherwise are to be found in the verb. You can test the verb for transitiveness in two ways: First, does the NP following the verb answer the question *what* or *whom,* as a direct object always does? And second, can you transform the sentence into the passive voice? The answer to both questions is "no"; these noun phrases answer adverbial questions, such as *where* and *when*. And obviously you cannot make the sentences passive:

> *Home was walked by us.
> *This evening was arrived by him.

Thus the sentences fail both tests for transitive verbs; they are intransitive Pattern VI sentences.

Exercise 41: Identify the sentence patterns of the following sentences.

1. The birds flew south.   *NP Vint*
2. I drank up the leftover punch.
3. We took the northern route.
4. I'll see you soon.   *NP, Vtr NPv*
5. The students were in line at the ticket window before dawn.   *NP, be ADV/TP*
6. They bought up all the tickets before noon.
7. My family is coming next week for a visit.   *NP, Vint*
8. They are in Canada now.   *NP, V,,*
9. I was awake the whole night.   *NP, be ADJ*
10. Bonnie will do the dishes next time.   *NP, Vtr NPv*

VERB PHRASES

The most common form of the verb in an adverbial role is the **infinitive,** the base form of the verb with *to:*

> The gymnast jumped up <u>to grab the horizontal bar.</u>
> I went home early <u>to get ready for the party.</u>
> Jennifer took on two paper routes <u>to earn money for camp.</u>

Note that the infinitives—*to grab, to get,* and *to earn*—are not simply verbs with *to;* they are entire verb phrases, complete with complements and modifiers. And even though they are not main, or **finite,** verbs, infinitives can be categorized as transitive or intransitive or linking, just as main verbs can; consequently, we can classify them according to their sentence patterns. Infinitives are, in effect, the predicate half of the sentence patterns, as the diagrams clearly show:

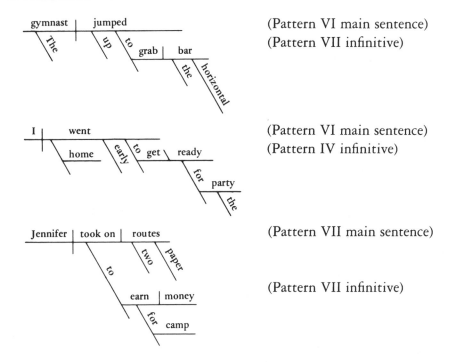

(Pattern VI main sentence)
(Pattern VII infinitive)

(Pattern VI main sentence)
(Pattern IV infinitive)

(Pattern VII main sentence)

(Pattern VII infinitive)

Note, too, that the subjects of the sentences are also the subjects of the infinitives.

In the third sentence, where the infinitive phrase follows a noun, *routes,* it may appear to be a modifier of that noun. The clue that says otherwise is the meaning "in order to" that underlies almost every adverbial infinitive; it answers the question *why* about the verb:

> The gymnast jumped up in order to grab the horizontal bar.
> I went home early in order to get ready for the party.
> Jennifer took on two paper routes in order to earn money for camp.

In fact, we often include *in order,* especially in introductory position:

> In order to earn money for camp, Jennifer took on two paper routes.

There are exceptions. Occasionally an infinitive functions adverbially without the meaning of "in order to," but such sentences are uncommon in speech:

> The detective glanced out the window only <u>to see</u> the suspect slip around the corner.
>
> I arrived at the auditorium only <u>to find</u> every seat taken.

These infinitives have an almost main-verb rather than adverbial quality. We could, and probably would, more often say:

> The detective glanced out the window <u>and saw</u> the suspect slip around the corner.
>
> I arrived at the auditorium <u>and found</u> every seat taken.

Other exceptions, which are fairly common idioms, occur with the verbs *come* and *live:*

> I've <u>come to believe</u> in UFOs.
>
> I've <u>come to understand</u> your point of view.
>
> You'll <u>live to regret</u> that remark.

The *-ing* verbs occasionally act adverbially, too, as in the following sentences:

> He drank his pitcher of beer <u>standing at the bar</u>. (*How?*)
>
> The kids came <u>running out of the house</u>. (*How? Where?*)
>
> Betsy went <u>swimming</u>. (*Where?*)

Dangling Infinitives. We noted that the subject of the sentence is also the subject of the adverbial infinitive. When this is not the case, the infinitive is said to "dangle," as in the following sentences, where the infinitive phrases have no stated subject:

> <u>To keep farm machinery in good repair</u>, a regular maintenance schedule is necessary.
>
> For decades the Superstition Mountains in Arizona have been explored in order <u>to find the fabled Lost Dutchman Mine</u>.

Certainly the problem with these sentences is not a problem of communication; no one is likely to misinterpret their meaning. But in both cases a kind of fuzziness exists that can be cleared up with the addition of a subject for the infinitive:

> A farmer needs a regular maintenance schedule to keep the farm machinery in good repair.
> For decades people [or adventurers or prospectors] have explored the Superstition Mountains in Arizona to find the fabled Lost Dutchman Mine.

Exercise 42: Underline all of the adverbial modifiers in the following sentences. Identify the sentence pattern of the main clause; then identify the sentence pattern of any adverbial verb phrases. Diagram the sentences.

1. Our cat often jumps up on the roof to reach the attic window.
2. Sometimes she even climbs the ladder to get there.
3. Last night the television set buzzed strangely after the ten o'clock news.
4. We were in the kitchen at the time.   *NP₁ be ADV TP*
5. We went downtown last Saturday to take advantage of the sidewalk sales.
6. First I bought the children winter boots at the new shoe store.
7. Afterwards we stayed home to watch the playoff game with Uncle Dick.

CLAUSES

What is a clause? When is a clause adverbial? The first question is fairly easy to answer, the second a bit more difficult. It will be helpful here to review the distinction between "sentence" and "clause" that we discussed in Chapter 1.

All sentences are (or include) clauses. In fact, Part I of this book could just as well be entitled "Clause Patterns" instead of "Sentence Patterns," because the basic sentence patterns underlie all clauses.

But not all clauses are complete sentences. Some are embedded in other clauses as adverbials, adjectivals, and nominals. Using the criterion of form, we will define **sentence** as a word or group of words that begins with a capital letter and ends with a period or other terminal punctuation. (In terms of spoken sentences, we would refer to terminal "juncture" rather than punctuation.) A more complete definition, one that includes the criterion of meaning as well as form, would read as follows:

> A **sentence** is a word or group of words based on one or more subject–predicate, or clause, patterns; the written sentence begins with a capital letter and ends with terminal punctuation.

This definition eliminates "Wow!" and "The very idea!" and "Rats!" as sentences, but it includes imperatives, such as "Help!" with its underlying clause "You help me."

All sentences, then, are clauses, but not all clauses are sentences. A clause introduced by a subordinating conjunction, for example, is not a sentence. The addition of *because* or *since* or *if* to a clause keeps it from being independent; it makes it dependent on another clause:

> <u>because</u> you were here
> <u>since</u> Joe went away
> <u>if</u> he knows the truth

The subordinating conjunctions are listed on page 136.

We use the term **independent clause** to denote a clause that can stand as a complete sentence. A sentence always contains at least one independent clause; when it contains more than one, we label it a **compound sentence.** The term **dependent clause,** on the other hand, refers to clauses like those listed above that do not stand alone as complete or independent sentences. When you read these clauses alone, the pitch of your voice will probably not drop at the end as it would if they were complete sentences. Try reading them as they are written above; then read them without the subordinating conjunction, as complete sentences:

> You were here.
> Joe went away.
> He knows the truth.

The difference you probably hear at the end—the more o.
pitch fading away in the dependent clause, as opposed to t.
pitch in the complete sentence—is the distinction between ...-
minal and terminal juncture in speech.

Look again at the sentence with a *when* clause at the beginning of
this chapter. Without *when* the clause would be independent. You can
hear the difference between the independent and the dependent clause
when you read them aloud:

> The magician thrust his sword into the box.
> When the magician thrust his sword into the box . . .

The addition of *when* turns the sentence into a dependent clause; a
sentence that includes a dependent clause is known as a **complex sentence**.

> The audience gasped when the magician thrust his sword into the
> box.

This example brings us to our second question: When is a dependent
clause adverbial?

The *when* clause above appears to be a straightforward adverbial of
time, just as *yesterday* or *then* or *at that very moment* would be, telling
"when" about the verb *gasped*. But it also seems accurate to say that
when relates the idea of the second clause to the entire first clause, not
simply to the verb. In the case of clauses introduced by such subordinating conjunctions as *since* or *because* or *if,* the issue is somewhat
clearer:

> I didn't expect to have a good time this week because you went
> away.

Here the condition introduced by *because* modifies more than the verb
didn't expect or even *didn't expect to have;* it is clearly related to the entire
idea "I didn't expect to have a good time this week." So a more accurate description of the function of the *because* clause here is "sentence
modifier" rather than "verb modifier," or adverbial.

Subordinate clauses, dependent clauses introduced by subordinating conjunctions, are traditionally classified as adverbial clauses. Certainly the meaning they add to the sentence is the same kind of information that adverbs and other adverbial structures contribute. The question is whether they belong in this chapter, "Modifiers of the Verb." For the majority of subordinate clauses, such as the *because* clause, the answer is probably "no"; they should be in the chapter entitled "Sentence Modifiers." But for some, such as the *when* clause about the magician and other clauses of place and time and manner, the issue is less clear-cut:

> After the Tigers won the World Series, the city of Detroit went wild.
> He held his partner on the dance floor as if she were made of glass.
> You should eat some food before you drink more wine.
> I usually take the subway home at night, even though my family disapproves.

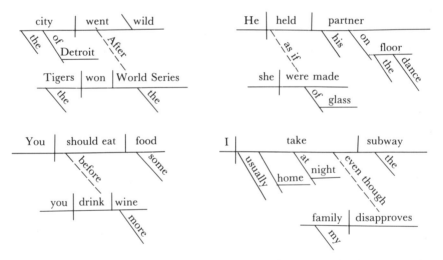

But no matter how we interpret such clauses—whether as verb modifiers or sentence modifiers—we can recognize them as contributors of adverbial information.

Adverbial clauses also function as modifiers in verb phrases that are themselves modifiers—such as the adverbial infinitive phrases we saw earlier:

> I went home early *to get ready for the party before the guests arrived.*

The underlined clause added to the infinitive phrase is clearly adverbial, telling "when" about *get ready;* it does not tell "when" about the verb *went,* the main verb, nor is it likely to be construed as a modifier of the whole sentence.

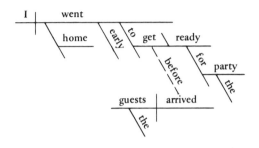

So even a clause that might normally be interpreted as a sentence modifier will act as a verb modifier when it is included in a nonfinite verb phrase, such as this adverbial infinitive phrase. (The term **nonfinite verb** refers to a verb that acts in some capacity other than as the main verb, as the adverbial infinitive phrase does here.) We shall see other such adverbial modifiers in participial phrases (Chapter 9) and in gerund phrases (Chapter 11). And in Chapter 12 we shall take up the subordinate clause in its role as sentence modifier.

SUMMARY

The term *adverbial* designates the function of any structure that modifies the verb—in other words, any structure that acts like an adverb, providing information of time, place, manner, reason, and the like. In this chapter we have looked at the various structures that provide such information. Adverbials come in many forms: adverbs, nouns and noun phrases, prepositional phrases, verb phrases, and clauses. It is sometimes difficult to decide if these structures—especially the clauses—are modifying the verb alone or the entire sentence; in the latter case, we would designate them as sentence modifiers. *gerund-verb used as a noun*

Exercise 43: Underline the adverbials in the following sentences. Identify each in terms of its form.

1. On Halloween all the neighbor children go out trick-or- *gerund* treating.

2. They expectantly ring every doorbell on the block to fill their bags with goodies.

3. A stranger on crutches was slowly walking his dog in the park last night.

4. The stranger walked on crutches with difficulty.

5. The couple upstairs remained friends after their divorce.

6. My neighbor's son is coming home for the holidays for the first time in over eight years.

7. The soprano sang beautifully at the opening performance of the new season.

8. After she sang so beautifully, the critics wrote rave reviews.

9. Diane must take fifteen credits to graduate this term.

10. Where were you when I needed a shove to get my car to the garage for repairs?

SENTENCES FOR PRACTICE

Underline the adverbials in the following sentences and identify their forms. For additional practice, identify the sentence patterns and ~~diagram the sentences.~~ Remember also to identify the sentence patterns of all adverbial verb phrases and clauses.

1. By the end of the fifth inning, the playoff game had become downright boring. *Prep. P.* *ADV* *NP V-lnk ADJ*

2. When the fall foliage shows its color in New England, thousands of tourists go there to enjoy nature's astonishing display.

3. At Mike's Halloween party a ghostly face appeared in the window at midnight.

4. This week's rally on Wall Street probably happened because of the optimistic news about interest rates.

5. Be silent always when you doubt your sense. (Alexander Pope)

6. Cowards die many times before their death. (Shakespeare)

7. During the month of December there will be dozens of holiday specials on television.

8. Whenever Henry becomes nervous, he gets a nasty skin rash behind his left ear.

9. Because of a rabies epidemic in Pennsylvania, fewer hunters applied for licenses in 1985.

10. On Monday Sue stayed home to fix a special gourmet dinner.

11. The subway was really crowded last night after work.

12. I always have a hard time when I put in a zipper.

13. In spite of my best efforts, I can never do it right the first time.

14. According to the Wall Street Journal, the deficit is considered our most serious domestic problem.

15. To give his kids a college education, my neighbor invests in the stock market.

QUESTIONS FOR DISCUSSION

1. Discuss the difference in the function of the infinitive phrase in the following sentences:

> I started to work on my math.
> I stopped to work on my math.

2. Consider the following pairs of sentences. Are they all grammatical? Does the difference between the adjective and the adverb represent a difference in meaning?

> Spread the paint thinly.
> Spread the paint thin.
>
> Spread the paint thickly.
> Spread the paint thick.

In thinking about the differences, be sure to make use of the sentence patterns.

3. Notice the idioms, or set expressions, in the following sentences: *put forward* and *shake loose.*

> Put your best foot forward.
> I can't shake this feeling loose.

Would you consider either of these expressions phrasal verbs? Why? Or why not? How do these two sentences differ? What are the patterns?

4. Think about the sentence pattern and the function of the prepositional phrase in the following sentence:

> The potato salad is for the picnic.

Is it possible that we may need another sentence pattern to account for this sentence?

5. How do you account for the difference in meaning of the following sentences? Why is "in the mountains" so important?

> After his retirement, Professor Jones lived for six months in the mountains.
> After his retirement, Professor Jones lived for six months.

6. The following sentence appeared in a letter to the editor of *Time*:

> I suggest the U.S. Government stop helping the Kremlin regime in its repressive actions by selling wheat to the USSR.

Why does the sentence require a second look? What is the source of the ambiguity?

7. As you know, single-word adverbs are often movable, producing a number of variations in a sentence. How many acceptable variations can you produce by adding the adverb *frequently* to the following sentence?

> I have had colds this year.

Are there any slots in the sentence where *frequently* is clearly unacceptable?

8. One of our most movable words in English is *only*. How many variations of the following sentence can you produce by inserting it?

> Joe eats raw vegetables for dinner on Sunday evenings.

Explain the difference in meaning that *only* produces by adding a negative clause to each version of your sentence, as shown in the following example:

> Only Joe eats raw vegetables for dinner on Sunday evenings; Mary doesn't.

9. Recently a banner was hung across the main street of a nearby city to recognize the local bus company's ten years of service to the community. On it was printed the company's name, followed by the verb phrase "serving our community" and, in bold print, these three words:

> SAFELY   ECONOMICALLY   FRIENDLY

What suggestion could you have made to the banner committee if they had asked for your advice?

9

Modifiers
of the Noun: Adjectivals

A noun phrase occupies at least one slot in every sentence pattern—that of subject. In six of the ten patterns, noun phrases occupy one or more slots in the predicate as well: direct object, indirect object, subjective complement, and objective complement; and in every prepositional phrase a noun phrase serves as the object of the preposition. Most of the NPs used in the sample sentences have been simple two-word phrases: *the students, a scholar, an apple, their assignment.* But in the sentences we actually speak and write, the noun phrases are frequently expanded with modifiers—not only with adjectives, the basic noun modifier, but with other nouns and noun phrases, with prepositional phrases, verb phrases, and clauses. We refer to the function of all such modifiers in the noun phrase as **adjectival.**

We can think of the noun phrase as a series of slots (in much the same way as we looked at the expanded verb), with the determiner and noun headword as the required slots and the modifiers before and after the headword as optional:

NP = <u>DETERMINER</u> ( ) ( ) <u>HEADWORD</u> ( ) ( ) ( )

Because of their frequency in the sentence and the variety of structures we use to expand them, noun phrases provide a remarkable range of possibilities for putting ideas into words. In this chapter we will look at these possibilities, and we will come to appreciate the systematic nature of modification in the noun phrase.

THE REQUIRED SLOTS

The Determiner. The **determiner** is the structure-word class that signals nouns. As we saw in Chapter 6, this class includes *articles, possessive nouns, possessive pronouns,* and *demonstrative pronouns,* as well as a variety of other common words. Like the other structure classes, determiners are learned early and used automatically; the native speaker rarely thinks about them. But when the writer begins to think consciously about language, an understanding of the determiner's role becomes important. For example, as the first word of the noun phrase, and thus frequently the first word of the sentence and even of the paragraph, the determiner can provide a bridge, or transition, between ideas. The selection of that bridge can make subtle but important differences in emphasis:

> <u>This</u> attempt at reconciliation proved futile.
> <u>The</u> attempt at reconciliation. . . .
> <u>Their</u> attempt. . . .
> <u>Every such</u> attempt. . . .
> <u>All of their</u> attempts. . . .
> <u>Those</u> attempts. . . .

In selecting determiners, writers have the opportunity not only to make such distinctions but also to help their readers move easily from one idea to the next in a meaningful way.

Some nouns, of course, are used without determiners: proper nouns (*John, Berkeley*), noncountable nouns (*salt, water*), abstract nouns (*justice, grief*), and sometimes plural count nouns (*apples, students*). The transformational linguists explain these undetermined nouns as actually having a determiner in the underlying meaning, which they label *null* or *zero* [∅].

```
              NP
            /    \
        DET        N

        the        boy
        my         hat
        ∅          John
        ∅          Berkeley
```

So as to emphasize the importance of determiners, we will follow the lead of these theorists and describe the noun phrase in terms of two required slots: determiner and headword.

The Headword. Filling the **headword** slot in the noun phrase is, of course, the noun, the word signaled by the determiner. We usually think of a noun as the name of a person, place, thing, event, concept, or the like—a meaning-based definition that works fairly well. But a more reliable criterion for identifying nouns, as we saw in Chapter 5, is that of form, signaled by the derivational and inflectional suffixes. Also, an understanding of the system of pre- and postnoun modifiers in the noun phrase will make the identification of the noun headword an easy matter.

Recognition of the headword of the noun phrase, incidentally, can be a help in preventing problems of subject–verb agreement. Such problems can arise when a postheadword modifier includes a noun itself:

*The stack *of instruction forms* were misplaced.

*The complicated instructions *on the new income tax
    form* really confuses me.

It is the number, either singular or plural, of the headword in the subject noun phrase that dictates the form of the verb in the present tense. In the preceding sentences, the writer has used the wrong noun in making the verb selection. *Stack* and *instructions* are the headwords; *forms* and *form* are simply parts of postnoun modifiers.

The stack was misplaced.

The *stack* of instruction forms was misplaced.

The instructions confuse me.

The complicated *instructions* on the new income tax form really
    confuse me.

THE PRENOUN MODIFIERS
Adjectives and Nouns. These two form classes generally fill the slots between the determiner and the headword. When the noun

phrase includes both an adjective and a noun as modifiers, they appear in that order; they cannot be reversed:

DETERMINER	ADJECTIVE	NOUN	HEADWORD
the	little		boy
the		neighbor	boy
the	little	neighbor	boy
a		marble	quarry
an	ancient	marble	bathtub
that	nervous	test	pilot
my	new	kitchen	table

The adjective slot frequently includes more than one adjective; all of them modify the headword:

the funny brown monkey

the little old man

You'll notice that there are no commas in the preceding noun phrases, even though there are several modifiers before the noun. But sometimes commas are called for. A good rule of thumb is to use a comma if it is possible to insert *and* between the modifiers. We would not talk about "a little and old man" nor "a funny and brown monkey." However, we would say "a strange and wonderful experience," so in using these two adjectives without *and,* we would use a comma:

a strange, wonderful experience

That comma represents juncture in speech—a pause and slight shift in pitch. Read the following pair of sentences aloud and listen to the difference in your voice:

On the table stood a little black suitcase.
On the table stood an ugly, misshapen suitcase.

In general, the system calls for a comma between two adjectives when they are of the same class, for instance, when they are both subjective qualities such as "strange" and "wonderful" or "ugly" and

"misshapen." However, in the earlier example—*funny brown monkey*—
the adjectives *funny* and *brown* are not alike: "funny" is a subjective,
changing quality; "brown" is an objective, permanent quality.

The adjective can also be qualified or intensified:

the extremely bright young lady

a really important career decision

In this situation we often have occasion to use a hyphen to make the
relationship clear:

a half-baked idea
the moss-covered stones
a Spanish-speaking community
a bases-loaded home run

Hyphens are especially common when the modifier in the adjective
slot is a participle (the *-ing* or *-en* verb), as in the previous examples:
baked, covered, speaking, and *loaded* are participles. And because participles are verbs, they are also commonly modified by adverbs:

a well-developed paragraph
the fast-moving train
the low-hanging clouds
this highly publicized event
a carefully conceived plan

The hyphen rule here is fairly straightforward: The *-ly* adverbs (such as
highly and *carefully*) and *-ly* intensifiers (such as *really* and *extremely*) do
not take hyphens; other adverbs in preparticiple position (such as *well*
and *fast* and *low*) do take hyphens.

Other classes of words also need hyphens when the first modifier
applies not to the headword but to the second modifier:

high-technology industries
two-word verbs
all-around athletes
free-form sculpture

In these modifiers, if the hyphen were eliminated, the reader would not know that *two* does not apply to *verbs,* nor *all* to *athletes,* nor *free* to *sculpture.*

Another occasion for hyphens in preheadword position occurs when we use a complete phrase in the adjective slot:

> an off-the-wall idea
> the end-of-the-term party
> a middle-of-the-road policy
> my back-to-back exams

When a phrasal modifier fills the subjective complement slot in the sentence pattern, however, the hyphens are generally omitted:

> Our party will be at <u>the end of the term</u>.
> My exams during finals week are <u>back to back</u>.

In certain idioms they would probably be retained:

> His idea seemed off-the-wall to me.
> The policy he subscribes to is strictly middle-of-the-road.

The position in the sentence can also affect the earlier hyphenated examples:

> The paragraph was well developed.
> The industry did research in high technology.

Nouns that fill the preheadword position are of two kinds: Some, such as *marble* in "an ancient marble bathtub," are simply modifiers of the noun; others actually combine with the headword to form a compound noun, as in "a marble quarry." The difference between "marble bathtub" and "marble quarry" can be heard in the stress pattern. The noun as modifier usually has weaker stress than the noun headword it modifies:

> The mârble báthtub

(The symbol / indicates primary stress or loudness; ∧ indicates secondary stress; \ indicates tertiary, or the third level of stress.)

Compare the preceding stress pattern with the stress pattern usually found in the compound noun, where the primary stress is on the first noun:

the márble quàrry

Many nouns in the preheadword slot are of this second kind—part of a compound structure, carrying the primary stress. Many such compounds have come to be written as single words: teacup, applesauce, doorknob, bookcase. Many are written as separate words, and some can be found both ways:

téa servìce	wíne glàss (wineglass)
tést pilòt	béef stèak (beefsteak)
táx shèlter	hóuse plànt (houseplant)
oíl revènue	

Nouns that serve simply as modifiers often describe the material the headword is made of:

mârble báthtùb	âpple píe	strâwbèrry shórtcàke
wîcker básket	bêef stéw	glâss bóttle

In other noun phrases with the *modifier* + *noun* stress pattern, the first noun often specifies a time or place:

wînter vacátion	schôol cafetéria
kîtchen táble	nîght bréeze
sûmmer wárdròbe	dâytime témperature

A fairly common practice is to turn these modified nouns and compound nouns into modifiers themselves:

a winter vacation plan
a school cafeteria policy
an oil revenue tax writeoff
a food service operation

Such strings can easily proliferate—and their meanings become obscure. For example, the committee in charge of the school cafeteria policy becomes the "school cafeteria policy committee" and their meetings then come to be known as the "school cafeteria policy committee meetings." In the case of all of these noun phrases with prenoun modifiers, the headword is the last noun in the string.

In the diagram of the noun phrase, no matter where in the sentence it appears and no matter how many modifiers it includes, the headword is on a horizontal line with the determiner, adjective(s), and modifying noun(s) sloping down from it:

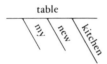

When the modifiers themselves have modifiers, either qualifiers or other nouns, the diagram will make that clear:

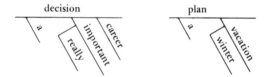

Incidentally, the noun acting as a preheadword modifier and the possessive noun in the determiner slot are the only nouns that do not appear on horizontal lines in the sentence diagram; these are the only cases when nouns are not headwords of noun phrases.

Exercise 44: Underline the determiner and the headword of each noun phrase in the following sentences. Identify the form of any modifiers that fill slots between them. Punctuate the noun phrases with commas and hyphens, if necessary.

1. The department's personnel committee met in the main office Monday night.
2. I am impressed with the new Sunday brunch menu at the Country Club.

3. I found an expensive looking copper colored bracelet in the subway station.
4. The committee has worked hard to make this year's homecoming celebration a really festive occasion.
5. The bicycle safety commission will discuss the new regulations at their regular meeting this noon.
6. Her lovely gracious manner was apparent from the start.
7. My poor old cat probably won't last through another extreme winter.
8. There was a splendid old table at the auction.
9. They served us delicious refreshing iced tea.
10. A commonly held notion among my cynical friends is that big business lobbyists run the country.

THE POSTNOUN MODIFIERS

The postheadword position in the noun phrase may contain modifiers of many forms; when there is more than one, they appear in this order:

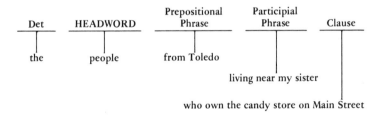

The other principal postheadword modifier is the **appositive**, a noun phrase that renames the headword. The position of the appositive is somewhat flexible in relation to the other structures:

my *uncle,* a butcher at Phil's Market, who makes his own salami

the funny little *man* who lives next door, a World War I veteran

In this section we will look at each of these structures that follow the headword, beginning with the most common postnoun modifier, the prepositional phrase.

Prepositional Phrases. The adjectival prepositional phrase, which modifies a noun, is in form identical to the adverbial prepositional phrase described in Chapter 8. In its adjectival role the prepositional phrase identifies the noun headword in relation to time, place, direction, purpose, origin, and the like:

> The *people* across the street rarely speak to the neighbors.
> The security *guard* in our building knows every tenant personally.
> I have always admired the lovely *homes* along Sparks Street.
> The *meeting* during our lunch hour was a waste of time.
> Jack is a *man* of many talents.

Because the prepositional phrase itself includes a noun phrase, the adjectival prepositional phrase demonstrates the recursiveness of the language—the embedding of one structure in another of the same kind:

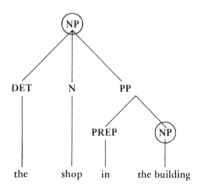

Such recursiveness occurs in many parts of the sentence: a sentence within a sentence, a noun phrase within a noun phrase, a verb phrase within a verb phrase. In the case of the adjectival prepositional phrase, we nearly always have a noun phrase within a noun phrase. And we needn't stop with one embedding; we could continue branching that NP at the bottom of the diagram with another D + N + PP, which would produce yet another NP:

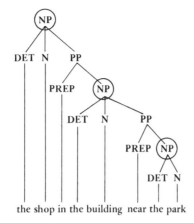

the shop in the building near the park

Such strings, though fairly common, especially at the end of the sentence, are sometimes open to ambiguity:

My sister manages the flower shop in the new brick building near the park on Center Street.

Our linguistic computer most readily associates a modifier with the nearest possible referent:

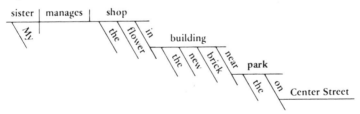

If a different meaning is intended—if, for example, it is the building rather than the park that is on Center Street—the writer must make that clear: "the flower shop in the brick building on Center Street that is near the park."

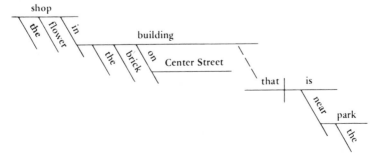

In the discussion of adverbial prepositional phrases in Chapter 8, we described another source of ambiguity—the modifier that could be either adjectival or adverbial:

They discussed their problems with the teacher.

Here the ambiguity arises because the adverbial phrase often comes at the end of the sentence, which is also a common position for the noun phrase modifier:

We followed the man in the park.

There are always alternatives to ambiguity, ways of recasting a sentence to make it clear:

We followed the man who was in the park.
or
We followed the man through the park.
or
We followed the man as he strolled in the park.

Unlike the adverbial prepositional phrase, which is often movable, the adjectival prepositional phrase always stays with the noun it modifies; and with few exceptions it follows the noun. Occasionally a prepositional phrase appears in prenoun position, as we saw earlier; in such cases it is usually written with hyphens; and because it is so rare, it always calls attention to itself:

the across-the-street neighbors
the club's after-hours activities
an out-of-the-way place
an off-the-wall idea

Exercise 45: Underline the adjectival prepositional phrases in the following sentences. If any of them are ambiguous, explain the reason for the ambiguity.

1. A young man with a cast on his left foot hobbled down the street.
2. I will meet you in the lobby of the museum near the visitors' information booth.
3. The party after the game at Bob's must have been a riot.
4. The field across the street is filled with beautiful wild flowers in spring.
5. The field is now ablaze with the colorful wild flowers of spring.
6. The textbook for my science course was written by a Nobel laureate from Stanford.

Participial Phrases. The participle—the *-ing* or *-en* form of the verb—is another of the nonfinite verbs, those forms of the verb in roles other than that of main verb. But because they are verbs in form, participles have all of the characteristics of verbs, including complements and adverbial modifiers. So even when verbs or verb phrases are adjectivals—noun modifiers—they can be thought of in terms of sentence patterns:

The *students* taking the law boards look nervous.

In form this postnoun modifier is a verb phrase, a participle. Underlying it is a Pattern VII sentence—NP_1 V-tr NP_2:

The students are taking the law boards.

The relationship of the noun headword to its participle modifier is always a subject–verb relationship: A participle modifies its own subject.

In the diagram the participle slopes down from its subject, the headword, and then becomes a horizontal line to accommodate any complements and/or modifiers it may have:

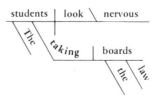

The diagram of the participle looks exactly like the verb half of the sentence that underlies it:

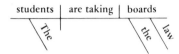

You'll notice that the only difference between the participle and the finite verb (the main verb) in the preceding diagram is a form of *be*.

As the example illustrates, participles that are formed from transitive verbs will take direct objects (taking *the law boards*), and all participles, just like verbs in all the sentence patterns, may be modified by adverbials of various forms:

The students *taking the law boards this morning* look nervous.

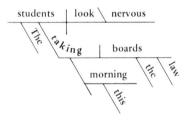

In the preceding sentence we have added an adverbial noun phrase, *this morning*. The adverbial modifying the participle may take the form of a subordinate clause too. Even those clauses that normally function as sentence modifiers rather than verb modifiers will be adverbial when they are a part of the participial phrase:

The old hound, *guarding the bone as though it were his very last meal,* growled fiercely at every stranger.

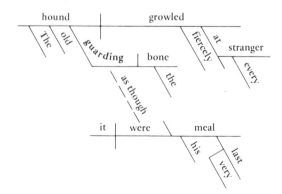

In the next example, a prepositional phrase modifies the participle:

I don't know the people *living across the hall.*

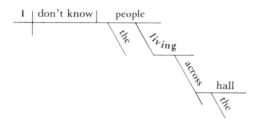

You'll notice, too, that in this sentence the participle modifies the direct object. Any noun phrase slot in the sentence, of course, can include participles as modifiers. The entire system for expanding the noun phrase described in this chapter applies to noun phrases in all positions.

Exercise 46: Turn each of the following sentences into a noun phrase with a postnoun participial phrase. Use that noun phrase in a sentence.

Example: Two dogs are fighting over the bone.
Sentence: I recognize those two dogs fighting over the bone.

1. An expensive sports car is standing in the driveway.
2. The students are cramming for their history test.
3. The baby is sleeping upstairs in the crib.
4. The fans are lining up at the ticket office.
5. A huge crowd is watching the parade.

Passive Participles. The participles we have seen so far are the *-ing* form of the verb (traditionally called the *present participle*); and the sentences underlying them are in the active voice. Another common form of the participle is the *-en* form, the past participle:

The houses <u>designed by Frank Lloyd Wright</u> are national treasures.
The car <u>driven by the front runner</u> has developed engine trouble.

We can figure out the sentences underlying these *-en* participles by again adding a form of *be:*

>The houses <u>were designed</u> by Frank Lloyd Wright.
>The car <u>was driven</u> by the front runner.

Both of these underlying sentences are passive transformations. (You will recall from Chapter 2 that in active voice verbs the auxiliary *be* is followed by the *-ing* form of the verb, not the *-en*.)

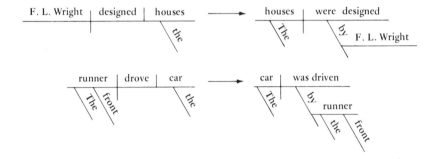

Remember, we produce a passive sentence by adding *be* + *-en* to the verb, so the passive verb is always the *-en* form. When we turn such sentences into participles, we will automatically have the *-en* form:

>We <u>stored</u> the record collection in the attic. (*Active*)
>The record collection <u>was stored</u> in the attic. (*Passive*)

This passive verb phrase will become a passive participle with the deletion of *was:*

>The record collection <u>stored in the attic</u> collected dust all summer long.
>I completely forgot the record collection <u>stored in the attic</u>.

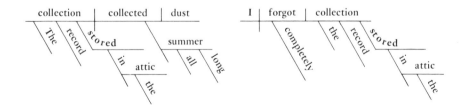

A participle derived from a passive Pattern IX or X sentence will include a subjective complement:

My brother is considered <u>the area's best foreign car mechanic</u>.

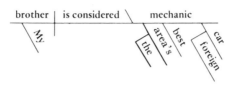

When we delete *is*, the result is a noun phrase with a postheadword passive participial phrase, which we can then use in another sentence:

My brother, <u>considered the area's best foreign car mechanic</u>, drives an old Chevy pickup.

Because these last two examples of passive participles are derived from regular verbs, the *-en* form ends in *ed* rather than *en*. The participles are obviously passive rather than active, however, because with few exceptions the active voice participle will be the *-ing* form.

Exercise 47: Transform the following active sentences into noun phrases with passive participles. Use each noun phrase in a sentence.

Example: The neighbor boys broke the garage window.
Passive: The garage window was broken by the neighbor boys.
Noun phrase: the garage window broken by the neighbor boys
Sentence: We should replace the garage window broken by the neighbor boys.

1. The bartender filled our mugs to the brim.
2. Betty made the costumes for the play herself.
3. The victim scrawled the murderer's name on the floor in lipstick.
4. The committee awarded Mary first prize for her charcoal sketch of an albatross.

Movable Participles. We can think of the postheadword slot in the noun phrase as the "home base" of the participle, as it is of the adjectival prepositional phrase. But unlike the adjectival prepositional phrase, the participial phrase can shift to the beginning or end of the sentence when it modifies the subject:

> Built by Frank Lloyd Wright in 1936, the Kauffman house at Fallingwater is one of Western Pennsylvania's most valued architectural treasures.
> Hoping for good weather, we planned our class picnic for Saturday.
> We planned our class picnic for Saturday, hoping for good weather.

The introductory slot is a common position for expanded participial phrases, those that include auxiliaries:

> Having found the camp deserted, we assumed that the hunters had returned to civilization.

Dangling Participles. This introductory participial phrase provides a good way to add variety to sentences, to get away from the standard subject opener. But it carries an important restriction: The participle can begin the sentence *only* if it modifies the subject—that is, when the subject of the participle is also the subject of the sentence and is in regular subject position. Otherwise, the participle dangles. Simply stated, a dangling participle is a verb in search of a subject:

> *Having swung his five iron too far to the left, Joe's ball landed precisely in the middle of a sand trap.

(The ball did not swing the five iron; Joe did.)

> *Still smiling blandly at the newsmen, a cream pie from somewhere in the crowd struck the senator squarely in the face.

(The cream pie was not smiling; the senator was.)

A common source of the dangling participle, and other kinds of dangling modifiers as well, is the sentence with a "delayed subject." Two common delayers are the *there* transformation and the generalized *it*. (They are described on pages 71–73 and 140–141.)

*Having moved all the outdoor furniture into the garage, there
    was no room left for the car.

In this *there* transformation, the subject of *having moved* does not appear
at all. But even when the subject is part of the sentence, the participle
will dangle if the subject is not in normal subject position:

*Knowing how much work I had to do yesterday, it was good of
    you to come and help.

In this sentence the subject of the participle, *you,* is there, but it
appears in the predicate rather than in the usual subject position. As
readers and listeners, we process sentences with certain built-in expectations. Our linguistic computers are programmed to attach an introductory participle to the first logical subject offered. The dangling
participle causes a malfunction in the program.

Incidentally, moving the participle to the end of the sentence does
not solve the problem of the dangler. Even there we expect the participle to modify the subject:

*Joe's ball landed precisely in the middle of a sand trap, having
    swung his five iron too far to the left.

Probably the most efficient way to revise such a sentence is to expand
the participial phrase into a complete clause. That expansion will add
the missing subject:

After *we* moved all the outdoor furniture into the garage, there
    was no room left for the car.
It was good of you to come and help yesterday when *you* learned
    how much work I had to do.

Another common source of the dangling participle is the passive
sentence:

*Having worked hard since 6 A.M., the project was completed
    before noon.

Here the problem arises because the passive transformation has deleted the agent, which is also the subject of the participle. Transforming the sentence into the active voice will solve the problem.

> <u>Having worked hard since 6 A.M.</u>, *we* completed the project before noon.

Exercise 48: Rewrite the following sentences to eliminate the dangling participles.

1. Having endured rain all week, the miserable weather on Saturday didn't surprise us.
2. Having hiked five miles uphill, my backpack must have weighed a ton.
3. Hoping for the sixth win in a row, there was great excitement in the grandstand as the band played "The Star Spangled Banner."
4. Guarding his bone as though it were his last meal, it was fascinating to watch the dog react to strangers.
5. Working ten hours a day, six days a week, John's first novel was completely finished in six months.
6. Exhausted by the hot weather, there was nothing to do but lie in the shade.
7. Wearing their new uniforms proudly, we watched the band march across the field and form a huge "O."
8. Having spent nearly all day in the kitchen, that superb gourmet dinner was worth the effort.

Prenoun Participles. Before leaving the participle, we should note that when a participle is a verb alone, a single word, with no complements or phrasal modifiers, it will usually occupy the adjective slot in preheadword position:

> Our <u>snoring</u> visitor kept the household awake.
> The <u>barking</u> dog next door drives us crazy.
> I should replace that <u>broken</u> hinge.
> The old hound growled at every <u>passing</u> stranger.

In this position, an adverb sometimes modifies the participle:

Our <u>loudly snoring</u> visitor kept the household awake.
The <u>peacefully sleeping</u> baby was a joy to watch.

Exercise 49: Write out the sentences that underlie the prenoun participles in the six examples preceding. Identify their sentence patterns.

1. snoring:
2. barking:
3. broken:
4. passing:
5. snoring:
6. sleeping:

Relative Clauses. Like the adverbial clause that modifies verbs, the **relative,** or **adjectival, clause** is a dependent clause; as a clause in form, it is a sentence pattern, complete with subject and predicate. The only difference between the relative clause and a complete sentence is the introductory word, the relative: It may be a relative pronoun (*who, whose, whom, which, that, whoever, whatever,* etc.) or a relative adverb (*where, when, why*).

The **relative pronoun** (1) renames the headword, which is the antecedent of the pronoun, and (2) plays the part of a noun in the clause:

The people <u>who live across the street</u> always share their surplus vegetables.

The traditional diagram clearly shows the relationship of the clause to the noun it modifies:

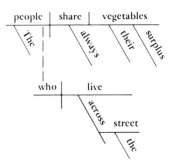

The broken line connects the pronoun to its antecedent, the headword of the noun phrase; the pronoun *who* fills the subject slot in its clause. In the next sentence, the relative pronoun *which* is the direct object in its clause:

> The solution, which Mary finally discovered after two hours of hard work, completely eluded me.

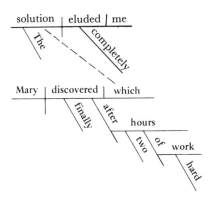

The commas around the *which* clause mean that it is not restrictive in relation to its headword. (The difference between restrictive and nonrestrictive modifiers is discussed in the next section.) In the next sentence the possessive relative pronoun, *whose,* acts as a determiner in the clause, the part that possessive pronouns usually play:

> The people whose car we bought gave us some good tips on fuel economy.

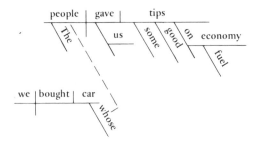

The broken line connects *whose* to its antecedent, *the people*—in other words, *the people's car.*

In the following sentence, the relative pronoun *that* acts as the subject of its clause:

The museum in Johnstown <u>that commemorates the city's fre-
quent floods</u> has some astonishing pictures.

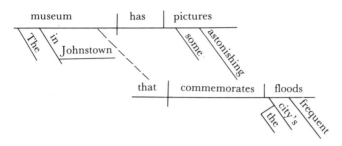

In the next sentence the relative pronoun *that* is the direct object in its
clause:

You choose a color <u>that you like.</u>

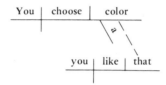

Note that this sentence would be equally grammatical without *that:*

You choose a color you like.

The relative *that* can be deleted only when it is an object in its clause,
not when it acts as the subject.

Like the relative *that,* the objective case relative, *whom,* can often be
deleted. The following *whom* clauses illustrate another principle: The
case of the relative is determined by the part it plays in its own clause:

The agent <u>[whom] we know as Mr. X</u> always gets his man.

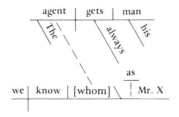

Even though the *whom* is deleted, it will have a place on the diagram; it is "understood." The deleted word can be shown in brackets, or it can be replaced by an x.

> King Edward VIII gave up the throne of England for the woman [whom] he loved.

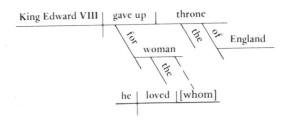

Sometimes we substitute *that* in order to avoid the awkwardness or formality of *whom*. Some writers, however, consider *that* unacceptable in reference to people:

> A man that I knew in the army called me last week.

In this example, we would be more likely to simply delete the relative. In the case of a nonrestrictive clause, however, the relative pronoun is required:

> Sergeant Major Miller, whom I knew in the army, called me last week.

In speaking this sentence we are more likely to say *who* instead of *whom;* most listeners wouldn't notice the difference.

Exercise 50: Underline the adjectival clauses in the following sentences. Identify (1) the role of the relative in its clause and (2) the sentence pattern of the clause.

1. The man I love loves me.
2. I don't like the new kitchen chairs that we bought.
3. The people whose farm we rent like to gossip about the neighbors.

4. Vitamin C, which some people consider a defense against the common cold, is relatively inexpensive.
5. My grandfather once knew a man who lived next door to the Wright brothers.
6. Our faithful dog, whom we all dearly loved, died last week at the age of seventeen.
7. Professor Black, who is here for a conference, will be the guest speaker in my history class today.
8. We're going to the concert that the string quartet is giving this afternoon on the lawn.

The expanded, or indefinite, relative pronouns also introduce adjectival clauses:

I will give the prize to <u>whoever scores the most points</u>.

On the surface this relative clause looks like a nominal, rather than an adjectival, clause; it looks like the object of the preposition. We include it here because of its underlying meaning, which is illustrated by the diagram that follows: "I will give the prize to [the person who] scores the most points." The expanded relatives are called *indefinite* because there is no specific noun they refer to, but there is an understood, or general, reference underlying these relatives.

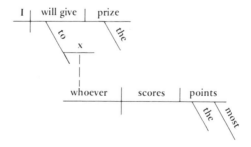

This sentence again illustrates the concept of case: The case of the relative pronoun is determined by its role in the relative clause, not by the role of the clause. In this sentence the clause follows the preposition; however, the relative pronoun is the subject of *scores* within its clause, so its form is subjective (*whoever*), not objective (*whomever*).

Exercise 51: Select the form of the relative pronoun in the following sentences.

1. Tell me the name of the man (who, whom) you are planning to marry.
2. The foreman gave bonuses to (whoever, whomever) the committee recommended.
3. John is the man (who, whom) I expect to win. ?
4. I will ask (whomever, whoever) I want to the party.
5. (Whoever, Whomever) leaves the room last must turn out the lights.
6. Our senator, (who, whom) we all believe to be an honorable man, seems reluctant to talk about his campaign funds.

All of the relative pronouns fill slots in the clauses that nouns normally fill. However, some adjectival clauses are introduced not by relative pronouns but by the relative adverbs *where, when,* and *why.* In these clauses the relative fills an adverbial slot in its clause. The relative adverb *where* introduces clauses that modify nouns of place:

Newsworthy events rarely happen in the small *town* where I was born.

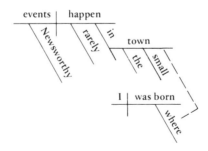

In the diagram note that the relative adverb *where* modifies the verb *was born* in its own clause; however, the clause itself is adjectival, modifying *town.*

When clauses modify nouns of time:

We are all looking forward to *Tuesday,* when results of the audi-
tion will be posted.

Why clauses modify the noun *reason:*

I understand the *reason* why Margo got the leading role.

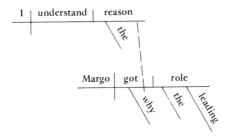

Where, when, and *why* clauses are often equally acceptable, and sometimes smoother, without the relative:

I understand the reason Margo got the leading role.
We are looking forward to the day the results are posted.

Sometimes *that* takes the place of the relative adverb:

I understand the reason that Margo got the leading role.
We are looking forward to the day that the results will be posted.

In diagramming these sentences, we would have to recognize the
underlying meaning of *that* as an adverbial. In the last example, "the
day that" it is another way of saying "the day on which"; the clause
itself, however, is adjectival, the modifier of a noun.

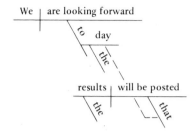

PUNCTUATION OF CLAUSES AND PARTICIPLES

The question regarding punctuation of clauses and participles is the question of restrictive versus nonrestrictive modifiers. The question put simply: Should I set off the phrase or clause with commas?

In answering this question, the writer must think about the referent of the noun being modified. Is it clear to the reader? In the case of a singular noun, is there only one possible person (or place or thing, etc.) to which the noun can refer? In the case of plurals, are the limits understood? If there is only one, the modifier cannot restrict the noun's meaning any further: The modifier is therefore **nonrestrictive** and will be set off by commas. It might be useful to think of these commas as parentheses and the modifier as optional; if it's optional, we can assume it's not needed to make the referent of the noun clear.

If the referent of the noun is not clear to the reader—if there is more than one possible referent or if the limits are not known—the purpose of the modifier is quite different: to restrict the meaning of the noun. Thus the modifier in this case is **restrictive** and is not set off by commas. You may find the terms *defining* and *commenting* easier to understand than *restrictive* and *nonrestrictive*.[1] Does the modifier define (restrict) the noun or does it merely comment on (not restrict) it?

Notice the difference in the punctuation of the following pair of sentences:

> The football players wearing shiny orange helmets stood out in the crowd.
> The football players, wearing shiny orange helmets, stood out in the crowd.

---

[1] These terms are used by Francis Christensen in *Notes Toward a New Rhetoric* (New York: Harper & Row, 1967), pp. 95 ff.

In the first sentence the purpose of the participial phrase is to define *which* football players stood out in the crowd. We could illustrate the situation by depicting a crowd of football players on the field, some of whom are wearing *shiny orange helmets;* they are noticeable—they *stand out in the crowd* of football players—because the others are wearing drab, dark helmets. In the second sentence the modifier merely comments on the players—it does not define them. An illustration of this situation might show a group of orange-helmeted football players signing autographs in a crowd of children; those players would stand out in that crowd with or without orange helmets. The modifier does *not* tell *which* football players stood out in the crowd; they *all* did. (And, incidentally, they were all wearing orange helmets.)

Context, of course, will make a difference. What does the reader already know? For example, out of context the clause in the following sentence appears to be restrictive:

> The president <u>who was elected in 1932</u> faced problems that would have overwhelmed the average man.

Ordinarily we would say that the noun phrase *the president* has many possible referents; the *who* clause is needed to make the referent clear; it defines and restricts *the president* to a particular man, the one elected in 1932. But what if the reader already knows the referent?

> Franklin Delano Roosevelt took office at a time when the outlook for the nation was bleak, indeed. The president, <u>who was elected in 1932</u>, faced decisions that would have overwhelmed the average man.

In this context the clause is simply commenting; the referent of the noun phrase *the president* is already defined by the time the reader gets to it. Many times, however, context alone is an insufficient determinant; only the writer knows if the clause defines or comments. The reader can only take the writer's word—or punctuation—at face value:

> The rain began with the first drumbeat. Only the band members <u>who were wearing rain gear</u> stayed reasonably dry. Everyone else at the parade, spectators and marchers alike, got wet.

Without commas the clause restricts the meaning of the noun phrase *the band members;* it defines those band members who stayed dry.

Francis Christensen emphasizes that the writer must also be aware of what the reader might infer from the restrictive clause or phrase. "When the modifier is restrictive, the sentence makes one statement and implies its opposite; and what it implies is just as important as what it states."[2] In other words, in the preceding sentence the clause *who were wearing rain gear* implies that some band members were *not* wearing rain gear and did *not* stay reasonably dry. In the case of the football players, the modifier in the first sentence, the one with the restrictive clause, suggests the presence of football players who were *not* wearing shiny orange helmets and did *not* stand out in the crowd. That implication is built into the restrictive modifier. If such an opposite statement is not true, the writer must be careful to avoid giving the reader the wrong impression. In writing the sentence with commas, the writer would no longer be identifying or defining a *subgroup* of dry band members or football players; with commas, the clauses become comments about the *entire group*.

So in reaching a decision about commas, the writer must take into account (1) what the reader knows (Is the referent clear without this information?) and (2) what the reader will infer if the modifier is restrictive.

Avoiding Comma Errors. The writer who uses commas at every pause in the sentence probably uses too many commas. In speech we often pause between the subject and the verb or between the verb and the direct object—that is, between the slots in the sentence pattern; but in writing we never separate these slots with commas. A simple pause, then, does not signal a comma. The pause that signals a comma usually includes a change in pitch.

Reading a sentence aloud as you would normally speak can be useful in identifying such changes. If you wanted to distinguish the dry band members from the wet ones, for example, you would probably speak the sentence with the loudest stress on *rain,* with secondary stress on *dry:*

The band members wearing rain gear stayed dry.

---

[2] Christensen, p. 98.

The line indicates the normal pitch or **intonation** contour, showing rising pitch over the loudest syllable and falling pitch at the end. The intonation contour of the sentence with a nonrestrictive modifier is quite different:

The bánd members, wearing raín gear, stayed drý.

The nonrestrictive modifier has an intonation contour separate from that of the main sentence, so that this sentence has three main stress points. In reading the sentence aloud, you'll especially notice a difference in the stress you give to *band;* it is longer and louder than it is in the other version, with its single intonation contour. And if you listen carefully to the words *members* and *gear,* you'll detect a slight rise in pitch at the very end of the words. That is the pitch rise that is often signaled by a comma.

Actually this sentence probably sounds strange when you hear yourself say it; it has an unnatural, stilted quality. That quality occurs because we rarely speak in sentences with nonrestrictive modifiers in postnoun position. This is an important difference between speaking and writing. In making punctuation decisions about such modifiers, the writer can take advantage of this difference by reading the sentence aloud.

In the case of participial phrases that modify the subject, the writer has another useful test: Can the modifier be shifted to the beginning or end of the sentence? If that shift does not change the meaning, the modifier is nonrestrictive. The restrictive participial phrase will remain within the noun phrase, whereas the nonrestrictive phrase can introduce the sentence and sometimes follow it:

Wearing rain gear, the band members stayed reasonably dry.

In the case of the relative clause, the relative pronoun provides some clues for punctuation:

1. The adjectival *that* clause is always restrictive; it is never set off by commas.
2. The *which* clause is generally nonrestrictive; it is set off by commas. For many writers this rule is invariable: The *which* clause is always nonrestrictive.

3. If the relative can be deleted, the clause is restrictive:

> The bus (that) I ride to work is always late.
> The woman (whom) I work with is always early.

The next two rules of thumb apply to both clauses and phrases:

4. After any proper noun the modifier will be nonrestrictive.
5. After any common noun that has only one possible referent the modifier will be nonrestrictive:

> My youngest sister, who lives in Oregon, is much more domestic than I.
> The highest mountain in the world, which resisted the efforts of climbers until 1953, looks truly forbidding from the air.

Exercise 52: Identify the postnoun modifiers in the following sentences as restrictive or nonrestrictive by adding commas if needed.

1. My parents who retired to Arizona in 1975 love the dry climate there.
2. My favorite teacher who always celebrates Fridays with cookies for the class will be leaving at the end of the term.
3. The driver of the bus that I take to work knows all of his passengers by name.
4. After our first assignment in economics class which everyone complained about, I'm not looking forward to the second.
5. The little log house that sits on the bank downstream from the dam always looks lonely to me.
6. That little house is occupied by our county's only known recluse whom I often see near the dam with a fishing pole in hand.

A PARTICIPIAL RESTRICTION

Sometimes for purposes of emphasis or variety, we switch the nonrestrictive modifier to the end of the sentence, especially if the sentence is fairly short. Even there, however, the modifier is set off by a comma, and it still modifies the subject of the sentence:

> The Boy Scout troop trudged up the mountain in search of a campsite, carrying all of their supplies on their backs.
> The audience stood and applauded, laughing uproariously.

The rule about nonrestrictive participial phrases at the end of the sentence may seem quite simple—and it is—but it's also a surprising rule. The nonrestrictive participial phrase is different from other nonrestrictive modifiers in being limited to the subject. Even when it's at the end of the sentence, it doesn't modify a noun in the predicate. For example, consider the following sentences:

> Bill washed the car standing in the driveway.
>
> Bill washed the car, standing in the driveway.

As the arrows indicate, in the first sentence the restrictive participial phrase modifies *car;* it's the car that's standing in the driveway. In the second, however, the phrase is nonrestrictive; it modifies *Bill.* Here's another illustration:

> Bill talked to the mailman coming up the walk.
> Bill talked to the mailman, coming up the walk.

Again, the subject of *coming* changes.

The rule is a surprising one because it doesn't apply to any other kind of noun modifier. If we were to turn those modifiers into clauses, for example, both would modify the object:

> Bill washed the car that was standing in the driveway.
>
> Bill washed the car, which was standing in the driveway.
>
> Bill talked to the mailman who was coming up the walk.
>
> Bill talked to the mailman, who was coming up the walk.

Understanding this tricky rule about participles will keep you from writing strange-sounding sentences like this one:

> Bill washed his car, covered with dust from the trip home.

You can express that idea by using a different form for the modifier:

> Bill washed his car, which was covered with dust from the trip home.
> Bill washed his dust-covered car.

MULTIPLE MODIFIERS

So far we have used examples of noun phrases with a single post-headword modifier, either a clause or a phrase. But we often have more than one such modifier, and when we do, the order in which they appear is well defined: prepositional phrase, participial phrase, relative clause:

> the security guard {in our building} {who checks out the visitors}
> the woman {from London} {staying with the Renfords}
> the DC-10 {on the far runway} {being prepared for takeoff} {which was hijacked by a group of terrorists}

In a traditional diagram, all of the noun modifiers in both pre- and postposition are attached to the headword:

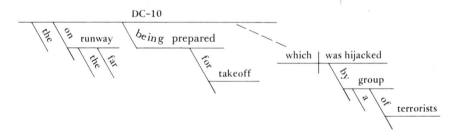

A change in the order of modifiers would change the meaning:

> the DC-10 being prepared for takeoff, which was hijacked by a group of terrorists on the far runway

Here the prepositional phrase no longer specifies *which* DC-10; it has become an adverbial modifier in the relative clause, modifying *was hijacked*. In this version *DC-10* has only two postheadword modifiers, not three:

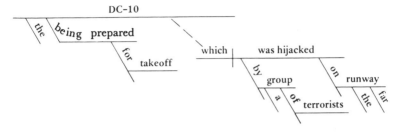

Just as ambiguity may result from a string of prepositional phrases, these multiple modifiers, too, are sometimes open to more than one interpretation:

> the driver of the bus standing on the corner
> a friend of my sister who lives in Livermore

In context these noun phrases may or may not be clear to the reader. In any case, the ambiguity is easily avoided:

> the driver of the bus who was standing on the corner
> the driver of the bus parked at the corner

> my sister's friend who lives in Livermore
> my sister in Livermore's friend (or, my sister in Livermore has a
>   friend who . . .)

OTHER POSTNOUN MODIFIERS

Appositives. In form the **appositive** is itself a noun phrase with the same referent as the headword; it renames the headword:

> my best friend, Meda
> Julia, a butcher at the A & P
> the security guard in our building, an ex-Marine who once played
>   professional football

the Bradleys, <u>the people living in the apartment across the hall</u>

And, as these examples show, the appositive can be expanded with modifiers just as any other noun phrase can be.

The appositive noun phrase is diagrammed in parentheses, with its headword next to the headword it renames:

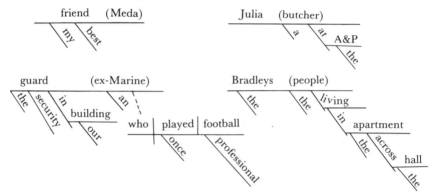

The appositive noun phrase has the same relationship to the head-word it renames as the subjective complement has to the subject it renames. In fact, we could turn these noun phrases into Pattern III sentences simply by adding a form of *be:*

My best friend <u>is</u> Meda.
Julia <u>is</u> a butcher at the A & P.
The security guard in our building <u>is</u> an ex-Marine who once played professional football.
The Bradleys <u>are</u> the people living in the apartment across the hall.

For the writer who overuses Pattern II and III sentences, who tends to fill the pages with forms of *be,* the appositive may offer a solution:

Apricots and raspberries are my favorite kinds of fruit. Unfortunately, the supermarket rarely has them.
Rewrite: Unfortunately, the supermarket rarely has apricots and raspberries, my favorite kinds of fruit.

Gallo is the world's largest winery. It bottles 250,000 cases of wine a day.

Rewrite: Gallo, the world's largest winery, bottles 250,000 cases of wine a day.

Because appositives rename nouns—and, in fact, can substitute for them—it is probably equally accurate and appropriate to classify appositives as nominals—that is, to call the appositive slot an NP slot. But because appositives fit into the noun phrase, adding descriptive information to the headword, we include the discussion of them here with the noun modifiers, the adjectivals.

The appositive shares the movability feature of the participial phrase; it can introduce the sentence when it modifies the subject:

An ex-Marine who once played professional football, the security guard in our building makes us feel secure, indeed.
The world's largest winery, Gallo bottles 250,000 cases of wine a day.

The appositive that modifies the subject can also come at the end of the sentence if the sentence is fairly short. In final position, the appositive gets special emphasis.

The wine glowed with a robust and seductive innocence, a veritable nymphet of wines.
The old house sat empty on the hill, a ghostly shell.

The explanatory appositive introduced by the expletive *or* does not share the movability feature of other appositives; it always follows the noun that it renames:

The study of sentences, or syntax, helps us appreciate the richness of our language.
The African wildebeest, or gnu, resembles both an ox and a horse.

Although most appositives are noun phrases in form, as we have seen here, other structures can also rename nouns, as the following examples show:

The Senate minority leader recently explained his party's priorities for the coming session: to curb spending and to bring the deficit down.

We went to so many places on Saturday night that I can hardly remember them all: to the movies, to the shopping mall, to the pizza parlor, to the party at Connie's, and then to the disco.

In the first example two verb phrases name the priorities; in the second a series of prepositional phrases names the places. In Chapter 11 we will see examples of appositives in their nominal roles.

Exercise 53: Underline all of the noun phrases that are functioning as appositives. Remember, an appositive noun phrase has the same referent as the headword it renames.

1. My sister Susan's husband, Bill, watches television every night of the week except Wednesday, his bowling night.
2. The president's latest economic proposal, a crackpot plan from the word *go,* was rejected out of hand by Congress.
3. Nearly all the way across Kansas we followed a pack of highway monsters, sixteen-wheelers carrying strange-looking machinery.
4. John Barth's first novel, *The Floating Opera*, is easy to read compared with his latest one, an exercise in mental gymnastics.
5. My son gave Snoots, his grand champion Chester White pig, very special care.
6. Black lung, an incurable disease of the respiratory system, affects countless coal miners in Pennsylvania and West Virginia.

Most appositives are nonrestrictive; those we have looked at so far are set off by commas. However, the issue of punctuation often does come up when the appositive is a proper noun:

My daughter <u>Barbara</u> lives in Upper Darby.
My husband, <u>Jack</u>, has been making wine for years.

In the first sentence the restrictive (defining) appositive makes one statement and implies its opposite. The reader can infer from the absence of commas the existence of another daughter whose name is *not* Barbara, who does *not* live in Upper Darby. If such is not the case, the reader has been misled, and the appositive needs commas. The second sentence includes no such implication of an opposite meaning.

Reading the two sentences aloud can make the distinction clear; the first has one main stress, one intonation contour; the second has three:

My daughter Bárbara lives in Upper Dárby. ⟍

My húsband, Jáck, has been making wine for yéars. ⟍

Incidentally, both of these sentences could be said with different main stress, depending on the emphasis—on *Darby,* for instance; and on *my* instead of *husband;* and on either *making* or *wine.* Such a change would not affect the contrast in meaning being illustrated here.

But we cannot read the second sentence with only one main stress:

My husband Jáck has been making wine for years. ⟍

—unless, of course, the writer of the sentence has another husband, perhaps named Tom or Dick or Harry, who *hasn't* been making wine for years!

Like the other nonrestrictive modifiers, the appositive that merely comments is rarely used in speech. We would be more likely to say either

My husband has been making wine for years.
or
Jack has been making wine for years.

depending on the knowledge of the listener. An understanding of the relationship between intonation and meaning can sometimes come to the rescue of the writer who is unsure of punctuation.

The Colon with Appositives. To understand appositives is to understand that tricky mark of punctuation, the colon. The structure that the colon signals is, in fact, an appositive, or—as is so often the case—a list of appositives.

Notice how the structure following the colon renames a noun phrase in the sentence:

> I'll never forget the birthday present my dad bought me when I was twelve: <u>a new three-speed bicycle</u>.
>
> Our visitor was a stranger with a long, jet-black beard and unexpected light blue eyes: <u>a real mystery man</u>.

Both of the foregoing sentences could be written with a comma instead of a colon. With the comma, however, there is less anticipation; the appositive gets less emphasis.

One of the most common uses of the colon is to signal a list:

> Three committees were set up to plan the convention: <u>program, finance, and local arrangements</u>.

Here the list is actually a list of appositives renaming the noun *committees*. The colon is a way of saying, "Here it comes, the list I promised." Sometimes the list following the colon includes internal punctuation other than commas:

> The study of our grammar system includes three areas: phonology, the study of sounds; morphology, the study of meaningful combinations of sounds; and syntax, the study of sentences.

Here the list includes three nouns, each of which has a nonrestrictive postnoun modifier of its own. This is one of the two occasions in our writing system that call for the semicolon. (The other, the joining of clauses in compound sentences, is discussed on pages 315–316.)

The end of the sentence is not the only place for an appositive, of course; those we looked at earlier directly follow the noun they rename. We could shift the appositives in these examples too if we wanted to change the emphasis:

> Our visitor, <u>a real mystery man</u>, was a stranger with a long, jet-black beard and unexpected light blue eyes.

When the appositive that we shift is a list, we use a pair of dashes to set it off:

Three committees—program, finance, and local arrangements—
were set up to plan the convention.

All three areas of our grammar system—phonology, morphology, and syntax—are covered in this book.

Dashes will add emphasis even when the appositive has no internal
punctuation; the dashes announce the appositive with a kind of fan-
fare:

Maria's latest purchase—a new Apple computer—has really
pleased her.

The main stress of the sentence, however, remains on the predicate.

Notice that dashes within the sentence always come in pairs. At the
end of the sentence, a single dash sometimes replaces the colon; it
represents a somewhat less formal colon:

I ordered my favorite flavor—pistachio nut.

Our visitor was a stranger with a long, jet-black beard—a real
mystery man.

Avoiding Punctuation Errors. The use of the colon with appositives is the source of a common punctuation error, but one simple rule
can resolve it:

A COMPLETE SENTENCE PRECEDES THE COLON.

Notice in the examples that the structure preceding the colon is a
complete sentence pattern, with every slot filled:

Three committees were set up to plan the convention.

The study of our grammar system includes three areas.

Because the colon so often does precede a list, the writer may assume
that every list should be preceded by one, but that is not the case. In
the following sentences, the colons are misused:

*The committees that were set up to plan the convention are:
program, finance, and local arrangements.

*The three areas of the grammar system are: phonology, morphol-
ogy, and syntax.

Your understanding of the sentence patterns will tell you that a subjective complement is needed to complete these sentences in which a form of *be* is the main verb.

One common variation for the sentence with a list includes the phrase *the following:*

> The committees that were set up to plan the convention are the following: program, finance, and local arrangements.

That noun phrase, *the following,* fills the subjective complement slot, so the sentence is indeed grammatical. But it is not necessarily the most effective version of the sentence. If you want to use a colon in such a sentence for purposes of emphasis, the earlier version is smoother and more concise:

> Three committees were set up to plan the convention: program, finance, and local arrangements.

Infinitives. The infinitive—the base form of the verb preceded by *to*—can serve as a modifier in the postnoun position. As a verb, it will have all the attributes of verbs, including complements and modifiers, depending on its underlying sentence pattern:

> the way to serve lobster
> the time to start
> the party after the play to honor the leading lady
> the best place in San Francisco to eat seafood

As the last two examples illustrate, the infinitive can be separated from the headword by another modifier. These examples also illustrate another common feature of the adjectival infinitive: Its subject may not be the noun it modifies; its subject is frequently just understood—the object in an understood prepositional phrase:

> That was a nice thing [for you] to do.
> Fishermen's Wharf is the best place in San Francisco [for one] to eat seafood.

The diagram of the adjectival infinitive looks exactly like that of the adverbial infinitive:

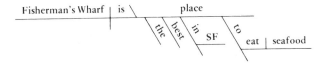

Noun Phrases. Nouns or noun phrases of time and place can follow the headword:

> the party <u>last night</u>
> the ride <u>home</u>

Note that even though these are nouns in form they are not appositives; they do not have the same referent as the headword.

Adjectives. Qualified adjectives and compound adjectives, which usually occupy the preheadword position, can follow the headword if they are set off by commas:

> the neighbors, <u>usually quiet</u>
> the neighborhood, <u>quiet and peaceful</u>

Like the appositives and nonrestrictive participles, these nonrestrictive adjectives can also introduce the sentence when they modify the subject:

> <u>Usually quiet</u>, the neighbors upstairs are having a regular brawl tonight.
> <u>Quiet and peaceful</u>, the neighborhood slept while the cat burglars made their rounds.

Adverbs. Even adverbs can occupy the postheadword position in the noun phrase:

> That was my idea <u>exactly</u>.
> The people <u>here</u> have no idea of conditions <u>there</u>.

SUMMARY

The noun phrase offers us a wide range of possibilities for adding information to our sentences. We can add modifiers before and after the headword in all of our noun phrases, and we do so in a highly systematic way. The system provides us with great versatility as writers and enables us to add depth and variety to our sentences.

Exercise 54: Diagram the following sentences. Identify the sentence patterns of the main clause and of all modifying verb phrases and clauses.

1. The little kids on our block who ride their skateboards around the parking lot every evening are driving the people downstairs absolutely crazy.
2. My mother, who cans two hundred jars of fruit every summer, will use only tree-ripened peaches picked at the peak of the season.
3. The little neighbor boy, who pitches for the Green Hornets, the local Little League championship team, threw an unbelievably wild pitch yesterday that crashed through our kitchen window.
4. The members of our wine-tasting club are planning a trip to the Napa Valley, which is considered by many experts the finest wine-growing region in America.
5. The meeting held by the Planning Commission that the editorial complained about was closed to the press.

Xerox

SENTENCES FOR PRACTICE

A. Draw vertical lines between the slots of the sentence patterns.

B. Mark the headword of each NP with an X, the determiner with a D; underline the pre- and postheadword modifiers; then label each according to its form.

C. Circle any pronouns that fill NP slots.

D. For further practice, identify the sentence patterns and diagram the sentences. Remember that all verb phrases and clauses functioning as adverbials and adjectivals also have identifiable sentence patterns.

1. The student in my history class whose written notes I borrowed has been absent since the midterm exam.

2. The initials engraved inside my ring are BFJ.

3. My neighbor's husband, a strong union man, would not cross the picket line that the clerical workers organized at the mill where he is a foreman.

4. The company's reorganization plan, voted down last week, called for the removal of all incumbent officers, a move that the stockholders considered grossly unfair.

5. My uncle, a successful businessman in Florida, who is now almost seventy, rides a bicycle to his office every morning.

6. Hurricanes along the eastern seaboard are commonplace in the fall.

7. The most exciting place I visited on my trip was Rome, the Eternal City, where the treasures of history blend with the attractions of a modern metropolis.

8. At midnight Cinderella's beautiful coach, in which she had been driven to the ball, suddenly became a pumpkin again.

9. When her son sent her an airline ticket, my aunt immediately made plans to spend March in New Mexico.

10. That old gentleman in Washington Square Park, whom I met last week, will talk to whoever will listen to him.

11. The play's the thing wherein I'll catch the conscience of the king. (Shakespeare)

12. Uneasy lies the head that wears the crown. (Shakespeare)

13. Rising tuition costs are becoming a serious burden for many college students.

14. Calling Pearl Harbor Day a day that would live in infamy, President Roosevelt asked Congress for a declaration of war.

15. Having been a police officer in downtown Atlanta for thirty years, my neighbor grew restless after he retired from the force.

16. The town where I lived until I reached my fifteenth birthday is in the foothills of the beautiful Ozarks.

QUESTIONS FOR DISCUSSION

1. Generate a noun phrase according to each of the following formulas:

A. det + adj + HEADWORD + participial phrase
B. det + adj + noun + HEADWORD + appositive + clause

C. det + adj + HEADWORD + prep phrase + part phrase
D. det + noun + HEADWORD + part phrase + clause

Use your NPs in sentences as follows:

Use A as the direct object of a Pattern VII sentence.
Use B as the object of a preposition.
Use C as an appositive.
Use D as the direct object in a relative clause.

2. In our description of the noun phrase we saw that the headword slot is filled by a word that is a noun in form. Would you consider these underlined noun phrases as exceptions to the rule?

The rich are different from other people.
I was late for our meeting.
You clean the upstairs, and I'll do the downstairs.

3. One of the sample sentences we used in this chapter has an ambiguous modifier. Explain the source of the ambiguity.

My brother is considered the area's best foreign car mechanic.

4. In this chapter we discussed the recursive quality of the noun phrase —that is, the embedding of one noun phrase in another. Give a sentence in which a relative clause is embedded in another relative clause; give another in which a participle is embedded in another participial phrase; another with an appositive in a relative clause; another with an appositive in another appositive.

5. Without this embedding quality of English we could not delight in "The House That Jack Built." Using either a branching diagram (see Chapter 10) or a traditional diagram, illustrate the embeddings in this sentence:

This is the cow with the crumpled horn that tossed the dog that worried the cat that killed the rat that ate the malt that lay in the house that Jack built.

Can you leave out any of the *that*'s?

6. We quoted Francis Christensen as saying that restrictive modifiers make one statement and imply the opposite. What opposite statement can you infer from the following?

All the students with an average of 90 or higher will be excused from
the final.
The flight controllers who saw the strange lights in the sky became
firm believers in UFOs.
The football players wearing white uniforms stood out in the crowd.

How would the meaning of these sentences change if the postnoun modifiers
were set off by commas?

7. What is the source of the ambiguity in the following sentences?

Tony buried the knife he found in the cellar.
Fred tripped his teammate with the baseball bat.

Diagram each in two ways to show its two possible meanings.

8. Is the *when* clause in the following sentence adverbial or adjectival?

The day will come when all men live together as brothers.

9. Speech can convey meaning that writing cannot. Consider the following sentence:

You mustn't serve the Arnolds any wine.

Read the sentence in three different ways to show the following meanings:

   a. The Arnolds are teetotalers.
   b. The Arnolds are wine connoisseurs.
   c. The Arnolds have a drinking problem.

Now restate the sentence in ways that will show those meanings unambig-
uously.

10. Picture this scene: A little girl hops off her bicycle and leans it
against the fence. In other words,

A little girl's bicycle is leaning against the fence.

How would you speak the same sentence (or is it the "same sentence"?) if you
simply came across the bicycle leaning there—a bicycle without a crossbar,
the kind built for girls?

A little girl's bicycle is leaning against the fence.

11. What is the source of the ambiguity in the following sentences? What are the two possible meanings of each?

> The painters' pants are lying on the floor.
> A little boy's jacket is lying on the floor.

12. As you know, a common form for the determiner is the possessive noun:

John's hat   my sister's husband

How would you diagram the noun phrases in Question 13?

> the painters' pants   a little boy's jacket

Can you diagram them in more than one possible way? What is the determiner? What does the possessive noun denote in these noun phrases? Ownership? Possession? How does the meaning of the possessive affect its function in the sentence?

13. Explain why the following sentence needs commas:

> Dad took my twin brother Bill and me to the circus.

Now explain why the sentence with commas becomes ambiguous:

> Dad took my twin brother, Bill, and me to the circus.

Rewrite the second sentence in two ways to show its two possible meanings.

14. Both of the following sentences include an adjectival infinitive as a modifier of *decision;* and in both, the expletive *as* introduces an objective complement. But there's an important difference between them. Diagram both sentences to illustrate the difference.

> The Jaycees are hailing the decision to admit women as a landmark.
> The Jaycees are hailing the decision to admit women as members.

15. In *The Book of Lists* (Morrow, 1977), David Wallechinsky et al. de-

scribe a comma "that cost the government two million dollars before Congress could rectify the error." Here's the expensive sentence:

All foreign fruit, plants are free from duty.

The clerk who wrote the rule was supposed to use a hyphen instead of a comma. Explain the difference.

16. In the summer of 1984 the writers of the Republican party's platform made headlines with their dispute about a comma. The first draft declared that Republicans "oppose any attempts to increase taxes which would harm the recovery and reverse the trend to restoring control of the economy to individual Americans."

The conservative wing of the party insisted on inserting a comma. Their version said that the Republicans would "oppose any attempts to increase taxes, which would harm the recovery and reverse the trend to restoring control of the economy to individual Americans."

Remember that a restrictive modifier says one thing and implies its opposite. What is the implication in the first version? Explain the difference between the two versions.

(P.S. The version with the comma was approved.)

17. Sometimes a verb phrase at the end of a sentence adds information that is more clearly adverbial than it is adjectival:

Pat spent the whole evening <u>cleaning house</u>.

Here the purpose of the verb phrase, rather than being simply to comment about Pat, is to tell "how" about the verb. In reading the sentence aloud, you will not hear the pause that signifies a comma.

Consider the following sentences. How should you punctuate them? The decision about whether to set off the final verb phrase is not always clear-cut. In making your decision, read the sentence aloud; then ask yourself how the verb phrase functions: Is it adverbial or is it adjectival? (You might try positioning the modifier elsewhere in the sentence. Does the meaning change?)

1. My uncle made his fortune selling real estate.
2. My uncle worked hard all his life selling real estate and insurance.
3. Pete spent the night sleeping in the car.
4. Gus crossed the finish line smiling at the judges and spectators.
5. Marcia came to visit me last night crying her eyes out.

6. The neighbors fled from their burning apartment making good use of their new fire escape.
7. The neighbors fled from their burning apartment carrying as many of their valuables as their arms would hold.
8. We ended the homecoming celebration singing around the bonfire.

CHAPTER

10

The Transformationalist's View of Noun Modifiers

The theory of **transformational generative grammar** (often abbreviated T-G or called simply transformational grammar) has itself gone through several stages of transformation since 1957, when it was first presented by Noam Chomsky in his book *Syntactic Structures* (The Hague: Mouton). But despite the changes, its goal remains the same: to account for the ability that native speakers of a language share in generating and processing sentences.

Although its origin is not pedagogical or practical like that of traditional and structural theory, transformational theory has practical value for the student of grammar. Many of the ideas in this book are taken directly from transformational grammar: the verb-expansion rule in Chapter 2, for example, and the idea of sentence transformations discussed in Chapter 3 and elsewhere.

One of the most useful concepts from transformational theory is the idea that a sentence has both a "deep structure" and a "surface structure." The **deep structure** consists of the semantic and grammatical relationships that underlie the surface structure; the **surface structure** is the form the sentence takes when we speak it. This concept of a deep structure underlying all of our sentences accounts for our ability to perceive more than one meaning when a sentence is ambiguous. Consider the following sentence:

Visiting relatives can be boring.

Who is doing the visiting, you or your relatives? The sentence is structurally ambiguous because there is more than one possible deep structure underlying it. In one, *relatives* is the subject of *visiting;* in the other, it is the object. The transformations that the two different deep structures go through result in the same surface structure:

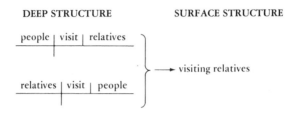

Exercise 55: Explain the source of the ambiguity in the following surface structures by giving two possible deep structures that underlie each.

1. Flying planes can be dangerous.
2. The shooting of the hunters was incredible.
3. I dislike burping babies.

The passive transformation illustrates the opposite situation—two different surface structures that mean the same thing:

Howard Hughes built "The Spruce Goose."
"The Spruce Goose" was built by Howard Hughes.

We are able to recognize these two sentences, these two different surface structures, as synonymous because they share the same deep structure. The relationship between Howard Hughes and "The Spruce Goose" remains the same no matter what the surface structure: Howard Hughes is the agent or actor (in this case, the builder); "The Spruce Goose" is the object of the action.

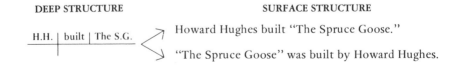

It was Chomsky's belief that the descriptive methods of the traditional and structural grammarians were simply inadequate to account for or explain this important aspect of language: this intuitive recognition of ambiguity and synonymy in sentences. One of his classic examples illustrates still another aspect of this inadequacy. The following sentences, neither ambiguous nor synonymous, are outwardly identical in structure:

> John is easy to please.
> John is eager to please.

A traditional analysis confirms their similarity:

But think about the underlying meaning. Think about the relationship of *John* and *please* in the two sentences. They are not the same. In one sentence John is doing the pleasing; in the other, someone is pleasing him. The first sentence can be paraphrased:

> It is easy to please John.

The second cannot:

> *It is eager to please John.

Transformational theory, then, is concerned with those underlying logical relations and the way in which the deep structure gets transformed into the outward surface structure. Deep structure is described in terms of *phrase-structure rules* such as the following:

> S → NP + VP

This rule says that a sentence can be rewritten as a noun phrase and a verb phrase. We used the branching diagram of this rule in Chapter 1 to describe the sentence patterns:

Another phrase-structure rule expands the verb phrase:

$$VP \rightarrow AUX + V + (COMP) + (ADV)$$

The VP rule describes how to generate a grammatical verb phrase; the required components are the auxiliary and the verb; the complement and the adverbial are optional, as indicated by the parentheses. The rule simply states in terms of a formula what you have learned about the sentence patterns: Some sentence patterns have a complement (a noun phrase or an adjective), and some don't, depending on the class of the verb.

You will understand why the AUX is shown as required instead of optional when you consider the next phrase-structure rule:

$$AUX \rightarrow T + (M) + (have + \text{-}en) + (be + \text{-}ing)$$

This rule should look familiar. It is, of course, the verb-expansion rule without the main verb slot at the end. In other words, it is the rule that describes how the auxiliary is generated. AUX is shown in the VP rule as required because, as you will recall from Chapter 2, every verb phrase includes tense, T. And in this rule, T is a component of the auxiliary.

In Chapter 2 we asked the following question in connection with the expanded verb: What rules and restrictions of our system would we have to include in a program for the computer in order for it to come up with all of the expanded verb strings in the language—to print out all of our possible variations of verbs? If we ask that question not just about verbs but about whole sentences, we are asking the question that the transformationalist asks. The resulting computer program would include the rules that generate deep structures as well as the transformational rules that turn those deep structures into surface structures.[1]

---

[1] Some current versions of transformational theory reject the concept of phrase-structure rules as the deep structure and suggest instead an underlying semantic component.

We certainly need not subscribe to, nor even comprehend, everything about transformational theory before using it in our study of sentences. In this chapter we are concerned with the transformational view of noun modification. Even the brief treatment that follows can be useful in understanding the source of dangling and misplaced and fuzzy modifiers that so often turn up in surface structures.

Here are the two phrase-structure rules that we will be concerned with in the study of noun modification—the one that rewrites the sentence and the one that rewrites the noun phrase:

$$S \rightarrow NP + VP$$
$$NP \rightarrow Det + N + (S)$$

Notice that an optional S (Sentence) has been added to the noun phrase. This means that a sentence can be embedded in a noun phrase; it is this embedded sentence in the deep structure that accounts for the modifiers of nouns in the surface structure.[2] *All* of the words and phrases and clauses that we use to modify nouns in both pre- and postheadword positions imply sentences in the deep structure:

the <u>noisy</u> neighbors
the <u>neighbor</u> boy
the people <u>across the street</u>
the people <u>living across the street</u>
the people <u>who live across the street</u>

Consider the clause modifying the subject in the following sentence:

The people <u>who live across the street</u> are noisy.

Who live across the street is clearly a sentence in form; we can pick out its subject and predicate; we can identify its sentence pattern; and in the traditional diagram we analyze it as a sentence, in form just like the

---

[2] A more accurate description of the NP rule would allow for multiple embedded sentences, given that noun phrases can have any number of modifiers. To keep the explanation simple, we will show one embedded S at a time.

main clause:

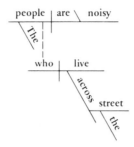

So we can easily recognize this noun phrase as Det + N + S:

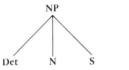

the people [the people live across the street]

The relative pronoun *who* is a feature of the surface structure only; its antecedent, *the people,* is what appears in the deep structure of the clause. Incidentally, the embedded S, the modifier, will always include an occurrence of the N headword, the noun being modified, although not necessarily as the subject. In the following sentence the N appears as the object in the embedded S:

The neighbors whom we met yesterday are nice.

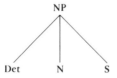

the neighbors [we met the neighbors yesterday]

Even when we leave out *whom* from the surface structure, as we probably would in this sentence, we recognize it as a part of the deep structure. The traditional diagram, too, you will recall, includes a slot for the relative pronoun even though it does not appear in the surface structure:

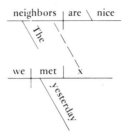

Not all modifiers in the noun phrase, of course, are clauses. The same information, or nearly so, can be conveyed with a participial phrase:

The people <u>living across the street</u> are noisy.

We can still identify the sentence pattern of the modifier, however, because sentence patterns are, in effect, verb phrase patterns; this one is Pattern VI, the intransitive verb pattern. Its subject is the noun being modified, *the people*. These two forms of modifiers, the clause and the participial phrase, have the same deep structure; only their surface structures are different. The participial phrase has undergone a transformational operation that deletes the subject.

The notion of the participle or participial phrase as a sentence should be obvious; earlier we identified the sentence patterns underlying both pre- and postnoun participles. And we saw that the diagram of the participial phrase looks just like the verb half of a sentence:

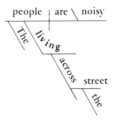

But even without a verb in the surface structure, transformational theory maintains that a complete sentence, that embedded S, underlies the modifier:

> The people <u>across the street</u> are noisy.

What is the sentence underlying the modifier *across the street*? It could be the same as that of the clause, *the people live across the street*. But because the verb, as well as the subject, has been deleted, we can't be sure. The surface structure of the noun phrase *the people across the street* doesn't tell us. Maybe the people don't live there; maybe they're just visiting; or maybe they're just walking by. Context, of course, may make the meaning clear; and it may not matter. But it could matter. And the writer should be aware of this potential source of ambiguity: a surface structure with more than one possible deep structure.

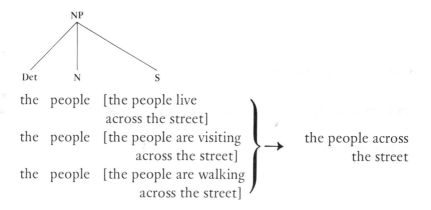

| DEEP STRUCTURE | SURFACE STRUCTURE |

Often, of course, prepositional phrases are completely unambiguous, even out of context:

> the clerk [who works] at Thrift Drug
> the meeting [that we had] during our lunch hour
> the security guard [who works] in our building
> the road [that goes] to Mandalay

Exercise 56: Show the deep structure of the underlined noun phrases in the following sentences. Write out the complete embedded sentence. Do any of the modifiers have more than one possible underlying sentence?

1. The man in the boat looked frightened.
2. The man standing in the boat is foolish.
3. The people upstairs are friendly.
4. The driver who delivered our furniture seemed very inexperienced.
5. The movies that Woody Allen makes simply amaze me.
6. I've known the people we visited in Utah all my life.
7. We took the children to the park behind the school.
8. The man I love loves me.

According to transformational theory, that S in the noun phrase accounts not only for postnoun modifiers but for those in prenoun position as well:

The noisy neighbors drive me crazy.

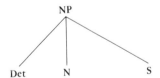

the   neighbors   [the neighbors are noisy]

The neighbor boy drives me crazy.

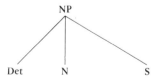

the   boy   [the boy is a neighbor]

Transformational theory describes the steps—the deletions and shifts—that transform the deep structure into the surface structure. For prenoun modifiers the steps include the deletion of the subject and

verb of the embedded sentence and a shift in position of the complement:

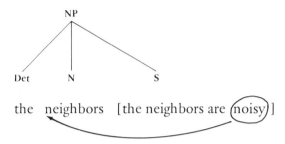

Recognizing the relationship between deep and surface structure
can help us understand the effect that misplaced and dangling modifiers can have. In the last chapter we saw dangling modifiers in opening position, participial phrases without subjects:

> *Having swung his five iron too far to the left, Joe's ball landed
> precisely in the middle of a sand trap.

Linguists don't, in fact, make any claims that transformational grammar actually describes what goes on in the mind of a speaker or listener. Nevertheless, the recognition of the difference between deep
and surface structure could account for reader expectation; it could
account for the source of interference that misplaced and dangling
modifiers introduce into the communication process. In the previous
sentence with a dangling participle, for example, the reader expects to
find a subject for the verb *having swung:* "the golfer," perhaps, or
"Joe."

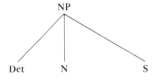

the   golfer   [the golfer swung his five iron . . . .]

So the reader does a double-take when *Joe's ball* shows up as the subject. The reader may understand the sentence with no problem, but
such double-takes are bound to interfere with readability.

Sometimes the reader is led astray because the path from surface to deep structure could go in either of two directions—an ambiguous sentence:

I know <u>the driver of the bus standing on the corner.</u>

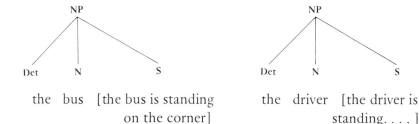

NP				NP		
Det	N	S		Det	N	S
the	bus	[the bus is standing on the corner]		the	driver	[the driver is standing. . . .]

And sometimes the modifier is merely misplaced—a temporary detour:

The doctor examined the patient lying in bed <u>with a stethoscope.</u>

Writers who are the clearest are the most effective. They will keep their readers moving smoothly along the path, and they will make the trip as fresh and interesting as possible with precise language, with sentence variety, with modifiers that add detail clearly and vividly. They will not hinder readers with unnecessary sidesteps nor misdirect them into paths that should be marked "wrong way" and "no exit."

SUMMARY

The theory of transformational grammar describes the sentence as having both a *deep* structure, its underlying meaning, and a *surface* structure, the form of the sentence as we speak it. The theory holds that all noun modifiers—single words, phrases and clauses—are complete sentences in the deep structure. This relationship of the embedded sentence to the headword of the noun phrase can help us understand the problems of misplaced and dangling modifiers.

QUESTIONS FOR DISCUSSION

1. In light of what we know about modifiers as embedded sentences, would the traditional diagram of a participial phrase make more sense if it looked like this?

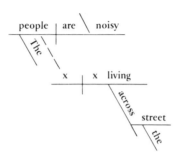

If so, how would you diagram the passive participle? What further step would be required to represent the deep structure?

2. Explain the ambiguity of the following sentence in terms of its deep structure:

We have James in control.

3. The phrase structure rule describing the VP looks like this:

VP → AUX + V + (COMP) + (ADV)

The following sentence includes both the complement and the adverbial:

The committee gave a trophy to the winner.

(a) What does AUX consist of? (Remember, the AUX is required.)
(b) In terms of its deep structure, what is the relationship of that sentence to the following one?

The committee gave the winner a trophy.

4. When the -*ing* form of the verb is used as a participle, it is in the active voice; the -*en* participle is generally passive. What is the sentence underlying

each of the *-en* participles in the following noun phrases? Are they active or passive? Do any of them seem ambiguous?

a vanished breed
the boy, grown tall,
my dear departed friend
Bill and Jane, married yesterday at City Hall,
a written guarantee

CHAPTER
11

The
Noun Phrase Functions:
Nominals

As you have discovered in the preceding chapters, the complete analysis of a sentence requires that we consider both form and function. We can call the slots in the sentence patterns by their "functional" names—that is, subject, direct object, subjective complement, and so on—but that label says nothing specific about the form of the structure that fills the slot. It's true, of course, that most subjects and direct objects are nouns or noun phrases in form; but in this chapter you'll discover other forms filling these slots, the slots that we call **nominal**. The label, as you can guess, is from the word *noun,* which means "name."

Even though the sentences in this chapter may look somewhat complicated compared with those you've seen before, the system for analyzing them is the same. The first step is to identify the sentence pattern. If you find that hard to do, perhaps it's because you don't know where the various slots begin and end. In that case, you might find it useful to substitute a pronoun such as *something* or *it* or *they* in the NP slots. For instance, in the first sample sentence demonstrating the gerund, *Living in Manhattan is very expensive,* you can figure out the sentence pattern easily if you say to yourself, *"It* is very expensive." The next step is to identify the form of the structure filling that "it" slot. You'll recognize the phrase *living in Manhattan* as a verb phrase (you can usually identify the form of a structure by looking at the first word). So again you'll ask yourself the question about its sentence pattern; in this case, where the verb is followed by an adverbial rather than by a complement, you will recognize it as intransitive, a Pattern

VI verb phrase. To diagram a verb phrase or clause in the NP slot, we use a vertical line, called a pedestal, to connect the structure to the main line.

To be consistent, we should probably begin the chapter on nominals with a discussion of the most common nominal, the noun phrase; you'll recall that we began the discussion of adverbials with the adverb. But because all the sentences we have considered up to now have had NPs filling the nominal slots, we will start right out with the structures that substitute for NPs—verb phrases and clauses.

VERB PHRASE NOMINALS

Gerunds. A common noun phrase substitute is the *-ing* verb; when the *-ing* verb functions as a nominal, it is known as a **gerund**. In form, gerunds and participles are identical; only their functions distinguish them. Participles modify nouns; gerunds act as nouns:

Living in Manhattan is very expensive.

In this sentence the underlined verb phrase fills the subject slot.

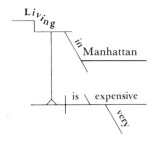

As the diagram shows, it is the entire gerund phrase that acts as subject.

Because they are noun-like, we can think of gerunds as names. But rather than naming persons, places, or things, as nouns generally do, gerunds, because they are verbs in form, name actions or behaviors or states of mind or states of being. In the sentence above, for example, *living in Manhattan* names an activity. Something is very expensive; the gerund phrase names that "something."

All of the sentence patterns can serve as the source of gerunds. And because they are verbs, the gerunds will include all of the complements and modifiers that main verbs include; in our example an adverbial prepositional phrase modifies the intransitive verb *living*, a Pattern VI gerund.

A Pattern I gerund, like the Pattern I sentence, will have an adverbial of time or place:

The teacher is here ⟶ the teacher's being here

Note that we convert *is* into the *-ing* form and its subject into the possessive case:

The teacher's being here surprised us.

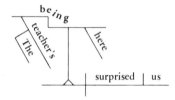

This gerund names an activity or state of being; that state is the "something" that surprised us. In this diagram the subject of the gerund is shown as a modifier; it has become a determiner of sorts, playing the same role that possessive nouns and pronouns ordinarily play: *John's* hat, *his* hat, *the teacher's* hat, *the teacher's* being here.

A gerund derived from a Pattern II sentence will include a subjective complement:

John's being angry surprised Mary.
                  or
His being angry surprised Mary.

Note that *angry* fills the subjective complement slot in the gerund phrase just as it did in the underlying sentence:

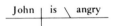

Exercise 57: Identify the sentence pattern of any gerund phrases and of the main clause.

1. Having measles is no fun.

2. Staying in the hospital for a week nearly drove me crazy.
3. Painting the kitchen cupboards purple was a big mistake.
4. Your complaining about the schedule will only make matters worse.
5. Being an actor seems glamorous to people outside the profession.
6. Studying math gives me a headache.
7. Jogging five miles every morning keeps me trim.
8. Jogging is good exercise.

In all of the above examples, the gerunds occupy the subject slot of the sentence, but they commonly occupy other NP slots as well:

Direct Object: My son enjoys <u>collecting stamps.</u>
Subjective Complement: His hobby is <u>collecting stamps.</u>

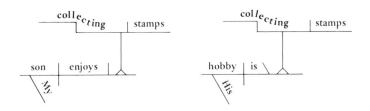

In these gerund phrases the underlying sentence is Pattern VII: *My son collects stamps.*

Object of Preposition: We gave the children a bigger allowance for <u>keeping their rooms spotless.</u>

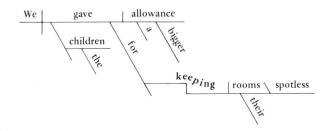

Here the sentence underlying the gerund phrase is Pattern IX: *The children keep their rooms spotless.*

Appositive: The favorite of all my son's hobbies, <u>building rockets</u>, is also the most expensive.

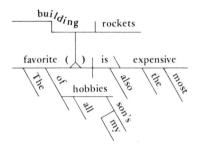

That was a great idea, <u>cooking steaks on the grill</u>.

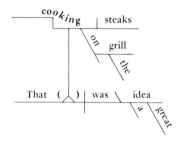

In these sentences the gerund renames, in the first, a noun phrase (*the favorite of all my son's hobbies*) and, in the second, a pronoun (*that*). In both cases a Pattern VII sentence underlies the gerund phrase: *He builds rockets; Someone is cooking steaks on the grill.*

You'll recall that we first took up the appositive in Chapter 9, where we discussed it as an adjectival; but even as a modifier in the noun phrase, its nominal quality is apparent, in that it renames another noun. In this chapter that quality is even more obvious; the verb phrases and clauses we are identifying here as appositives are clearly functioning as nominals.

Exercise 58: Identify the sentence pattern of each gerund phrase and the part that the gerund phrase plays in the sentence.

1. After clearing the courtroom, the judge admonished the lawyers.
2. I got stopped for going through a red light.
3. I really dislike weeding the garden.
4. My hobby is growing roses.

5. Finding Japanese beetles in my prize roses simply ruins my day.
6. My neighbor is helping me with my roses.
7. It is nice being here with you.
8. The landlord obviously enjoys giving people a bad time.

The Subject of the Gerund. In the last five examples, the subject of the gerund is not a part of the gerund phrase itself. In *My son enjoys collecting stamps,* the subject of the sentence is the subject of the gerund as well; in *His hobby is collecting stamps,* the subject is understood from the determiner *his.* In the sentence illustrating the gerund as the object of the preposition, its subject is the indirect object *children.* But in the last example above, *cooking steaks on the grill,* the subject is not stated at all. The subject will generally be left unstated when it names a general, rather than a particular, action or behavior:

> Raising orchids requires patience.
> One of the most popular forms of exercise in our neighborhood is
>   jogging.
> Becoming a lawyer is not easy.

As we saw in earlier examples, when the subject of the gerund is part of the gerund phrase, it will often be in the possessive case:

> The teacher's being here surprised us.
> John's being angry surprised Mary.

Although the possessive case may sometimes sound excessively formal or even incorrect, it is the form considered correct in formal writing.

When the subject of the gerund includes postheadword modifiers, we generally omit the possessive inflection. We would say

> I appreciated his giving me a lift
>   *or*
> I appreciated Bill's giving me a lift,

but we would probably not say

> I appreciated the man next door's giving me a lift.

Instead we would say simply

>   I appreciated <u>the man next door</u> giving me a lift.

It's not unusual to hear people say,

>   I appreciated *him* giving me a lift,

but, technically, this version makes the man himself, rather than his action, the object of the appreciation.

Exercise 59: Identify the subject of all the gerunds in the following sentences.

1. Do you mind my speaking out on the subject?
2. For an hour John tried starting the car.
3. I disapprove of him dating my daughter.
4. Before starting to bake a cake, make sure that you have all the ingredients on hand.
5. The dog's barking is driving me crazy.

Dangling Gerunds. Like the dangling participle, the dangling gerund occurs when its subject is neither stated nor clearly implied. This situation arises at times when the gerund serves as the object in an opening or closing prepositional phrase:

>   After <u>cooking the snails in white wine</u>, none of the guests would eat them.
>   In <u>filling out the form</u>, an original and two copies are required.
>   The rust spots must be carefully sanded and primed before <u>giving the car its final coat of paint</u>.

We certainly have no problem understanding such sentences; the message comes through. In fact, "dangling" may be too strong a word; these sentences don't have the obvious weakness of those with dangling participles. Of the three sentences preceding, the first is probably the least acceptable; here the activity named by the gerund is a specific, one-time event, and we expect the subject of the gerund to be the first available noun. So it appears that *none of the guests* did the cooking. One alternative is to expand the opening phrase into a clause, turning *cook* into the main verb of the clause:

> <u>After I cooked the snails in white wine</u>, none of the guests would eat them.

Another version would leave *cooking* as a gerund, but its subject is now clearly stated:

> <u>After I went to all the trouble of cooking the snails in white wine</u>, none of the guests would eat them.

But even when the verbs refer to general, rather than specific, activities, there tends to be a vagueness in these dangling gerund phrases, simply because we are programmed to expect the subject of the sentence to serve as the subject of the gerund as well, as in the following revisions:

> <u>After cooking the snails in white wine</u>, *I* couldn't get any of the guests to eat them.
> <u>In filling out the forms</u>, *you* will need an original and two copies.
> <u>Before giving the car its final coat of paint</u>, sand the rust spots carefully and paint them with primer.

In the last example the subject of both the gerund and the main clause is the understood *you*.

Exercise 60: Improve the following sentences by providing a clear subject for the gerund.

1. Before starting to bake a cake, the ingredients should be assembled.
2. Heavy meals should be avoided before swimming.
3. In making a career decision, my counselor was a big help.
4. After storing the outdoor furniture in the garage, there was no room left for the car.

Infinitives. Another fairly common nominal is the **infinitive phrase**—the base form of the verb with *to*. We have already seen infinitives functioning as adverbials (Chapter 8) and as adjectivals (Chapter 9); as nominals they often act as subject, direct object, subjective complement, or appositive. In their nominal roles, infinitives, like gerunds, name actions or behaviors or states of being. And like the gerunds, infinitives can be derived from all of the sentence patterns. In the following sentence, a Pattern VII infinitive fills the subject slot in a Pattern III sentence:

Subject: To fly a helicopter is one of my ambitions.

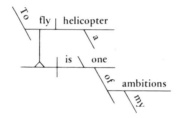

At first glance you may confuse the infinitive with a prepositional phrase, such as *to school* or *to the store;* to appears in both constructions, and the traditional diagrams are similar. But there is an important difference in form: In the prepositional phrase, a nominal—usually a noun or noun phrase—follows *to;* in the infinitive a verb phrase follows *to.*

Direct Object: Since ancient times, people have attempted to fly.

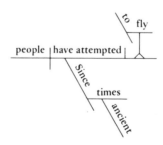

Note that the infinitive *to fly* is intransitive in this sentence: a Pattern VI infinitive. In the previous example the same infinitive has a direct object: Pattern VII.

Subjective Complement: My neighbor's goal in life is <u>to give me a bad time</u>.

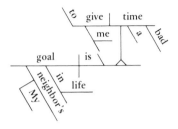

In this example the infinitive is derived from a Pattern VIII sentence (*My neighbor gives me a bad time*), so that the infinitive phrase has both an indirect object (*me*) and a direct object (*a bad time*).

Appositive: My parents aren't very enthusiastic about my plans for the term break, <u>to hitchhike to Florida</u>.

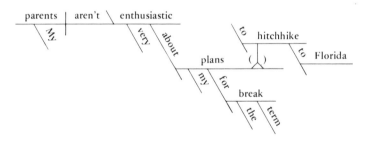

Here the idea stated in the infinitive renames the object in the prepositional phrase, *plans*.

Appositive: It would be exciting <u>to be a helicopter pilot</u>.

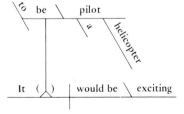

In the preceding sentence the infinitive is the actual subject; the *it* is an expletivelike word that allows us to delay the subject for greater emphasis. The diagram distorts the word order of the sentence, but it clearly shows the underlying meaning: *To be a helicopter pilot would be*

exciting. This use of *it* is sometimes called the anticipatory *it* (see page 140).

Hamlet's famous infinitive phrase is in apposition to *that:*

To be or not to be, that is the question.

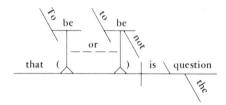

Exercise 61: Underline the nominal infinitives in the following sentences. Identify the sentence pattern of the main clause; identify the sentence pattern of the infinitive phrase; identify the function of the infinitive.

1. Today's pioneers hope to venture into outer space.
2. Hoping to fly stand-by, Jane waited at the ticket counter all afternoon.
3. Her plan was to fly to California to get a job at Disneyland for the summer.
4. It was embarrassing to see myself on television in speech class this morning.
5. I didn't want to stand up in front of the camera.
6. To survive midterms is my only goal at the moment.

Catenative Verbs. We have seen both gerunds and infinitives in the direct object slot of Pattern VII sentences:

My son enjoys collecting stamps.
Since ancient times, people have attempted to fly.

Enjoy and *attempt* are two of the verbs we call **catenatives,** or verbs that can take other verbs as objects. The label *catenative* comes from the verb *catenate,* which means "to form into a chain or linked series." We can, in effect, form a chain of verbs:

Not all transitive verbs, however, will take other verbs as objects. We wouldn't find *eat* and *hit* and *read,* for instance, in such sentences. There is no grammatical way to complete these diagrams:

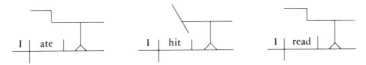

The verbs that do take other verbs as objects generally describe mental activities or processes, unlike such physical activities as *hit* and *eat* and *read.*

There is a certain arbitrariness in the way catenatives work. For example, we can use the verb *like* with either a gerund or an infinitive as its object:

My son likes <u>collecting stamps</u>.
My son likes <u>to collect stamps</u>.

Other catenatives that take both forms are *start, try, continue, attempt,* and *hate.*

But some verbs, such as *decide, want, expect, forget, dare,* and *agree,* take only the infinitive, not the gerund:

I have decided <u>to exercise every morning</u>.
*I have decided <u>exercising every morning</u>.
I want <u>to ride to work</u>.
*I want <u>riding to work</u>.

Other catenative verbs, such as *dislike, enjoy,* and *avoid,* take only the gerund:

I avoid <u>exercising</u>.
*I avoid <u>to exercise</u>.

You'll notice that in all of the catenative sentences so far the subject of the sentence is also the subject of the infinitive or gerund that fills the direct object slot. But we have another class of verb in which the direct object of the sentence is the subject of the following infinitive:

I want the boys to mow the lawn.

Actually, the entire phrase *the boys to mow the lawn* is the direct object, not just *boys*. In order for the diagram to show that meaning, the entire phrase is attached to the direct object slot with a pedestal; the infinitive is shown as a continuation of its subject, not as a modifier, with a vertical line between them to show the subject–predicate relationship—that is, to show *boys* as the subject of the verb *mow*:

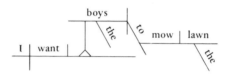

A few of these verbs, like *want,* pattern with the infinitive in both ways—with either its subject or its object as the subject of the infinitive:

I want to go home.

I want you to go home.

Other verbs that work both ways are *expect* and *dare:*

I expect to finish the job before noon.

I expect the carpenters to finish the job before noon.

I don't dare [to] take a chance.

I dared him to take a chance.

Infinitives following certain verbs, such as *let* and *make,* appear without the *to:*

The coach let the team choose its own captain.

The editors made the reporters check their facts thoroughly.

Infinitives following *dare* may also be grammatical without *to:*

I don't <u>dare take</u> a chance.

With or without *to* we recognize the verbs as infinitives, and we diagram them the same:

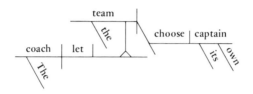

Although the catenative verbs are transitive—remember, they do have direct objects—many of them are restricted from the passive transformation. We would probably not say,

*Collecting stamps is liked by my son.
*Exercising is avoided by me.
*To exercise every morning has been decided.

Certainly some of them are acceptable in the passive voice:

Collecting stamps is enjoyed by many people.
Exercising is avoided by great numbers of people.

There is one group of catenatives, however, that is fairly common in the passive voice, in the group we looked at last, in which the subject of the infinitive is the direct object in the sentence, that direct object becomes the subject of the passive sentence, with the infinitive retained as the object:

Active: I expect the carpenters to finish the job before noon.
Passive: The carpenters are expected to finish the job before noon.

Active: I asked the boys to mow the lawn.
Passive: The boys were asked to mow the lawn.

> **Active:**   The editors required the reporters to check their own facts.
>
> **Passive:** The reporters were required to check their own facts.

Again, not all of the sentences of this form are acceptable in the passive:

> *The boys were wanted to mow the lawn.
> *The reporters were made to check their own facts.
> *The team was let to choose its own captain.

There's no apparent system here; whether or not the passive is acceptable seems to be strictly arbitrary.

The form that can follow catenatives provides another illustration of the sometimes arbitrary nature of English. As native speakers we are programmed to avoid such sentences as

> *My son enjoys to collect stamps.

We need the gerund, not the infinitive, following *enjoy.*

> *The coach let the team to choose its own captain.

Interestingly, the verb *allow,* with essentially the same meaning as *let,* would be ungrammatical *without* the *to; let* is ungrammatical *with* it.

In the absence of any systematic way to identify the various classes of catenatives, the nonnative speaker must simply learn by reading and listening the way each of the verbs works.

Exercise 62: Diagram the following sentences.

1. Frank has decided to join the debate team.
2. Debating is the ideal activity for people who like to argue.
3. Frank really enjoys arguing.
4. Do you like being a business major?
5. My mother plans to start selling real estate next month.

6. At first my father didn't particularly want my mother to start working.
7. Now he has decided to give her encouragement.

Complementary Infinitives. We should mention one other use of the infinitive, even though it is not a nominal: the so-called **complementary infinitive**, a completer of the verb. We take it up here simply because it looks so much like the nominal infinitive following a catenative verb:

I am going to eat less sugar.

This sentence not only resembles but also means very much the same as

I plan to eat less sugar.
or
I am planning to eat less sugar.

However, in the first sentence *eat* is the main verbal idea—*am going* actually serves as a modal-like sign of the future, whereas in the second, *plan* is the main verb, and the infinitive is the direct object: *To eat less sugar* is the "something" that I plan. The diagrams demonstrate the difference.

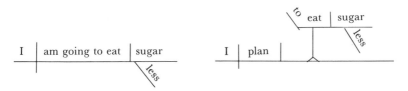

The verbs *be* and *have* sometimes take complementary infinitives too:

The parade is to start at noon.
The marchers have to arrive by eleven.

Here the main verbal ideas are *start* and *arrive,* not *is* and *have.*

There is a modal-like quality in all of these complementary infinitives; *will* could easily substitute for *is to* or *am going to* and *must* for *have to* with little change in meaning. In fact, in Chapter 6, the list of marginal modals includes *have to*.

CLAUSE NOMINALS

In the preceding sections we have seen examples of verb phrases—gerunds and infinitives—filling NP slots. In this section we will see that complete sentences, clauses, can do so as well:

> I wonder <u>what our history midterm will cover.</u>
> I suspect <u>that it will be hard.</u>

In each of these examples, the underlined clause fills the direct object slot in a Pattern VII sentence:

> I wonder <u>something.</u>
> I suspect <u>something.</u>

The clause names the "something."

These two sentences illustrate the two kinds of introductory words that signal **nominal clauses** (sometimes called "noun clauses"): interrogatives, such as *what,* and the expletive *that.* The diagrams will show a basic difference between them:

The interrogative *what* fills a grammatical role in the clause that it introduces—in this case, that of direct object; the expletive *that* does not.

The Expletive That: As you may recall, the term **expletive** refers to a sentence element that plays no grammatical role itself; the expletive is an operator of sorts, an added element that enables us to manipulate a structure for reasons of emphasis and the like. The expletive *that* enables us to embed one sentence as a nominal in another sentence. In the example above, the Pattern II sentence "It [our history midterm] will be hard" becomes a direct object. We should note that this clause introducer sometimes goes by other names: It is sometimes called a "nominalizer," which is certainly an accurate label; it is sometimes called a "subordinator." The term that we are using here, "expletive," emphasizes its role outside of the clause itself. The diagram illustrates that added-on quality. (See also pages 141–142.)

Incidentally, the expletive *that* should not be confused with the relative pronoun *that,* which we saw as an adjectival clause introducer in Chapter 9:

You choose a color that you like.

In this sentence the adjectival clause acts as a postheadword modifier in the noun phrase *a color; that* is a relative pronoun renaming its antecedent, *color.* Unlike the expletive *that,* the relative pronoun does play a part in its own clause—in this case, as the direct object:

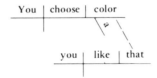

The expletive *that* can turn any declarative sentence into a nominal clause:

Tim loves to play poker ⟶ I know that Tim loves to play poker.
You choose a color that you like ⟶ I hope that you choose a color that you like.

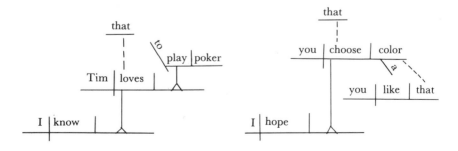

When the *that* clause fills the direct object slot, as in the preceding examples, the sentence may be grammatical without the expletive:

> I know <u>Tim loves to play poker</u>.
> I hope <u>you choose a color that you like</u>.

But when the clause is the subject, the expletive is required:

> <u>That he loses often</u> is no secret.
> *<u>He loses often</u> is no secret.

The expletive *that* also enables us to turn a direct quotation into an indirect one:

> **Direct Quotation:** He said, "<u>I will get to the gym soon</u>."
> **Indirect:** He said <u>that he would get to the gym soon</u>.

Note the change in the tense of the verb. It is common to change present tense to past when transforming a direct quotation into indirect discourse. If the verb in the direct quotation is already past tense, we would probably add *have* + *-en,* our usual verb form for indicating a past completed action, or, in this case, a past completed statement:

> **Direct:** He said, "<u>I polished off the cake yesterday</u>."
> **Indirect:** He said <u>that he had polished off the cake yesterday</u>.

But we could also use the simple past in the indirect version:

> He said that he <u>polished</u> off the cake yesterday.

In these direct quotations following the verb *say,* the expletive *that* could be omitted, but after verbs such as *reply, explain,* and *state,* the *that* is usually retained:

> He said he had polished off the cake yesterday.
> He explained <u>that</u> he had polished it off himself.

Exercise 63: Identify the function of each *that* clause in the following sentences. If adjectival, what noun does it modify? If nominal, what NP slot does it fill? (Remember: The relative pronoun *that* plays a part in its own clause; the expletive does not.)

1. Part of the crowd that lined up for concert tickets had been there all night.
2. I couldn't believe that anyone would wait all night to buy a ticket.
3. The reason that Mary gave for her strange behavior made no sense to me.
4. We hope that you can come for the weekend.
5. I suspect that riding on the bus for three hours was really tiring.
6. Andy has assured me that the party that his frat is having on Saturday makes the long trip worthwhile.

Punctuation of Nominal Clauses. In this chapter we have seen some fairly long phrases and clauses filling NP slots. With one exception, the punctuation of these sentences remains exactly the same as the punctuation of the basic sentence: no commas between the sentence pattern slots. The exception occurs when the direct object is a direct quotation. The usual convention calls for a comma between a verb like *say* or *reply* and the quote:

He said, "I will get to the gym as soon as I can."

Interrogatives. All of the interrogatives that introduce questions can also introduce nominal clauses: *who, whose, whom, what, which, where, when, why, how, how much, how often,* and so on. Unlike the expletive, the interrogative always plays a grammatical role in its own clause. In an earlier example we saw the interrogative *what* as the direct object in its clause:

I wonder *what* our history midterm will cover.

In the following sentence the interrogative adverb *where* acts as an adverb in the clause:

Where you are going is no business of mine.

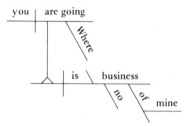

The simple question "Where are you going?" would be diagrammed exactly the same as the nominal clause:

In these question sentences, the adverb does not provide the adverbial information as other adverbials do; rather it asks for it—or, in the case of the noun clause, simply refers to it.

The interrogative pronoun *who* will be the subject in its own clause:

Tell me *who* will be at the party.

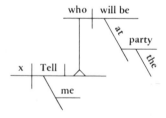

Who can also be the subjective complement:

I don't know *who* that stranger is.

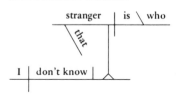

What can act as subject, subjective complement, or object in its clause:

Subject: I wonder *what* will happen now.

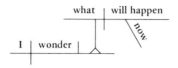

Subjective Complement: I finally learned *what* the problem was.

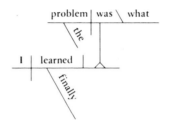

Direct Object: I can't believe *what* the teacher expects us to do for an A.

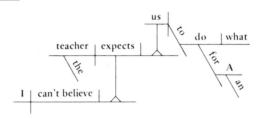

At first glance it may appear that *what* is the subject of the clauses in the last examples as well as in the first, but as soon as you pick out *was* and *expects* as verbs, you will recognize *problem* and *teacher* as their subjects on the basis of both meaning and position. The interrogative word introduces the clause no matter what part it plays in the clause.

In the following sentences *what* and *which* are determiners:

I wonder *which* brand of yogurt has the most calories.

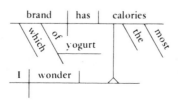

I wonder *what* brand I should buy.

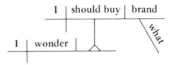

The interrogative pronoun *whose,* the possessive case of *who,* also acts as a determiner in its clause:

Tell me *whose* car you borrowed.

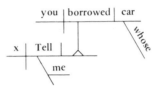

The interrogative *whom* will act as an object in its clause; when it is the object of a preposition, it may not be the first word in the clause, as in the famous line by John Donne:

Ask not for *whom* the bell tolls.

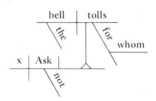

In everyday speech we rarely introduce a clause with *for whom* or *to whom* or *by whom;* we are more likely to use *who* instead of *whom* and to end the clause with the preposition:

> Bill told me who he bought the flowers for.
> I wonder who Mary is going to dance with.
> Don't ask who the bell is tolling for.

At the beginning of the clause, *who* seems a more logical form, perhaps, because *who* is the subjective case form and the subject generally fills the opening position. But the diagrams clearly show *he* and *Mary* and *the bell* as the subjects and *whom* in the prepositional phrase:

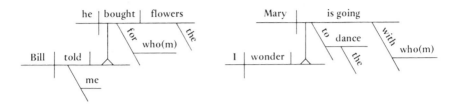

Even though *whom* may sound awkward or too formal for everyday speech, the conventions of edited English call for *whom* in formal writing. If you want to avoid the formality of

> Bill told me whom he bought the flowers for,

there are always alternatives:

> Bill told me the name of the lady he bought the flowers for.
> Bill said he bought the flowers for Kathy.

In the discussion of nominal clauses introduced by the expletive *that*, we saw examples of indirect discourse with verbs such as *say:*

> He said that we would leave soon.

The same system applies with the interrogative clauses following such verbs as *ask* and *inquire:*

> He asked, "Where are you going?"
> He asked where we were going.
> He inquired what our motives were.
> "What are your motives?" he inquired.

A verb like *say* would not be used with the interrogative clause simply because of the nature of the interrogative. There is a question involved, so only verbs that denote a question, such as *ask* or *inquire,* appear in this structure.

Exercise 64: Identify the nominal clauses in the following sentences. What part does the interrogative play in the clause it introduces? (Remember, the same words can introduce adjectival clauses.)

1. I wonder <u>where I put my math book.</u>
2. <u>How you spend your money</u> is no business of mine.
3. The instructor couldn't remember <u>who had volunteered to do the presentation in class today.</u>
4. Do you know the man <u>who picked Joanne up this evening?</u>
5. Have you decided <u>which gym class you're going to take?</u>
6. I sometimes wonder <u>how the students who register late ever catch up.</u>

Yes/No Interrogatives. Besides the questions introduced by interrogatives that ask for specific information, we also ask questions that call for a yes or no response. We form these questions simply by moving the first word in the auxiliary—or in some sentences *be*—in front of the subject:

The students have finished their assignment.

The basketball season was a success.

The interrogative clauses based on yes/no questions are introduced by two expletivelike elements, *if* and *whether (or not):*

> I can't remember if I turned off the television.
> Whether or not I turned it off doesn't matter.

We consider these introductory words as expletives because, unlike other interrogatives, they play no part in the clause. They simply act as operators that allow us to use yes/no questions as nominal clauses:

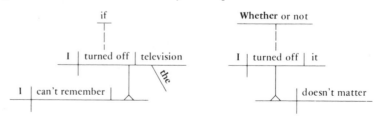

Functions of Nominal Clauses. All the nominal clauses we have seen so far fill either the direct object or the subject slot in the sentence. Another fairly common function is that of appositive:

> The idea <u>that our powerful defense couldn't stop the Cornhuskers</u> was unthinkable.

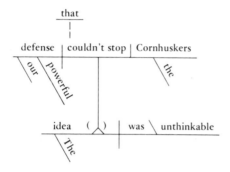

Like many appositives, the *that* clause could actually replace the head-word, *idea:*

> <u>That our powerful defense couldn't stop the Cornhuskers</u> was unthinkable to the fans.

An alternative position for the appositive clause is at the end of the sentence, as a "delayed subject":

> It was unthinkable to the football fans <u>that our powerful defense couldn't stop the Cornhuskers.</u>

Note that these appositives are restrictive; they are not set off by commas.

Another slot that the nominal clause can fill is that of subjective complement. The subject would, of course, have to be the kind of noun phrase that could be renamed by a sentence, a complete idea. *Reason* is such a noun:

> The reason for our defeat was <u>that the Cornhuskers' backfield outsmarted us on every play.</u>

The nominal clause can also be the object of the preposition:

> At halftime the coaches talked to the linebackers about <u>how they could stop those tailbacks.</u>

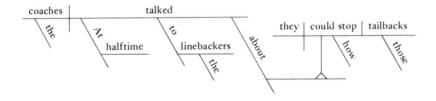

THE SUBJUNCTIVE *THAT* CLAUSE

In Chapter 2 we discussed a variation of the verb called the subjunctive mood, which is expressed in certain *that* clauses conveying strong suggestions or resolutions or commands:

> We suggested <u>that Mary go with us.</u>
> We insisted <u>that Bill consult the doctor.</u>
> The doctor recommended <u>that Bill stay in the hospital.</u>
> I move <u>that the meeting be adjourned.</u>

Note that these clauses do not contain modal auxiliaries; instead the mood is indicated by the base form of the verb—even for a third-person singular subject, which would normally take the *-s* form of the verb, and for the past tense. In the preceding sentences the *that* clauses fill the direct object slot; other verbs that commonly take clauses in the subjunctive mood are *command, demand, ask, require, order,* and *propose.*

The subjunctive *that* clause can also act as a restrictive appositive when it modifies a noun related to commands, suggestions, and the like:

> The suggestion that Bill see the doctor was a good one.
> The doctor's insistence that Bill stay in the hospital took us by surprise.

THE *THAT* CLAUSE AS ADJECTIVE COMPLEMENT

Most clauses introduced by the expletive *that* fill NP slots in the sentence patterns, but they can also act as complements, or completers, of certain adjectives that express feelings or attitudes. When these adjectives—among them, *aware, afraid, hopeful, pleased, sure, happy, glad, certain, positive, sorry, doubtful*—fill the subjective complement slot, they are commonly followed by *that* clauses:

> The committee was certain that the dance marathon would be a success.
> They were pleased that so many couples entered.
> John and Claudia were doubtful that they could last the entire forty-eight hours.

In most cases the expletive introducing the clause is optional:

> I was sure (that) they could last to the end.
> We were happy (that) they made it.

Some of these adjectives are either derived from verbs or are closely related to them. Notice the similarity between the *that* clause as adjective complement and the *that* clause as direct object:

> I was hopeful that they would win.
> I hoped that they would win.

> I was doubtful that they would last for forty-eight hours.
> I doubted that they would last for forty-eight hours.

I was afraid they would collapse on the dance floor.
I feared they would collapse on the dance floor.

Most of the adjectives that take *that* clauses as complements can take prepositional phrases as well; some can also take infinitive phrases:

They were afraid of falling down.
They were certain to win.
We were aware of the problem.
We were happy about their victory.

SUMMARY

In this chapter we have looked at the verb phrases and clauses that fill noun phrase slots in the sentence patterns. Because they are themselves either verb phrases or clauses, the gerunds and infinitives and nominal clauses have all the features of the sentence patterns they are based on, including complements and modifiers.

Exercise 65: Diagram the following sentences. Identify the sentence pattern of the main clause and the sentence patterns of the nominal verb phrases and clauses.

1. I have always wanted to fly a helicopter.
2. I suspect that flying a helicopter is difficult.
3. The visiting astronomer who gave the lecture in our class today assured us that the chances of a comet's striking the earth are very remote.
4. Astronomers have discovered that life on Venus, where the temperature reaches 900°F, would be impossible.
5. The discoveries that scientists make with their telescopes never cease to amaze me.
6. I haven't figured out which Shakespeare play is my favorite.
7. It is obvious that our professor considers *Hamlet* the greatest work of the English language that any human mind could ever create.
8. Wouldn't it be extraordinary to know someone who could write a play like that?

SENTENCES FOR PRACTICE

Draw vertical lines to show the sentence slots. Label the form of the structure that occupies each slot. Identify the sentence pattern of each verb phrase and clause. Diagram the sentences.

1. I wonder what Jeff's problem is.
2. I think that I know what the solution to Jeff's problem is.
3. The friend who called last night said that she would call back today.
4. Speaking before Congress last week, the president announced that he will recommend that tax reform be made a priority.
5. Where you will be in ten years is a question you probably think about sometimes.
6. I told my nephew to stop asking our neighbor how old she is.
7. Greta Garbo used to say, "I want to be alone."
8. Having been allergic to tomatoes all my life, I finally quit eating them.
9. For some students the cost of going to college is moving out of reach.
10. Ask not what your country can do for you.
11. To fly through the air—to soar like a bird—has always been a dream of mine.
12. Letting their children make their own mistakes is often a very hard thing for parents to do.
13. Being a good homemaker has been the goal of most women in our culture for many generations.
14. Many people on our campus have the job of helping students make wise decisions.
15. Before they are finally successful, some people try many times to stop smoking.
16. My roommate, who will graduate this month, wonders why finding a job in his field, petroleum engineering, is so difficult.

QUESTIONS FOR DISCUSSION

1. Consider the modifiers in the following noun phrases. What is the sentence underlying each of them? Would you classify them as adjectives, participles, or gerunds? On what basis do you make your classification? Are any of them ambiguous?

a walking stick   a rocking chair
a drinking fountain   a fishing pole

a dancing partner	a meeting place
a dining room	an interesting topic
his unwashed hands	the warning bell

2. Show by a diagram how the sentences in the following sets are different. Identify their sentence patterns.

My brother is getting into trouble again.
My problem is getting into law school.

I went to work.
I want to work.

3. The traditional grammarian would label the *who* clause in this famous line by Shakespeare as an adjectival clause. Why? Why is it not nominal? How would you as a twentieth-century speaker word this statement?

Who steals my purse steals trash.

4. What is the source of the ambiguity in the following sentence?

I disapprove of her smoking.

If the smoker were male instead of female, how would the sentence be stated? Would it still be ambiguous?

5. Identify the sentence patterns of the five verbs that appear in the following sentence. What label would you give to the noun phrase substitutes, the nominals—gerund, infinitive, or nominal clause?

All I did before hitting Joe was tell him to mind his own business.

6. Consider the differences in meaning in these two pairs of sentences. How do you account for the differences? Do the differences involve different sentence patterns?

Mel stopped to talk to Walt.
Mel stopped talking to Walt.

Mel started talking to Walt.
Mel started to talk to Walt.

7. What are the two possible meanings of the following ambiguous sentence?

The shooting of the hunters was a wanton act.

In what way is the traditional diagram inadequate to account for that ambiguity?

8. One of the most common roles for nominals is as object of the preposition. In the following sentences, identify the form of that object in the underlined prepositional phrases:

1. This afternoon I took a nap after exercising.
2. Before starting my exercise program, I had a thorough physical examination.
3. Until recently, I did very little exercise.
4. After my physical, I began doing calisthenics gradually.
5. From then on, I began to be careful about my diet too.
6. For the truly obese, strenuous exercise can be dangerous.

9. Using your understanding of sentence patterns, subordinate clauses, and nominals, explain why the following sentences are often considered ungrammatical. Do you agree with that judgment?

The reason we are late is because we couldn't get the car started.
Happiness is when the professor cancels class on Friday afternoon.

10. In Chapter 9 we saw examples of both active and passive participles. Can gerunds and infinitives be passive?

11. Identify the underlined *that* in terms of both its form and its function.

1. I know that you're busy.
2. The time that we have together is much too short.
3. We must use that time well.
4. He left so that I could do my homework.
5. To be that tall must be a problem.

12. In speech a fairly common way of expressing purpose is the use of the infinitive *to try* with *and:*

I'm going to try and finish my homework before lunch.

Given what you know about catenative verbs, how would you judge the correctness (perhaps *precision* is a better word than *correctness*) of "try and finish"? How does the structure differ from *go and see* in the following sentence?

> We should go and see what they're doing.

13. The similar surface structures of the following sentences might lead you to think that the two are alike. Knowing what you know about *-ing* verbs as adjectivals and nominals, explain how the sentences differ:

> I had a hard time choosing the right color.
> I have a good thing going for me.

In considering the difference, think about the subject of the *-ing* verb.

14. In the discussion of the catenative verbs in this chapter, we note that not all transitive verbs will take other verbs as objects. We wouldn't find *eat* and *hit* and *read*, for example, with other verbs as their direct objects. If this is true, then how do we account for such sentences as the following:

> We ate his cooking.
> Tom hit his pitching.
> I read her writing.

In considering this question, you might find it useful to think about the sentence pattern of *cook, pitch,* and *write.*

15. In this chapter we looked at some sentences with catenative verbs in which the passive transformation retained the infinitive as the object:

> I expect <u>the carpenters</u> to finish the job before noon.
> <u>The carpenters</u> are expected <u>to finish the job before noon.</u>

Compare these passive sentences with those you studied in Chapter 2. What sentence pattern do they most nearly resemble? In what respect do they differ?

16. In Chapter 3 we looked at cleft sentences, variations that change the focus of the sentence. Some of the resulting sentences have nominal clauses; others have adjectival clauses. Identify the grammatical function of the clause in the following cleft sentences. One way to demonstrate that function is to diagram the various cleft sentences. Then see how many other ways you can vary the focus of each.

Our boat capsized in high winds off Point Loma.
Cleft: It was off Point Loma that our boat capsized in high winds.
Cleft: What caused our boat to capsize off Point Loma was high winds.

Harold quit smoking last New Year's eve.
Cleft: It was last New Year's eve that Harold quit smoking.
Cleft: What Harold did last New Year's eve was to quit smoking.

12

Sentence Modifiers

Like the modifiers of nouns and verbs, modifiers of the sentence as a whole also come in the form of single words, phrases, and clauses. In general, these modifiers resemble adverbials: The information they contribute is, for the most part, adverbial information—time, place, manner, and the like; and most single-word sentence modifiers are adverbs in form. The choice of whether to call a certain phrase or clause a sentence modifier or a verb modifier is, in fact, sometimes hard to make; there are few definitive rules. Within a sentence the sentence modifier will usually be set off by commas, but at the beginning or end of the sentence it may not be. As a result, often the only structures classified as sentence modifiers are those that are clearly parenthetical or independent in meaning or those in which an obvious contrast exists, as in the following pair:

Clearly, he did not explain the situation.
He did not explain the situation clearly.

This contrast in meaning shows the difference between the two functions of *clearly:* It is a **sentence modifier** in the first sentence but an adverbial in the second.

You'll notice that there are no diagrams in this chapter to help you visualize the sentence modifiers. There's a good reason for that omission: With a traditional diagram the only way of showing a structure that is related to the sentence as a whole is to diagram it separately. For example, there is no way of diagramming the differing meanings of *clearly* in the foregoing examples. One method that does work well, however, is the system known as "immediate-constituent analysis."

I-C analysis, as it is called, is based on the premise that the sentence and the structures within the sentence are binary in nature—that is, they have two parts. That division in the case of the first example with *clearly* would identify the parts as *sentence modifier* + *sentence:*

Clearly	he did not explain the situation

In the sentence where *clearly* is an adverbial, the I-C analysis would show the two parts as *subject* + *predicate:*

He	did not explain the situation clearly

Here the analysis makes it obvious that *clearly* is part of the verb phrase.

(I-C analysis is shown in detail in Appendix B.)

The single-word sentence modifier is often set off by a comma. We can usually identify its relationship to the sentence as a whole even without the obvious contrast in meaning that a word such as *clearly* illustrates:

Increasingly, college students are taking practical courses that will prepare them for the job market.

Invariably, the dress or pair of shoes I like best is the one with the highest price tag.

Luckily, the van didn't get a scratch when it hit the ditch.

But not all sentence modifiers are separated by commas:

Perhaps the entire starting lineup ought to be replaced.

Here it is fairly clear that *perhaps* raises a question about the idea of the sentence as a whole. If it were moved to a position within the sentence, it would probably be set off by commas:

The entire starting lineup, perhaps, ought to be replaced.

So the absence of a comma after an introductory modifier does not rule it out as a sentence modifier; but neither does the presence of a comma rule it in. As we saw in the earlier chapters on noun and verb modifiers, both adjectivals and adverbials can sometimes be shifted to the opening position. That shift does not in itself make them sentence modifiers. For example, in the following sentences the introductory phrases are adjectival, modifiers of the subject:

> <u>Hot and tired</u>, we loaded the camping gear into the station wagon for the long trip home.
> <u>Limping noticeably</u>, the runner rounded third base and managed to beat the throw at home plate.

Verb modifiers in introductory position are somewhat more open to interpretation as sentence modifiers, because adverbials do tend to add information that relates to the whole idea. In Chapter 8 we classified phrases like the following as modifiers of the verb, although admittedly the designation is somewhat arbitrary; a case could be made for such modifiers to be classified as sentence modifiers rather than adverbials:

> <u>To polish his skills for his trip to Las Vegas</u>, Tim plays poker every night.
> <u>Almost every Monday morning</u>, I make a vow to start counting calories.
> <u>On a day like today</u>, I prefer to stay in bed.

The less clearly a modifier is related to a particular part of the sentence, the more clearly we can classify it as a modifier of the sentence as a whole. English has many idiomatic expressions—unvarying formulas that have an independent or parenthetical quality—that are clearly sentence modifiers. Unlike the three adverbial examples earlier, the introductory modifiers in the following sentences are not added for information such as *when* or *where* or *why:*

> <u>Frankly</u>, I didn't expect sailing to be so much work.
> <u>Speaking of the weather</u>, let's decide on the place for our picnic.
> <u>To tell the truth</u>, I have never read *Silas Marner.*
> <u>To our amazement</u>, the driver of the Corvette walked away from the accident.

NOUNS OF DIRECT ADDRESS: THE VOCATIVES

Another structure set off by a comma is the noun or noun phrase of direct address, known as a **vocative.**

> <u>Ladies and gentlemen</u>, please be seated.
> <u>Jennifer</u>, your date is here.

Although the vocative is not a modifier in the same sense that other structures are, in that it does not modify the meaning of the sentence, it does have a relationship to the sentence as a whole. And like other modifiers, it can come at the beginning, middle, or end of the sentence:

> We certainly hope, <u>my dear friends</u>, that you will visit again soon.
> I promise you won't see me here in court again, <u>your honor</u>.
> Tell us, <u>Mr. President</u>, how your new tax plan will benefit the poor.

The purpose of the vocative, as the term "direct address" implies, is to direct the writer's or speaker's message to a particular person or group. Further, as the choice of words in the foregoing examples illustrate, the vocative can express the attitude of the writer or speaker and reflect the tone, whether formal or informal, serious or light, familiar or distant. In that sense, certainly, the vocative is a "sentence modifier" of sorts: It can affect the meaning of the words.

INTERJECTIONS

The **interjection**—usually a single word or short phrase—can also be considered as a modifier of the sentence as a whole:

> <u>Oh</u>, don't frighten me like that!
> <u>Ah</u>! That's exactly what I expected.

The traditional view of grammar treats the interjection as one of the parts of speech, probably because there is no other way to categorize such "nonwords" as *oh* and *ah.* However, many words that we recog-

nize as nouns and verbs are also used as exclamatory sentence modifiers
of this kind:

Heavens, I don't know what to say.
Good grief! Don't confuse me with the facts!
My word! This will never do.

It would seem logical to consider these as interjections of the same
kind as *oh* and *ah;* however, we do not put all such "interjections" into
a single parts-of-speech class, as the traditional grammarians do; such
a classification distorts the principle on which we make judgments
about word categories. Except for *oh* and *ah* and *whew* and a few others,
we recognize interjections strictly by their exclamatory, or emotional,
function in the sentence. It's true, of course, that the familiar definitions given to the traditional eight parts of speech are not necessarily
consistent in their criteria; for example, nouns and verbs are defined
according to their meaning (as names and as actions) and adjectives
and adverbs by their function (as modifiers). Nevertheless, out of all
eight traditional "parts of speech," only the interjection category is
denoted strictly by sentence function, rather than as a word type; that
is, the other seven traditional parts of speech (noun, verb, adjective,
adverb, pronoun, preposition, and conjunction) are names of word
classes. It is for this reason that the interjection is not included in our
inventory of structure words, described in Chapter 6, but rather is
included here as one kind of sentence modifier.

Exercise 66: Underline any sentence modifiers in the following sentences.

1. Amazingly, the money held out until the end of the month.
2. The twins look amazingly alike.
3. Well, I plan to stay, myself.
4. Myself, I plan to stay well.
5. Strangely, he seemed to look right through me.
6. I thought he looked at me strangely.
7. Without a doubt our team will win the league championship.
8. We will no doubt win the league championship.

9. I told my friend I was not interested in his scheme.
10. I told you, my friend, that I am not interested.

SUBORDINATE CLAUSES

In Chapter 8 we looked at the adverbial clauses, recognizing that they, too, often seem to relate to the sentence as a whole rather than to the verb specifically. Those introduced by *where, when, before,* and *after* seem to be the most "adverbial" of all in that they convey information of time and place about the verb; but certainly we could make an equal case for classifying even these as sentence modifiers. Clauses introduced by subordinators such as *if, because, since, as,* and *although* seem even more clearly to modify the idea of the whole sentence, because the subordinator explains the relationship of one idea to another:

> *If* you promise to be there, I'll go to Sue's party.
> I'll go to the party *because* you want me to.
> I'll go with you, *although* I would rather stay home.
> We'll have scrod for dinner *if* the fish market has it at a reasonable price.
> *Because* you prefer it, we'll have scrod instead of sole.

The phrasal subordinators, too, may relate one complete clause to another:

> *Provided that* the moving van arrives on schedule, we'll be ready to leave by three o'clock.
> All the members of the city council, *as far as* I know, voted in favor of the new dog ordinance.

(See page 136 for a list of the simple and phrasal subordinators.)

Punctuation of Subordinate Clauses. In opening position the subordinate clause is always set off by a comma; in closing position, punctuation is related to meaning. As a general rule, when the idea in the main clause is conditional upon or dependent upon the idea in the subordinate clause, there is no comma. For example, the idea of the main clause—the opening clause—in the following sentence will be realized only if the idea in the subordinate clause is carried out; thus here the main clause depends on the *if* clause:

> I'll go to Sue's party if you promise to be there.

But in the next sentence the subordinate clause does not affect the fulfillment of the main clause:

> I'm going to the party that Sue's giving on Saturday night, even though I know I'll be bored.

In general *even though* and *although* are preceded by commas; *if* and *because* are not. The point to be made here is that the subordinator relates the idea in its clause to the idea in the main clause, so the subordinate clause clearly functions as a modifier of the sentence as a whole—even though it is not preceded by a comma. But in opening position, the clause is always followed by a comma. The use of the comma with final subordinate clauses is probably one of the least standardized of our punctuation rules. The final criterion must be readability and clarity for the reader.

Exercise 67: Add commas to the following sentences, if necessary.

1. We left the party as soon as we politely could.
2. Jim agreed to leave the party early and go bowling with us although he was having a good time.
3. When the storm is over we can head for home.
4. We might as well put on the coffee since we're going to be here for another hour.
5. I know that Jerry and I will never be able to afford that much money for rent even if it does include utilities.
6. I won't be able to stay in this apartment if the rent goes any higher.
7. I won't be able to stay in this apartment even if the rent stays the same.

Elliptical Clauses. Many subordinate clauses are **elliptical**—that is, certain understood words are left out:

<u>While</u> [we were] <u>waiting for the guests to arrive</u>, we ate all the
good hors d'oeuvres ourselves.
<u>When</u> [you are] <u>in doubt about home-canned vegetables</u>, be sure
to bring them to a boil before you taste them.

In these clauses the missing words could be included; both versions are
acceptable sentences.

In most cases the subject of the elliptical clause will also be the
subject of the main clause, as in the two preceding sentences. But that
understood element may also be the source of an illogical sentence,
similar to one with a dangling gerund or participle. In the following
sentences, for example, you'll notice that the subject of the main
clause fails to meet the reader's expectations set up by the elliptical
clause:

<u>When late for work</u>, the subway is better than the bus.
<u>If kept too long in hot weather</u>, mold will grow on the bread.
<u>While waiting for the guests to arrive</u>, there were a lot of last-
minute details to take care of.

As with many of the dangling structures we have seen, the message of
the sentence may be clear; but there's simply no reason for a writer to
set up a situation in which the reader must make the connections—
and must do so in a conscious way. Those connections are the writer's
job.

In the case of some subordinate clauses, only the elliptical version is
grammatical:

I'm a week older <u>than Bob</u>.
My sister isn't <u>as tall as I</u>.
or
I'm a week older <u>than Bob is</u>.
My sister isn't <u>as tall as I am</u>.

We would never include the entire clause:

*I'm a week older <u>than Bob is old</u>.
*My sister isn't <u>as tall as I am tall</u>.

In both of these examples, we are comparing an attribute of the subjects of the two clauses. But the ellipses in such comparisons can produce ambiguity when the main clause has more than one possible noun phrase for the subordinate clause to be compared with:

> The Rangers beat the Dolphins worse <u>than the Broncos.</u>
> Joe likes Mary better <u>than Pat.</u>

In these sentences we don't know whether the comparison is between subjects or objects because we don't know what has been left out. We don't know whether

<table>
<tr><td>The Rangers beat the Dolphins worse <u>than</u></td><td>}</td><td>the Rangers beat the Broncos.
or
the Broncos beat the Dolphins.</td></tr>
</table>

<table>
<tr><td>Joe likes Mary better <u>than</u></td><td>}</td><td>Joe likes Pat.
or
Pat likes Mary.</td></tr>
</table>

Exercise 68. Rewrite the three sentences on page 293, including a subject in the elliptical clause. You may have to make changes in the main clause as well.

A. When late for work, the subway is better than the bus.
B. If kept too long in hot weather, mold will grow on the bread.
C. While waiting for the guests to arrive, there were a lot of last-minute details to take care of.

Now rewrite the following sentences, supplying the words missing in the elliptical clauses. Are the sentences clear?

1. I picked up a Midwestern accent while living in Omaha.
2. My accent is not as noticeable as Mary's.
3. Holmes hit Ali harder than Norton.
4. If necessary, strain the juice before adding the sugar.
5. While waiting at the train station in Lewistown, there was no place to sit.
6. If handed in late, your grade will be lowered ten percent.

ABSOLUTE PHRASES

The **absolute phrase** (also known as the *nominative absolute*) is a structure independent from the main sentence; in form the absolute phrase is a noun phrase that includes a postnoun modifier. The modifier is commonly an *-en* or *-ing* participle or participial phrase, but it can also be a prepositional phrase, an adjective phrase, or a noun phrase. The absolute phrase introduces an idea related to the sentence as a whole, not to any one of its parts:

> Our car having developed engine trouble, we stopped for the
>   night at a roadside rest area.
> The weather being warm and clear, we decided to have a picnic.
> Victory assured, the fans stood and cheered during the last five
>   minutes of the game.

Absolute phrases are of two kinds—with different purposes and different effects. (Moreover, both are structures generally used in writing, rather than in speech.) The preceding sentences illustrate the first kind: the absolute that explains a cause or condition. In the first sentence, the absolute phrase could be rewritten as a *because, when,* or *since* clause:

> When our car developed engine trouble,
> *or*
> Since our car developed engine trouble,   } we stopped for
>   the night. . . .
> *or*
> Because our car developed engine trouble,

The absolute construction allows the writer to include the information without the explicitness that the complete clause requires. In other words, the absolute phrase can be thought of as containing all the meanings in the three versions shown here rather than any one of them.

In the following sentence the idea in the *because* clause could be interpreted as the only reason for the picnic:

> Because the weather was warm and clear, we decided to have a
>   picnic.

The absolute construction, on the other hand, leaves open the possibility of other reasons for the picnic:

The weather being warm and clear, we decided to have a picnic.

It also suggests simply an attendant condition rather than a cause.

In the second kind of absolute phrase, illustrated by the sentences following, a prepositional phrase (*above his head*), adjective phrase (*alert to every passing footstep*), or noun phrase (*a dripping mess*), as well as a participle (*trembling*), may serve as the postnoun modifier. This second kind of absolute adds a detail or point of focus to the idea stated in the main clause:

Julie tried to fit the key into the rusty lock, her hands trembling.
The old hound stood guard faithfully, his ears alert to every passing footstep.
Hands above his head, the suspect advanced cautiously toward the uniformed officers.
Her hair a dripping mess, she dashed in out of the rain.

One interesting difference between the two kinds of absolute constructions is the kind of paraphrase each can undergo. As we saw earlier, the first kind—the absolute of cause or condition—can be expanded into a subordinate clause introduced by such words as *because* or *since* or *when*. But if the absolute phrase of detail or focus—the second kind—is expanded into a clause, it will become the main clause of the sentence, not the subordinate one:

Julie's hands trembled as she tried to fit the key into the rusty lock.
The old hound's ears were alert to every passing footstep as he faithfully stood guard.
The suspect held his hands above his head as he advanced cautiously toward the uniformed officers.

This underlying meaning suggests that the idea in the absolute construction may be the main focus of the sentence, even though grammatically and structurally it occupies a subordinate role.

Another way of paraphrasing the absolute construction is to make it the object of the preposition *with:*

> Julie tried to fit the key into the rusty lock <u>with her hands trembling</u> (or <u>with trembling hands</u>).
> The old hound stood guard <u>with his ears alert to every sound.</u>

This paraphrase gives the former absolute phrase the role of manner adverbial, a role that may not render the meaning accurately. Again, the absolute construction enables the writer to avoid that specific adverbial suggestion and to sharpen the impact of the sentence by focusing on a detail of the whole.

This technique of focusing on a detail allows the writer to move the reader in for a close-up view, just as a filmmaker uses the camera. The absolute phrase is especially effective in writing description. Notice how the authors of the following passages use the main clause of the sentence as the wide lens and the absolute phrase as the close-up:

> There was no bus in sight and Julian, <u>his hands still jammed in his pockets and his head thrust forward</u>, scowled down the empty street.
> —FLANNERY O'CONNOR, *Everything That Rises Must Converge*

> The man stood laughing, <u>his weapons at his hips.</u>
> —STEPHEN CRANE, *The Bride Comes to Yellow Sky*

> He smiled a little to himself as he ran, holding the ball lightly in front of him with his two hands, <u>his knees pumping high</u>, <u>his hips twisting in the almost girlish run of a back in a broken field.</u>
> —IRWIN SHAW, *The Eighty-Yard Run*

> Soon afterwards they retired, <u>Mama in her big oak bed on one side of the room</u>, <u>Emilio and Rosy in their boxes full of straw and sheepskins on the other side of the room.</u>

> Soon the canyon sides became steep and the first giant sentinel redwoods guarded the trail, <u>great round red trunks bearing foliage as green and lacy as ferns.</u>
> —JOHN STEINBECK, *Flight*

Silently they ambled down Tenth Street until they reached a stone bench that jutted from the sidewalk near the curb. They stopped there and sat down, <u>their backs to the eyes of the two men in white smocks who were watching them.</u>

—TONI MORRISON, *Song of Solomon*

William Faulkner's style of writing depends heavily on the use of the absolute phrase. Probably no writer uses it more frequently or more effectively in setting scenes and describing characters. The following passages are from *Barn Burning*:

Then his father was gone, <u>the stiff foot heavy and measured upon the boards, ceasing at last.</u>

From the woodpile through the rest of the afternoon the boy watched them, <u>the rug spread flat in the dust beside the bubbling wash-pot,</u> <u>the two sisters stooping over it with a profound and lethargic reluctance,</u> while the father stood over them in turn, implacable and grim, driving them though never raising his voice again.

This time the sorrel mare was in the lot before he heard it at all, <u>the rider collarless and even bareheaded, trembling, speaking in a shaking voice as the woman in the house had done,</u> <u>his father merely looking up once before stooping again to the hame he was buckling,</u> so that the man on the mare spoke to his stooping back.

Notice that both of the absolute constructions in the preceding passage include subordinate—in this case, adverbial—clauses, the first introduced by *as,* the second by *so that.*

APPOSITIVES

You'll recall that one of the modifiers in the noun phrase described in Chapter 9 is the appositive, a structure that in form is itself a noun phrase:

Our visitor, <u>a grey-haired lady of indeterminate age,</u> surprised us all when she joined in the volleyball game.

In this example, the appositive renames the subject of the sentence. But sometimes we use a noun phrase to rename, or, more accurately, to capsulize the idea in the sentence as a whole. We call these structures sentence appositives; we often punctuate them with a dash:

> The musical opened to rave reviews and standing-room-only crowds—<u>a smashing success</u>.
> A pair of cardinals has set up housekeeping in our pine tree—<u>an unexpected but welcome event</u>.

Like the absolutes, which are also noun phrases in form, these sentence appositives are related to the sentence as a whole, but their purpose is quite different: They simply label, or restate, the idea of the main clause; they do not introduce a new, subordinate idea, as both kinds of absolute phrases do.

Exercise 69: Underline any absolute phrases in the following sentences. Is the modifier of the headword an adjective, a prepositional phrase, a noun phrase, or a participle?

1. The cat lay by the fire, purring contentedly, her tail moving from side to side like a metronome.
2. Chuck and Margie kicked their way through the fallen leaves, their arms draped across each other's shoulders.
3. The rain having persisted for over an hour, the game was officially stopped in the sixth inning.
4. With the Grand Tetons looming majestically above, Jackson Hole, Wyoming, looks like a picture postcard.
5. Julie sat in the principal's office, waiting nervously, her eyes cast to the floor.
6. Hands on hips, the team stood waiting for the signal to begin their routine.
7. Having slipped on the ice three times already, I decided to wear sensible boots for a change.
8. Then the boy was moving, <u>his bunched shirt and the hard, bony hand between his shoulder-blades</u>, his toes just touching the floor, across the room and into the other one, past the sisters sitting with spread heavy thighs in the two chairs over the cold hearth, and to

where his mother and aunt sat side by side on the bed, the aunt's arms about his mother's shoulders. (WILLIAM FAULKNER)

RELATIVE CLAUSES

Most relative clauses are modifiers of nouns, and most are introduced by a relative pronoun that refers to that noun:

Joe's car, which he bought just last week, looks like a gas guzzler to me.

In this sentence the antecedent of *which* is the noun *car;* the noun is modified by the clause.

But in some sentences *which* refers not to a particular noun but to a whole idea; it has what we call *broad reference.* In the following sentence, the antecedent of *which* is the idea of the entire main clause:

Joe bought a gas guzzler, which surprised me.

All such broad-reference clauses are introduced by *which,* never by *who* or *that,* and all are nonrestrictive—that is, they are set off by commas:

Tom cleaned up the garage without being asked, which made me suspect that he wanted to borrow the car.

This summer's heat wave in the Midwest devastated the corn crop, which probably means higher meat prices for next year.

Many writers try to avoid the broad-reference relative clause, instead using *which* only in the adjectival clause to refer to a specific noun. In inexperienced hands the broad-reference *which* clause often has the vagueness associated with dangling modifiers:

I broke out in a rash, which really bothered me.

In this sentence the referent of *which* is unclear; *which* could refer to either the *rash* or the *breaking out.* There are a number of alternatives in which the meaning is clear:

> Breaking out in a rash really bothered me.
> The rash I got last week really bothered me.

Even though they are not particularly vague, the earlier examples, too, can be paraphrased in ways that avoid the broad-reference *which:*

> When Tom cleaned up the garage without being asked, I suspected that he wanted to borrow the car.
> Tom's cleaning up the garage without being asked made me suspect that he wanted to borrow the car.
> This summer's heat wave in the Midwest, which devastated the corn crop, probably means higher meat prices for next year.

Exercise 70: Rewrite the following sentences to eliminate the broad-reference *which*.

1. I had to clean the basement this morning, which wasn't very much fun.
2. Otis didn't want to stay for the second half of the game, which surprised me.
3. The president criticized the Congress rather severely in his press conference, which some observers considered quite inappropriate.
4. The first snowstorm of the season in Denver was both early and severe, which was not what the weather service had predicted.
5. We're having company for dinner three times this week, which probably means hot dogs for the rest of the month.

SUMMARY

Sentence modifiers relate ideas to sentences in a variety of ways. Some sentence modifiers are difficult to distinguish from adverbials, modifiers of the verb; in fact, the decision to classify certain structures as sentence modifiers is somewhat arbitrary. But many subordinate clauses, certain idiomatic expressions, as well as absolute phrases, are clearly related to the whole sentence rather than to any particular part.

The absolute phrase is an especially effective way to add descriptive details to the sentence.

SENTENCES FOR PRACTICE

Draw vertical lines to set off sentence modifiers; identify them by form. If the sentence modifier is, or includes, a verb phrase or clause, identify its sentence pattern.

1. My brother will finish basic training next month if everything goes smoothly.

2. Last week stock prices scored surprisingly strong gains as Wall Street experienced one of the busiest periods in the market's history.

3. If you don't mind, I want to be alone.

4. Speaking of travel, would you like to go to Seattle next week to see the Seahawks play?

5. Incidentally, you forgot to pay me for your share of the expenses.

6. The weather being so beautiful last Sunday, we decided to go to Silver Creek Falls for a picnic.

7. The invitations having been sent, we started planning the menu for Maria's birthday party.

8. Jennifer stayed in bed all day, her fever getting worse instead of better.

9. If bread is kept too long in hot weather, mold will begin to grow on it.

10. The giant redwoods loomed majestically, their branches filling the sky above us.

11. Because the weather turned cold suddenly, we decided to postpone our Saturday morning walk.

12. Luckily, Sunday was a nice day, so we didn't miss our weekly hike.

13. Freddie suggested we take a taxi instead of the subway—a splendid idea.

14. Old Town was festive, indeed—the stores decorated with bright colored banners, the air alive with music, the streets crowded with people.

QUESTIONS FOR DISCUSSION

1. Many of the simple and phrasal subordinators listed in Chapter 6 introduce clauses that could be interpreted as either sentence modifiers or verb

modifiers. How would you classify the underlined clauses in the following sentences—as sentence modifiers or as verb modifiers? Why?

1. I'll return your book <u>as soon as I finish it.</u>
2. He'll lend me the money <u>provided that I use it for tuition.</u>
3. The dog looked at me <u>as if he wanted to tell me something important.</u>
4. Nero fiddled <u>while Rome burned.</u>

2. The following sentences are both illogical and ungrammatical. What is the source of the problem? Correct the sentences and diagram them, showing the deep structure of the elliptical clauses.

1. The summer temperatures in the Santa Clara Valley are much higher than San Francisco.
2. The Pirates' stolen base record is better than the Cardinals.

3. Consider the pronouns in these elliptical clauses. Are they the correct form? Is it possible that both sentences are correct?

I think my little sister likes our cat better than me.
I think my little sister likes our cat better than I.

4. A common subject for discussion among people who think about language and usage is the "problem" of *hopefully*. The following sentences are, in fact, avoided by many speakers and writers.

Hopefully, we will get to the theater before the play starts.
Hopefully, this play will be better than the last one we saw.

Is the adverb *hopefully* used incorrectly in these sentences? Should it be used only as a manner adverb? Or can it function as a sentence modifier? Make a case for both sides of the issue. (In considering *hopefully*, think also about other adverbs as sentence modifiers, such as *clearly, luckily,* and *admittedly*.)

5. Rewrite the following sentences, turning the underlined absolute phrases into complete clauses. Note whether the clauses are main clauses or subordinate. Do any of the sentences offer a choice between the two?

1. The fans surged onto the field, <u>their shouts of victory filling the stadium like the roar of an avalanche.</u>
2. The catamarans skimmed across the water, <u>their sails billowing like low-flying clouds.</u>

3. The garage being full of outdoor furniture and garden equipment, we had no room for the car.

6. In Chapter 9, we saw several examples of noun modifiers that could open the sentence:

An ex-Marine who once played professional football, the security guard in our building makes us feel secure, indeed.

Having found the camp deserted, we assumed that the hunters had returned to civilization.

Quiet and peaceful, the neighborhood slept while the cat burglars made their rounds.

How do these structures differ from the absolute phrases discussed in this chapter?

7. How do you explain the difference in meaning between the following sentences, which appear so similar on the surface? Discuss the effect of the understood elliptical clause in the second sentence. Are both sentences negative?

I have never been happy with our living arrangement.

I have never been happier with our living arrangement.

8. You will probably agree that one of the sentences in each of the following pairs is ungrammatical, or at least questionable. What makes it so? State the rule that a native speaker follows in avoiding such sentences.

Although she was tired, Alice picked blackberries all afternoon.

She was tired, but Alice picked blackberries all afternoon.

Since they worked extra hard, Tom and Jane earned a bonus of five dollars.

They worked extra hard, and Tom and Jane earned a bonus of five dollars.

CHAPTER

13

Coordination

In the five preceding chapters we have examined a variety of ways to expand sentences—by adding modifiers and by using verb phrases and clauses as nominals. Another common technique is **coordination:** joining two or more structures to form a pair or series.

All parts of the sentence can be coordinated—subjects, main verbs, auxiliaries, complements, modifiers, prepositions, objects of prepositions—as well as whole sentences. In Chapter 6 we looked at the conjunctions, the structure words that do the connecting; in this chapter we will look further at *how* they do this job.

COORDINATING PARTS OF THE SENTENCE

Within a sentence both coordinating and correlative conjunctions do the job of connecting parts. In the following sentence, for example, both the subject and the adverbial prepositional phrase are coordinate structures. The coordinating conjunction *and* connects the compound subject; the correlative *both–and* connects the two adverbial prepositional phrases of place.

John and Tim worked out on Saturday, both in the weight room and in the gym.

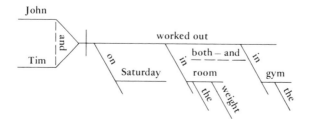

305

The diagram illustrates both the role of the coordinate structure and its form, with two or more lines in a particular slot instead of just one; a broken line for the conjunction connects them.

The sentences that follow illustrate coordination in other sentence slots:

Compound Subjective Complement: Molly's dessert was simple yet elegant.

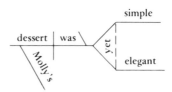

Compound Prenoun Adjective: Molly served a simple but elegant dessert.

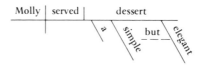

Compound Auxiliary: He can and should finish the job before dark.

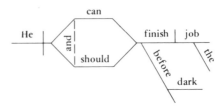

Compound Verb: The whole gang laughed and reminisced at the class reunion.

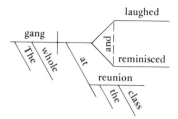

Note that in the last sentence the adverbial prepositional phrase modifies both verbs, so in the diagram it is attached to a line that is common to both. In the following sentence each verb has a separate modifier; the conjunction connects complete verb phrases, not the verbs alone. The introductory prepositional phrase modifies both verb phrases, so it is shown on a line common to both.

Compound Verb Phrase: On Homecoming weekend our frat party started at noon and lasted until dawn.

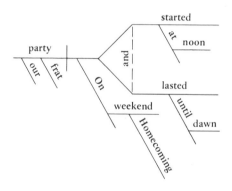

Punctuation of Coordinate Structures Within the Sentence. Pairs of words, phrases, or clauses within the sentence need no commas with the conjunctions, as the preceding sentences illustrate; this rule applies even when the elements are long. For example, in the following sentence a pair of nominal clauses fills the direct object slot. Even though the clauses are long ones—and even though the reader might pause for a breath at the conjunction—the object is simply a compound structure within the sentence like those we have seen before; the sentence has no place for a comma:

He said that he would get here sooner or later and that I shouldn't start the rehearsal without him.

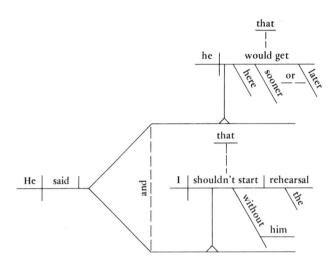

An exception to this rule against commas with compound elements occurs when the conjunction is *but:*

> I have visited a lot of big cities, but never Los Angeles.
> I worked hard all night, but just couldn't finish my project.
> My new white dress is beautiful, but not very practical.

There's a clear disjunction with *but,* resulting, of course, from its meaning; it introduces a contrast of one kind or another. Further, the phrase introduced by *but* could almost be thought of as an elliptical clause, another reason that the comma seems logical:

> I worked hard all night, but [I] just couldn't finish my project.
> My new white dress is beautiful, but [it is] not very practical.

Another exception to the comma restriction occurs when we want to give special emphasis to the last element in a coordinated pair:

> I didn't believe him, and said so.
> My new white dress is beautiful, and expensive.

This emphasis will be even stronger with a dash instead of a comma:

> I didn't believe him—and said so.
> My new white dress is beautiful—and expensive.

We also use commas with a series of three or more elements:

> We <u>gossiped, laughed, and sang</u> together at the class reunion, just like old times.

These commas represent the pauses and slight changes of pitch that occur in the production of the series. You can hear the commas in your voice when you compare the two—the series and the pair. Read them aloud:

> We gossiped, laughed, and sang. . . .
> We laughed and sang. . . .

You probably noticed a leveling of the pitch in reading the pair, a certain smoothness that the series did not have. In the series with conjunctions instead of commas, you'll notice that same leveling:

> We gossiped <u>and</u> laughed <u>and</u> sang together at the class reunion, just like old times.

When conjunctions connect all of the elements, we use no commas.

In the series of three, some writers—and some publications as a matter of policy—use only one comma, leaving out the serial comma, the one immediately before *and:*

> We gossiped, laughed <u>and</u> sang together at the class reunion, just like old times.

Perhaps they do so on the assumption that the conjunction substitutes for the comma. But it really does not. In fact, this punctuation misleads the reader in two ways: It implies a closer connection than actually exists between the last two elements of the series, and it ignores the pitch change, however slight, represented by the comma. The main purpose of punctuation, after all, is to represent graphically the meaningful speech signals—pitch, stress (loudness), and juncture (pauses)—that the written language otherwise lacks. That small pitch change represented by the comma can make a difference in emphasis and meaning.

Exercise 71: Punctuate the following sentences.

1. Pete sanded the car on Friday and painted it with undercoating on Saturday.
2. Even though the car's new paint job looks terrific now I suspect it will be covered with rust and scratches and dents before next winter.
3. I spent a fortune on new tires shock absorbers and brake linings for the car last week.
4. The car that my father had back in the 1930s and 1940s a 1929 Whippet required very little maintenance and no major repairs during the ten or more years he drove it.
5. I have decided to park my car until gas prices go down and to ride my bicycle instead.
6. I don't suppose I'll ever be able to afford the down payment or the interest or the insurance on a new Corvette the car of my dreams.

Subject–Verb Agreement. When nouns or noun phrases in the subject slot are joined by *and* or by the correlative *both–and,* the subject is plural:

My friends and relatives are coming to the wedding.

However, the coordinating conjunction *or* and the correlatives *either–or* and *neither–nor* do not have the additive meaning of *and;* with *or* and *nor* the relationship is called disjunctive. In compound subjects with these conjunctions, the verb will be determined by the closer member of the pair:

Neither the speaker nor the listeners were intimidated by the protestors.
Either the class officers or the faculty advisor makes the final decision.
Do the class officers or the faculty advisor make the final decision?
Does the faculty advisor or the class officers make the final decision?

If the correct sentence sounds incorrect or awkward because of the verb form, you can simply reverse the compound pair:

> Either the faculty advisor or <u>the class officers make</u> the final decision.

When both members of the pair are alike, of course, there is no question:

> Either <u>the president</u> or <u>the vice-president</u> is going to introduce the speaker.
> Neither <u>the union members</u> nor <u>the management representatives</u> were willing to compromise.

For most verb forms, you'll recall there is no decision to be made about subject–verb agreement; the issue arises only when the -*s* form of the verb or auxiliary is involved. In the following sentences, there is no -*s* form:

> Either the class officers or the faculty advisor <u>will make</u> the final decision.
> Either the faculty advisor or the class officers <u>will make</u> the final decision.

Another situation that sometimes causes confusion about number—that is, whether the subject is singular or plural—occurs with subjects that include a phrase introduced by *as well as* or *in addition to*:

> *The sidewalk, in addition to the driveway, need to be repaired.
> *The piano player, as well as the rest of the group, usually join in the singing.

These additions to the subject are parenthetical; they are not treated as part of the subject. To make the subject compound—to include them—the writer should use a coordinating conjunction, such as *and*:

> The sidewalk <u>and</u> the driveway <u>need</u> to be repaired.
> The piano player <u>and</u> the rest of the group usually <u>join</u> in the singing.

Parallel Structure. An important requirement for coordinate structures is that they be **parallel**. A structure is parallel when all of the coordinate parts are of the same grammatical form. The conjunctions must join comparable structures, such as pairs of noun phrases or verb phrases or adjectives:

> The little white-haired lady *and* her blonde poodle seemed to belong together.
> The stew smells delicious *and* tastes even better.
> The entire cast gave powerful *and* exciting performances.

Unparallel structures occur most commonly with the correlative conjunctions: *both–and, either–or, neither–nor,* and *not only–but also.* For example, in the following sentence, the two coordinators introduce structures of different forms:

> *Either* they will fly straight home *or* stop overnight in Dubuque.

Being able to picture the diagram can be helpful in preventing such unparallel structures. With the sentence above, you'll discover that the conjunction line would connect a complete sentence (*they will fly straight home*) and a verb phrase (*stop overnight in Dubuque*). As the two structures are not parallel, the diagram simply won't work.

A diagram of the following sentence won't work either:

> I'll *either* take a bus *or* a taxi.

The conjunction line would have to connect a verb phrase and a noun phrase; again the two structures are not parallel.

Such problems are easy to correct. It's just a matter of shifting one part of the correlative pair so that both introduce the same kind of construction:

> They will *either* fly straight home *or* stop overnight in Dubuque.
> I'll take *either* a bus *or* a taxi.

You might find it helpful to review the uses of the correlative conjunctions in Chapter 6; note the exception to the rule of parallelism on page 137 in connection with *either–or* and *neither–nor* as sentence connectors.

Exercise 72: Rewrite the following sentences, paying particular attention to correcting unparallel structures.

1. I can't decide which activity I prefer: to swim at the shore in July when the sand is warm or jogging along country roads in October when the autumn leaves are at their colorful best.
2. I almost never watch television. There is either nothing on that appeals to me or the picture disappears at a crucial moment.
3. I neither enjoy flying across the country nor particularly want to take the train.
4. The recipe was either printed wrong, or I misread it.
5. Other people can become frail and break, but not parents.
6. The coach announced an extra hour of drill on Saturday and that the practice on Sunday would be canceled.
7. Aunt Rosa has promised to fix her famous lasagna for my birthday dinner and will also bake my favorite cake.

COORDINATING COMPLETE SENTENCES

The section on conjunctions in Chapter 6 explains two methods of joining independent clauses to produce compound sentences: (1) using coordinating conjunctions and (2) using the semicolon, either with or without conjunctive adverbs.

Conjunctions. The compound sentence with a coordinating conjunction such as *and* shows up at an early stage of the writer's development:

We went to the fair, <u>and</u> we had a good time.
Robby is mean, <u>and</u> I don't like him.

Such sentences can, of course, be effective when they are used sparingly, but they will strike the reader as immature when overused. The compound sentence is most effective when the coordinate ideas have relatively equal importance—when the two ideas contribute equal weight:

> I disapprove of his betting on the horses, <u>and</u> I told him so.
> The curtain rose to reveal a perfectly bare stage, <u>and</u> a stillness settled over the audience.
> Pete filled the bags with hot roasted peanuts, <u>and</u> I stapled them shut.

Note that the punctuation rule that applies to the compound sentence differs from the rule regarding internal coordinate constructions. Between the sentences in a compound sentence we do use a comma with the conjunction; between the parts of a coordinate structure within the sentence we do not. When the clauses of a compound sentence are quite short and closely connected, however, we sometimes omit the comma. The following sentence, for example, would probably be spoken without the pitch change we associate with commas:

> October came <u>and</u> the tourists left.

The coordinators *and* and *or* can link a series of three or more sentences:

> Pete filled the bags, <u>and</u> I stapled them shut, <u>and</u> Marty packed them in the cartons.
> The kids can wait for me at the pool, <u>or</u> they can go over to the shopping center and catch the bus, <u>or</u> they can even walk home.

In these two sentences, the first conjunction can be replaced by a comma:

> Pete filled the bags, I stapled them shut, <u>and</u> Marty packed them in the cartons.

But usually joins only two clauses:

> Bill wanted me to wait for him, <u>but</u> I refused.

But can introduce the final clause when *and* or *or* joins the first two:

> Pete filled the bags, <u>and</u> I stapled them, <u>but</u> Marty refused to lift
> a finger.
> The kids can wait for me at the pool, <u>or</u> they can walk to the bus
> stop, <u>but</u> I really think they ought to walk home.

Semicolons. When a semicolon connects two coordinate clauses,
the conjunction can be omitted:

> Pete packed the hot roasted peanuts into bags; I stapled them
> shut.
> The curtain rose; a stillness settled over the audience.

The semicolon is also used when a conjunctive adverb introduces the
second clause. Note, too, that the conjunctive adverb is set off by a
comma:

> We worked hard for the Liberal Party candidates, ringing door-
> bells and stuffing envelopes; <u>however,</u> we knew they didn't
> stand a chance.

> We knew our candidates didn't have a hope of winning; <u>never-</u>
> <u>theless,</u> for weeks on end we faithfully rang doorbells and
> stuffed envelopes.

Of all the adverbial conjunctions, only *yet* and *so* can be used with a
comma instead of a semicolon between clauses:

> Several formations of birds were flying northward, <u>so</u> I knew
> spring was on the way.
> Several formations of birds were flying northward, <u>yet</u> I suspected
> that winter was far from over.

In both of these sentences, a semicolon could replace the comma, depending on the writer's emphasis. The semicolon would put extra emphasis on the second clause. *So* and *yet* straddle the border between the
coordinating conjunctions and the conjunctive adverbs; they are often

listed as both. In meaning, *so* is similar to *therefore* and *yet* to *however;* but unlike these conjunctive adverbs, *so* and *yet* always introduce the clause, so in this respect they are perhaps closer to the conjunctions. Sometimes we use both the conjunction and the adverbial: *and so; but yet*.

As we noted in Chapter 6, most conjunctive adverbs differ from the simple conjunctions in being movable, appearing in the middle of the clause or at the end, as well as at the beginning:

> . . . ; <u>however</u>, we knew they didn't stand a chance.
> . . . ; we knew, <u>however</u>, they didn't stand a chance.
> . . . ; we knew they didn't stand a chance, <u>however</u>.

Other common conjunctive adverbs are listed on page 136.

Diagramming the Compound Sentence. In the diagram a broken line connects the two verbs, with the connector on a solid line approximately halfway between the two clauses:

> Pete filled the bags, and I stapled them shut, but Marty refused to lift a finger.

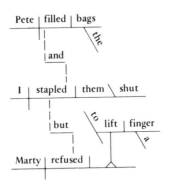

Exercise 73: Combine the following groups of sentences into compound structures, using conjunctions of your choice. In each case there are a number of possible ways to combine them, depending on the emphasis.

1. The library closes at noon on Thursdays.
   It is open until 9:00 P.M. on Fridays.

2. The food at the new French restaurant is exceptionally good.
   The prices are exceptionally high.
3. I am going to take piano lessons this fall.
   I may take guitar lessons, too.
4. My first-period students are bright.
   They are wide awake at 8:00 A.M., too.
5. Our trip across Kansas was long and straight and uneventful.
   The trip across Kansas took an entire day.

SUMMARY

The conjunctions in our store of structure words allow us to combine sentences and their parts in a variety of ways. We use the coordinating and correlative conjunctions both within and between sentences; we use conjunctive adverbs to combine sentences with an adverbial emphasis. An important consideration in all coordinate constructions is parallelism—keeping the parts of the coordinate structures equal.

SENTENCES FOR PRACTICE

Underline the sentence slots that have coordinate structures; circle the conjunctions. For further practice, identify the sentence patterns and diagram the sentences.

1. Despite the economic recovery, many auto workers in Detroit and many steelworkers in Pennsylvania are still unemployed.
2. I lent my son and daughter-in-law a sizable sum of money.
3. They have recently moved to Ohio and will soon be buying a new house.
4. To get your rebate, simply fill out the coupon and mail it to the company's headquarters in Michigan.
5. I have battled beetles and aphids and tent caterpillars for the entire summer.
6. Next month many students and tourists will be going to our nation's capital either to visit the historical monuments or simply to stroll along the streets and enjoy that beautiful city.

7. My friends and I, finding the movie boring, left at intermission and adjourned to our favorite hangout.

8. The new sofa that we bought this month with our income tax refund is both uncomfortable and unattractive.

9. A broad cross section of Americans, united by a deep and urgent concern about the proliferation of nuclear weapons, have given both their money and their time to the freeze movement.

10. The hundreds of separate groups that make up the nuclear-freeze movement are demonstrating to get the support of their fellow citizens and their legislators.

11. Having found an apartment that was inexpensive, roomy, and close to the subway, we made a split-second decision and rented it on the spot.

12. The woods are lovely, dark, and deep,
   But I have promises to keep,
   And miles to go before I sleep.
                                            —ROBERT FROST

QUESTIONS FOR DISCUSSION

1. In the following sentences the coordinate ideas are unparallel in form. Do some seem more acceptable than others? Rank them in order of acceptability. Rewrite those that can be improved.

1. Almost every lineman on the squad was overweight and out of condition when the season started.
2. She volunteered her services at the Senior Citizens' Center frequently and with boundless enthusiasm.
3. The old man, broke and having no friends to turn to, simply disappeared from the neighborhood.
4. I have always loved sports of all kinds and jog regularly.

2. Does a semicolon separate the clauses of a compound sentence or does it join them? A recent handbook describes a semicolon as taking the place of the period between two complete sentences. Would it be equally accurate, or perhaps more accurate, to say instead that the semicolon takes the place of the conjunction?

3. Consider the following compound sentences. Are they parallel? Can you find a way to improve them? What is their special problem?

1. I fixed three bowls of popcorn for the party, but it was eaten up before most of the guests even got there.

2. Burglars broke into the art museum last night, and three valuable paintings were stolen.

3. The television lost its sound last week, but luckily it got fixed before the World Series started.

4. Explain the deep structure that underlies the prenoun compound modifier in the following noun phrase:

the red and blue banners

Is there more than one possible deep structure? In other words, is this modifier ambiguous?

5. Explain why the verbs or auxiliaries in the following sentences would not be the -s form even though the subject headwords *crime* and *stamina* are singular.

Blue collar and white collar crime are on the increase.

Both physical and mental stamina are required for long-distance running.

IV

USAGE

T HE first three sections of this book describe the grammar of English, that unconscious system of rules that enables a speaker of the language to produce grammatical sentences. To emphasize the automatic and unconscious nature of those internalized rules, we have been comparing the native speaker to a computer and the rules of grammar to a computer program that generates sentences.

In Part IV we take up the subject of usage, a term that refers to rules of another kind. Rules of usage produce not sentences, but judgments about sentences and words; they are rules based on social and cultural criteria; they are closely bound up with status, with relative and fluctuating norms.

Such rules are often mistaken for "grammar rules." For example, you may have assumed that pronouncements about *ain't* result from a grammar rule—but they don't. Certainly, the word itself, the contraction of *am not,* is produced by a grammar rule, the same rule that gives us *aren't* and *isn't.* However, our judgment about using or not using *ain't* is strictly a matter of usage. If the network newscasters and the president of the United States and your teachers started to use *ain't* on a regular basis, its status would quickly change. The late linguist Paul Roberts made the idea of usage clear when he said that teachers and newscasters and presidents don't avoid using *ain't* because it's nonstandard; it's nonstandard because such people avoid it.

Standards and usage are matters of taste and habit. Tastes and habits, as we all know, change. They vary from place to place, from time to time, from one social group to another.

In Chapter 14 we ask, "What is 'Good English'?" This question is a question about usage; the answer, you'll discover, is "It depends." The chapter also includes other questions and answers dealing with usage: The first two, concerning prepositions at sentence end and split infinitives, are leftovers from a time when so-called experts not only prescribed but actually invented rules for writers and speakers; the other two questions deal with real issues of usage that trouble writers, issues related to our pronoun system. The chapter ends with a short glossary of usage.

14

What Is "Good English"?

"Good English" has many voices. In Pittsburgh you might hear someone say, "The car needs washed." In a black neighborhood a speaker may tell you, "Joe not here; he be working." And in communities throughout the South you can hear, "We might could go." All of these speakers are using "good English." Theirs may not be the "good English" that you speak or that you're used to hearing; it's not the "good English" of presidential candidates campaigning on college campuses or the "good English" of network broadcasters reading the nightly news; nor do these quotations reflect Standard Written English, the "good English" of most books and magazines and term papers. But in using the standard spoken dialect of their particular communities, those speakers are using "good English."

"Good English" is relative. The language that is appropriate in one region may be highly inappropriate in another. And "good English" is relative to the situation as well. The language that broadcasters use on the air is not the same as the language they use at the breakfast table. And in a Southern community, "We might be able to go" would probably replace "We might could go" at a business conference. Different situations call for different language.

Every speaker learns this principle of human behavior at an early age. Children understand that the language they use with their playmates is different from the language they use with adults. The negative "huh-uh" on the playground becomes "No thank you" when a friend's parent is asking the question. And the vocabulary that a child uses at home with the family is different from the vocabulary for school. Even within the school there are differences: What is appropriate in the cafeteria may not be appropriate in the classroom or in the principal's office. Most of the time we understand what is appropriate in a given situation, and we have no trouble shifting from one mode of language to another.

In the written language, too, what is appropriate or correct in one situation may be inappropriate or incorrect in another. The message scrawled on the kitchen bulletin board and the informal note to a friend are both noticeably different from the language of the job application letter. As with speech, the purpose and the audience make all the difference. Most of the papers you write in college—term papers and essay exams and lab reports and compositions for English class— are closer to the formality of the job application than to the informality of the hasty note. This formal level or style of writing is known as **Standard Written English.**

The grammar system described in this book is, of course, grounded in speech. We have defined grammar as the set of internal rules that native speakers somehow follow in speaking and in listening. The rules we have looked at are those that produce the sentences of the majority dialect—what we call Standard English. This is the dialect on which Standard Written English is based.

The three speakers quoted at the opening of this chapter were using speech patterns that, although standard and therefore "good English" in their own speech communities, are nonetheless not the standard for the majority of Americans. The verbs in "He be working" and "We might could go" cannot be generated from the standard verb-expansion rule described in Chapter 2. This is not to say that these nonstandard verb strings are unsystematic; on the contrary, they are generated by highly systematic rules that belong to the grammar of a great many native speakers of English in this country. But these particular verb strings—no matter how systematic, no matter how appropriate at a particular place or time—do not conform to Standard English and are generally not effective (and are therefore not used) in formal speech or in formal writing. Even though they are part of the local dialect, they are generally not used on local news broadcasts or in local newspapers, where Standard Written English predominates.

So not only do we have differences in speech—differences between speakers of various dialects and, for individual speakers, variations dependent on the occasion—we also have differences between speech and writing. For the speaker of a nonmajority dialect, there are many more speech/writing differences than there are for the speaker of the majority dialect. As we noted, even the verb-expansion rule may be different. But speakers of the majority dialect, too, have adjustments to make and rules to learn about the conventions of Standard Written English.

In the preceding chapters we have commented on punctuation and other conventions of writing. We have also looked at some of the differences between speech and writing, noting in particular the structures rarely used in speech, such as absolute phrases and nonrestrictive clauses. But the most important consideration is effectiveness. How can the writer achieve the precision of style, tone, clarity, and diction that makes a piece of writing effective? Certainly, an understanding of grammar can help the writer achieve that goal. A conscious knowledge of the grammar system can illuminate the wide range of choices that the language provides for putting words and sentences and paragraphs together.

An understanding of grammar can also help the writer answer questions about usage and standards of correctness. Some of the old do's and don't's—those persistent issues of "grammar etiquette" we still hear about—can be especially troublesome for the student writer. In the pages that follow we will take up some of the questions about "good English" that writers ask:

- Is it good English to end a sentence with a preposition?
- Is it good English to split an infinitive?
- In good English do pronouns like *everyone* and *everybody* always have singular referents?
- Is it good English to use *he* in reference to a person of unknown gender, or is that usage sexist?

IS IT GOOD ENGLISH TO END A SENTENCE WITH A PREPOSITION?

In his short story "An Outpost of Progress," Joseph Conrad (who, incidentally, was not a native speaker of English) goes out of his way to avoid a *to* at the end of a sentence:

> Besides, the rice rations served out by the Company did not agree with them, being a food unknown to their land, and to which they could not get used.

To avoid writing "which they couldn't get used to," Conrad has produced what can only be labeled an ungrammatical sentence—"ungrammatical" insofar as a native speaker would never say "to which they could not get used." It's even hard to pronounce.

Most books of grammar and usage no longer include this absurd warning against ending sentences with prepositions. As a result, people may conclude that the rule has changed through the years, that standards have deteriorated, or that teachers and textbook writers are getting more liberal. Those conclusions would be wrong. Nothing has changed.

The so-called rule never existed.

Grammarians in the eighteenth and nineteenth centuries who made pronouncements about prepositions at the end of the sentence were attempting to make English conform to the system of Latin. They decided that what was correct in Latin ought to be the rule in English as well. Unfortunately, they disregarded reality.

Here are some examples of reality:

> Did you turn the light out?
> Laziness is something I won't put up with.
> It's something I'm simply not used to.

These sentences may look as if they end with prepositions, but in fact the *out* and *with* and *to* that end them are not prepositions at all. They are particles—part of the phrasal verbs *turn out, put up with,* and *be used to.* When sentences with such phrasal verbs undergo transformations that turn them into questions or clauses, or that alter word order in some other way, the verb or part of it often ends up as the last element in the sentence.

There is nothing ungrammatical about such phrasal verbs. If we can say

> That's something I won't tolerate.

then we can also say

> That's something I won't put up with.

The first may be more effective in some situations; it may even be clearer; it is undoubtedly more formal. It is *not* more grammatical.

As we saw in Chapter 1, such phrasal verbs can be both transitive and intransitive. In a Pattern VI sentence, which has no complement, the verb can easily be the last word in the sentence, even without a transformation:

> It's time to turn in.
> Last night at the party, Mark and Karen made up.

Phrasal verbs are not the only source of the phenomenon. Many times such words at sentence end are, indeed, prepositions—part of prepositional phrases in which the noun phrase has been shifted:

> Chocolate is a flavor I'm especially fond of.
> What kind of music are you interested in?
> Nothing else happened that I'm aware of.

These sentences include adjectives that commonly pattern with phrases or clauses as complements: *fond, interested, aware*. In these particular transformations the object of the preposition has shifted while the preposition has remained with the adjective at the end of the sentence.

For a teacher to suggest that such sentences are ungrammatical because they end with prepositions is absurd. Perhaps the writer could improve on "Chocolate is a flavor I'm especially fond of" by being more straightforward, more concise:

> I like chocolate.
> I'm especially fond of chocolate.
> Chocolate is my favorite flavor.

The teacher might want to suggest that "Chocolate is a flavor . . ." is unnecessarily redundant. The alternatives are shorter and tighter; they may be more effective. But they are *not* more grammatical.

The "what for" question will also produce an end preposition:

> What did you say that for?

This, of course, is another way of asking

> Why did you say that?

What for may be less formal than *why,* but it is certainly *not* less grammatical.

The "who" question is a somewhat stickier problem because it often introduces another "grammatical error":

> Who are you going with?

This common structure illustrates a genuine difference between speaking and writing. Anyone who would correct the speaker, insisting on

> Whom are you going with?
> > *or*
> With whom are you going?

does not understand communication. Neither of these "corrected" versions represents the language as it is spoken by the masses.

The form the question should take in Standard *Written* English is another matter. Rather than use *who,* most writers would either use *whom* or would reword the sentence to avoid the problem altogether. But in conversation, "Who are you going with?"—in spite of its end preposition and its subjective *who*—is "good English."

IS IT GOOD ENGLISH TO SPLIT AN INFINITIVE?

We could say that technically it is impossible to "split an infinitive," because the infinitive is simply the uninflected form of the verb: *be, go, see, hear, consider.* The notion of the split infinitive assumes that the *to* is a part of it. In Old English, the infinitive was inflected with *-an* or *-n.* When that was dropped, the preposition *to* became the signal; it is now called the "sign of the infinitive," but the infinitive is the verb itself. Actually, there are a number of constructions in which the *to* is not used with the infinitive. With certain verbs that take infinitives as complements, for example, the *to* is either missing or optional:

> I expect Joe to mow the lawn.

I helped Joe <u>mow</u> the lawn.
The coach let the players <u>choose</u> their own captain.
I don't want <u>to drive</u> to the city alone.
I don't <u>dare</u> (to) <u>drive</u> to the city alone.

And there are a few other constructions, such as *rather–than, but,* and *except,* that occur with the bare infinitive:

I would rather <u>go</u> with you than <u>stay</u> here alone.
Mike did nothing today but <u>complain</u>.
I did everything you asked me to except <u>mow</u> the lawn.

However, most occurrences of the infinitive do require the *to:*

Jogging is a good way <u>to keep fit</u>.
I decided <u>to lose five pounds before the holidays</u>.
I went home <u>to get ready for the party</u>.

These infinitive constructions consist of entire verb phrases, not simply the base form of the verb. Such infinitives are actually the predicate half of sentences, complete with complements and modifiers:

to keep fit (Pattern IV)

to lose five pounds before the holidays (Pattern VII)

to get ready for the party (Pattern IV)

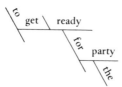

What then is a "split infinitive"? The "split" occurs when an adverbial—usually a single adverb—comes between the *to* and the verb. Is that "good English" or not?

As you know, adverbials can occupy a number of slots in the sentence patterns, including the slot before the verb:

> I <u>finally</u> understand algorithms.
> Ted <u>simply</u> stopped attending class.
> Our neighbors <u>never</u> watch television on Sunday.

Any predicate phrase can be turned into an infinitive phrase for use as a nominal or adjectival or adverbial in a sentence. When that predicate phrase includes an adverbial in the preverb slot, then so will the infinitive phrase. It's that simple.

> It is such a relief to <u>finally</u> understand algorithms.
> To <u>simply</u> stop attending class as he did was a real mistake on Ted's part.
> To <u>never</u> watch television on Sunday is to miss the week's best programs.

Most infinitives do not have preverb modifiers simply because most sentences do not. Adverbials are more likely to fill other slots, at the beginning or the end of the sentence. But certain adverbs often do fill the preverb slot; it makes no sense to say they cannot do so in infinitive phrases. The preceding "split infinitive" examples would sound unnatural if the adverb were shifted from its preverb position. And, what is more important, the adverb–verb relationship would lose its emphasis.

The warnings against splitting the infinitive are aimed not at logical adverbials, such as those in the examples above, but rather at awkward and ineffective constructions and also, perhaps, at the overuse of *really,* which finds its way so frequently into the sentences of student writers. *Really* is the culprit in a great many split infinitives:

> We promise to <u>really</u> try hard.
> This weekend we're going to <u>really</u> hit the books.

Other adverbials, too, are generally more effective outside the infinitive:

> It was unusual of the dog to all of a sudden snap at the children like that.
> We want to certainly help if we can.
> The police expect to quickly apprehend the culprit.

Most adverbials, like these, belong outside of the infinitive. But it makes no sense to produce awkward and unnatural infinitive phrases because of that long-standing but misguided prescriptive rule against splitting them. Blindly following that rule, a network newscaster recently came out with the following statement:

> The issue concerns the people's right freely to choose.

By refusing to do what comes naturally, the newscaster missed his chance to put the sentence stress on *freely*, the most logical place for it.

Does "good English" include split infinitives? Certainly. It always has.

IN GOOD ENGLISH DO PRONOUNS LIKE *EVERYONE* AND *EVERYBODY* ALWAYS HAVE SINGULAR REFERENTS?

The pronouns *everyone* and *everybody* are, in form, singular; as subjects, they take the -*s* form of the verb or auxiliary in the present tense:

> Everyone is leaving the room at once.

An illustration of the scene described by this sentence would show more than one person—more than two or three, probably—leaving the room, even though the form of *everyone* is singular. In spite of this anomaly, the issue of subject–verb agreement is not a problem.

But often such a sentence calls for a possessive pronoun:

> Everyone picked up his books and left the room.

If there are no females among the group designated by *everyone,* then this sentence makes some logical and grammatical sense. But with a mixed group, or if the writer is referring to people of unknown gender, then *his* is not logical. A common solution in current writing is to use both *his* and *her:*

Everyone picked up <u>his or her</u> books and left the room.

But even more common is the plural, in spite of the singular form of *everyone.* The plural, in fact, makes much more sense; in terms of meaning, it is the only logical choice:

Everyone picked up <u>their</u> books and left.

It is interesting to discover that the problem arises only with the possessive pronoun. No one would dispute the correctness of the subjective case, *they:*

The teacher asked everyone to leave, and <u>they</u> did.

Certainly *he* would make no sense at all, nor would *he and she.* The objective case, too, requires the plural:

Everyone cheered when I told <u>them</u> to leave the room.

In fact, if *him* were used in this sentence, the meaning would change.

There is simply no logic in insisting on the singular for the possessive case when both logic and good grammar call for the plural in every other situation.

It's true that in form *everyone* is singular; this is also true of collective nouns, such as *crowd* or *group.* But these nouns call for plural pronouns when the members of the collection are seen as individuals:

The group picked up <u>their</u> books.
The crowd began to raise <u>their</u> voices.

It is in this collective noun sense that *everyone* is plural in spite of its form. To label as ungrammatical "Everyone picked up *their* books and left" makes no sense at all.

But tradition dies hard. To avoid both the "ungrammatical" *their* and the sexism of *his* and the awkwardness of *his or her*, the writer can simply find a substitute for *everyone* in this situation:

All the students picked up their books and left.

More difficult than the problem of *everyone/their*, where the underlying referent of *everyone* is actually plural, is the problem of *one* or *someone* or *a person*, where meaning is actually singular and the gender is unknown.

IS IT GOOD ENGLISH TO USE *HE* IN REFERENCE TO A PERSON OF UNKNOWN GENDER, OR IS THAT USAGE SEXIST?

An invitation to membership recently sent by the Smithsonian Institution included a "registered number" for the addressee only, along with the following statement:

This registered number is not transferable. If a friend wishes to become a member, please ask them to write for information.

The gender of *a friend* is unknown, but its referent is clearly singular, so in terms of agreement *them* appears ungrammatical. To avoid *him*, with its masculine designation—and apparently to avoid the awkwardness of *him or her*—the Smithsonian has chosen to use *them* with an indefinite, singular meaning.

A few years ago neither the Smithsonian's writer nor anyone else would have hesitated to use *him*:

If a friend wishes to become a member, please ask him to write for information.

Long-established usage in English calls for the masculine pronoun to refer to either sex in this structure, just as the word *man* has long been used in reference to both sexes in such words as *mankind* and such statements as "*Man* is the thinking animal." This custom was even institutionalized by an Act of Parliament in 1850 with "An Act for shortening the language used in acts of Parliament," which announced that in all acts words importing the masculine gender shall be deemed and taken to include females, and the singular to include the plural, and the plural the singular, unless the contrary as to gender and number is expressly provided.[1]

But times and attitudes change. We have come to recognize the power of language in shaping attitudes. So an important step in reshaping society's view of women is to eliminate the automatic use of *he* and *his* and *him* when the person referred to could just as easily be female:

> <u>Someone</u> should lend <u>his</u> coat to the accident victim.
> Ask <u>a friend</u> to get <u>his</u> own number.

This situation comes up time and time again, in writing as well as in conversation. In some cases, the choice of the pronoun is fairly automatic in our society:

> "My son's <u>kindergarten teacher</u> just called."
> "What did <u>she</u> want?"

> "My <u>doctor</u> just called me."
> "What did <u>he</u> want?"

> "The <u>nurse</u> just called me."
> "What did <u>she</u> want?"

The second speaker has no problem in responding, even though the gender of the person referred to is not known. In such conversations, however, if the doctor is a woman or the nurse a man, the first speaker can simply correct the error.

But what should the writer do? The pronoun system simply does not provide a singular version of *they/their/them* in reference to people. For inanimate nouns and for animals we can use *it;* sometimes we even

---

[1] Quoted in Robert C. Pooley, *The Teaching of English Usage* (Urbana, Ill.: The National Council of Teachers of English, 1974), p. 86.

use *it* for very small babies of unknown gender:

> "Isn't it cute!"
> "When is it due?"

In reference to grownup people we seem to have two choices: Like the Smithsonian, we can become language liberals and use *they* or we can be awkward and use *he or she* (*his or her*) or, as some writers do, *s/he* (which has no possessive or objective case so far):

> Someone should lend their coat to the victim.
> Someone should lend his or her coat to the victim.

Eventually, perhaps, the plural pronoun will be common for both singular and plural. There's a precedent for this change: In the second person (*you/your/you*) we no longer make a distinction between singular and plural. We say "Are you coming?" to one person as well as to more than one; it would not be unreasonable to do the same in the third person. But such changes come about very slowly.

Meanwhile, what shall the writer do who wants to be not only logical and conservative but nonsexist as well? A number of current publications have adopted a policy of nonsexism in their pages, and more and more books are doing so as well, so it obviously can be done.

One alternative that often works in reference to students or teachers or people in general is the use of plural. The Smithsonian could easily have avoided the issue:

> If you have friends who wish to become members, please ask them to write for information.

The plural will not solve the problem in the sentence about the coat: "Someone should lend their coat." But sometimes in such cases another determiner can be substituted for the possessive pronoun:

> Someone should lend a coat to the victim.

The authors of the following passages could easily have found ways to avoid the masculine pronoun:

Of all the developments in the history of ~~man~~ _the human race_, surely the most
remarkable was language, for with it ~~he was~~ _our ancestors were_ able to pass on ~~his~~ _their_
cultural heritage to succeeding generations who then did not have
to rediscover how to make a fire, where to hunt, or how to build
another wheel.[2]

For thousands of years philosophers have been pondering the meaning of "meaning." Yet, everyone who knows a language can understand what is said ~~to him~~ and can produce strings of words which
convey meaning.[3]

It has been said that whenever ~~a person~~ _people_ speak~~s~~, ~~he is~~ _they are_ either mimick-
ing or analogizing.[4]

It is a rare sentence, indeed, that cannot be stated in an alternative
way. English is enormously versatile; we almost always have a choice.

[2] Charles B. Martin and Curt M. Rulon, _The English Language, Yesterday and Today_ (Bos-
ton: Allyn and Bacon, Inc., 1973), p. 1.

[3] Victoria Fromkin and Robert Rodman, _An Introduction to Language_ (New York: Holt,
Rinehart and Winston, Inc., 1974), p. 100.

[4] Charles F. Hockett, "Analogical Creation," in Wallace L. Anderson and Norman C.
Stageberg, eds., _Introductory Readings on Language_, 3rd Edition (New York: Holt, Rinehart
and Winston, Inc., 1970), p. 101.

Glossary
of Usage

As you read in the introduction to Part IV, the judgments we make about usage vary according to time and circumstances. In fact, some of the words and phrases in this glossary are in that state of flux, in the very process of change. Many of the entries are listed because they are common in colloquial English but not a part of Standard Written English. This list is by no means complete; there are dozens—perhaps hundreds—of other entries we could have included, words and phrases that are commonly misused and usages that writers may have questions about. The items selected for this glossary, however, are limited to usage issues that can be explained on the basis of their grammar.

Accept/Except.   *Except* is sometimes a verb (meaning "exclude"), but it is more often a preposition with a meaning like "but"; *accept* is the verb meaning "receive with consent":

> He should <u>accept</u> help if he needs it. (verb)
> I like all vegetables <u>except</u> squash. (preposition)

Understanding the meanings of *acceptable* and *exception* may help you to remember *accept* and *except*.

Affect/Effect.   Both can be either a noun or a verb, but the common noun of the two is *effect*. (*Affect* is rare as a noun.)

> The overall <u>effect</u> of the movie was depressing. (noun)

The common verb of the two is *affect:*

> The movie <u>affected</u> us all. (verb)

337

The verb *effect* means "to cause" or "to bring about"; it often has a noun like *change* as its direct object:

> The new treatment effected a change in the patient's condition.

Among/Between. The traditional rule specifying *between* to show a relationship between two and *among* for three or more is nearly always accurate. However, in some situations we do use *between* with numbers larger than two, as in the following example concerning discussions between individuals in the larger group:

> Discussions were held between all the Common Market representatives.

Amount of/Number of. These adjectival phrases signal nouns; *amount of* goes with noncountables (the *amount of* food; the *amount of* money) and *number of* goes with countables (the *number of* accidents; the *number of* dollars). The same distinction determines the use of *fewer* (countable) and *less* (noncountable): *fewer* dollars, *less* money. (See page 104).

Bad/Badly. The subjective complement slot in a Pattern IV sentence is filled by an adjective: The soup tastes *salty;* He looks *sleepy.* Yet it is fairly common, especially in speech, to use the adverb *badly* instead of the adjective *bad* after the verb *feel:*

> *I feel *badly* about that.

In other sentences, with other adjectives, it's obvious that the adjective, not the adverb, is the form to use: I feel *sad* (not *sadly*); I feel *hungry* (not *hungrily*). There is no reason to change the rule in the case of *bad:*

> I feel bad about that.

Different from/Different than. Standard American usage calls for the preposition *from* following the adjective *different:*

> My new diet is different from all the others I've tried.

We use *than* with the comparative form of adjectives:

> The new diet is easier to follow than the old one.

However, for the sake of economy we often do use *than* when a clause follows the word *different:*

It was <u>different than I expected it to be.</u>

In British English *different than* is more common in both situations.

Due to/Because of. The distinction between these two structures is blurred because in meaning they are so close. In terms of their parts of speech, however, the difference is clear: *Due* is an adjective meaning "ascribable," and it is used with a *to* prepositional phrase; *because of* is a phrasal preposition that functions adverbially. The prescriptive rule warning against beginning a sentence with *due to* makes sense: We rarely begin sentences with adjectival phrases. But we do begin sentences with adverbial prepositional phrases explaining cause:

<u>Because of overproduction by the OPEC nations,</u> oil prices will
  probably go down next winter.
Experts are predicting a cut in oil prices <u>due to overproduction by
  the OPEC nations.</u>

In the second sentence, the adjectival phrase with *due* modifies *cut.* The diagrams of these two sentences illustrates the difference.

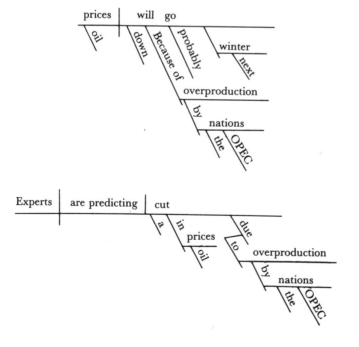

One of the confusing aspects of this pair is that a prepositional phrase with *because of* can come at the end of the sentence as well as at the beginning. It will still be adverbial, however:

> Experts are predicting a cut in oil prices <u>because of overproduction by the OPEC nations.</u>

The adjectival *due to* phrase often serves as a subjective complement in a Pattern II sentence:

> His delay was <u>due to a traffic jam.</u>
> Many of the advances in high-tech industries are <u>due to bright, young computer specialists.</u>

A *because of* phrase in that position would have the same ungrammatical structure as sentences with "The reason is because . . ." (see page 342).

Fewer/Less. We use the adjective *fewer* with countable nouns and *less* with noncountables:

> Apples have <u>fewer calories</u> than avocados.
> People with hypertension should eat <u>less salt</u> than other people.

An exception to this usage occurs in comparisons involving numbers where *than* is not separated by a noun; in this instance we tend to use *less than* even with countables:

> We have <u>less than two</u> weeks to get ready for opening night.
> We have <u>less than ten</u> dollars to last until payday.

(See also **Amount of/Number of,** page 338.)

Had better. This is an informal version of the modal auxiliary *should:*

> You <u>had better</u> wear your boots today.

In writing this, be sure to include *had,* even in the contracted form:

> You'd <u>better</u> be going.

The colloquial expression without *had*—"You better go"—is not used in Standard Written English.

Is when/Is where.   A clause can function as a nominal in the NP slot following *be* in Pattern III sentences:

My biggest problem is <u>that I don't budget my time.</u>

As a subjective complement, of course, this clause renames the subject. A *when* or *where* clause, however, which generally adds adverbial information, will not rename the subject:

Good manners are <u>when people respect the feelings of others.</u>
Sportsmanship is <u>where both winners and losers respect each other.</u>

These sentences appear to say that good manners are a time and sportsmanship is a place. Probably the easiest way to improve them is to replace the Pattern II with a different sentence:

Good manners express the consideration that people have toward one another.

or

People with good manners consider the feelings of others.
Sportsmanship requires that both winners and losers respect each other.

Lie.   This is an intransitive verb with two meanings: "to prevaricate" and "to recline." The first is a regular verb:

I <u>lie</u> about my age quite often.
Yesterday I <u>lied</u> about my age.
I have <u>lied</u> about my age frequently.

The second is an irregular verb:

I <u>lie</u> in the sun every chance I get.
Yesterday I <u>lay</u> in the sun.
I have <u>lain</u> in the sun every afternoon this week.

In speech, the verb meaning "recline" is used almost interchangeably with the transitive verb *lay:*

*I'm going to <u>lay</u> in the sun this afternoon.
*I <u>laid</u> in the sun too long yesterday.

If we want to retain the distinction between *lie* and *lay*, we will have to label the previous two sentences as ungrammatical. (*Webster's Ninth New Collegiate Dictionary* cites *lay* as a nonstandard version of the intransitive verb *lie;* the very fact that it is cited is evidence of how widespread the usage has become.)

Lay, being transitive, requires an object:

> The workmen will <u>lay the carpet</u> this afternoon.
> I know that I <u>laid my wallet</u> right here, but now it's gone.

Maybe/May be.   The single-word form is an adverb meaning "perhaps." The two-word version is the modal auxiliary used with the verb *be*. If you can substitute *might be,* you'll know that the two-word version is correct:

> We <u>may</u> (<u>might</u>) <u>be</u> going soon.
> <u>Maybe</u> (perhaps) we'll have a good time.

Passed/Past.   These two homonyms are different parts of speech. *Passed* is always a verb; it is the *-ed* and *-en* form of the verb *pass* (We *passed* the garage sale without stopping). *Past,* however, plays many roles, but not the role of verb: It can be a noun (*Your past* is your own business); an adjective (This *past month* has been busy); a preposition (We drove *past the garage sale* without stopping); and an adverb (We *drove past* but did not stop).

Reason is because.   The earlier discussion of "is when/is where" pointed out the problem with adverbial clauses filing the nominal slot in Pattern III sentences. The *because* clause introduces the same problem:

> The reason for the delay is <u>because the car wouldn't start.</u>

A *because* clause normally contributes adverbial information to a sentence; it answers the "why" question. However, in the foregoing example the *because* clause fills that nominal subjective complement slot. There are two ways to fix such sentences: (1) You can substitute a nominal clause:

> The reason for the delay is <u>that the car wouldn't start.</u>

Or (2) you can retain the causal information with an adverbial clause:

> We <u>were late because</u> the car wouldn't start.

Try and.   *Try* is a catenative verb, one that takes another verb as its direct object. In most cases that object is an infinitive in form:

> I tried <u>to help</u> the accident victim.
> I'm going to try <u>to help</u> the victim.

A variation that is common in colloquial English substitutes *and* for *to,* the sign of the infinitive:

> I'm going to try <u>and help</u> the victim.

In this case *and* is simply inaccurate; the usage is inappropriate in Standard Written English.

GLOSSARY
OF GRAMMATICAL TERMS

(For further explanation of the terms listed here, check the index for page references.)

Absolute phrase.   A noun phrase related to the sentence as a whole that includes a postnoun modifier (often a participial phrase). One kind of absolute explains a cause or condition (*"The weather being warm,* we decided to have a picnic"); the other adds a detail or a point of focus to the idea in the main clause ("He spoke quietly to the class, *his voice trembling"*).

Accusative case.   The Latin term for objective case.

Active voice.   A feature of transitive verb sentences in which the subject is generally the agent and the direct object is the goal or objective of the action. Voice refers to the relationship of the subject to the verb. See also *Passive voice.*

Adjectival.   Any structure, no matter what its form, that functions as a modifier of a noun—that is, that functions as an adjective normally functions. See Chapter 9.

Adjectival clause.   See *Relative clause.*

Adjective.   One of the four form classes, whose members act as modifiers of nouns; most adjectives can be inflected for comparative and superlative degree (*big, bigger, biggest*); they can be qualified or intensified (*rather big, very big*); they have characteristic derivational endings such as *-ous* (*famous*), *-ish* (*childish*), *-ful* (*graceful*), and *-ary* (*complementary*).

Adverb. One of the four form classes, whose members act as modifiers of verbs, contributing information of time, place, reason, manner, and the like. Like adjectives, certain adverbs can be qualified (*very quickly, rather fast*); some can be inflected for comparative and superlative degree (*more quickly, fastest*); they have characteristic derivational endings such as *-ly* (*quickly*), *-wise* (*lengthwise*), *-ward* (*backward*), and *-like* (*snakelike*).

Adverbial. Any structure, no matter what its form, that functions as a modifier of a verb—that is, that functions as an adverb normally functions. See Chapter 8.

Adverbial objective. The traditional label given to the noun phrase that functions adverbially: "Joe went *home*"; It was cold *last night.*"

Affix. A morpheme, or meaningful unit, that is added to the beginning (prefix) or end (suffix) of a word to change its meaning or its grammatical role or its form class: (prefix) *un*likely; (suffix) unlike*ly.*

Agent. The initiator of the action in the sentence, the "doer" of the action. Usually the agent is the subject in an active sentence: "*John* groomed the dog"; "*The committee* elected Pam."

Agreement. (1) Subject–verb. A third-person singular subject in the present tense takes the *-s* form of the verb: "*The dog barks* all night"; "*He bothers* the neighbors." A plural subject takes the base form: "*The dogs bark*"; "*They bother* the neighbors." (2) Pronoun–antecedent. The number of the pronoun (whether singular or plural) agrees with the number of its antecedent. "*The boys* did *their* chores"; "*Each boy* did *his* best."

Allomorph. A variation of a morpheme, usually determined by its environment. For example, the three allomorphs of the regular plural morpheme are determined by the final sound of the nouns to which they are added: /s/ *cats;* /z/ *dogs;* and /əz/ *churches.*

Ambiguity.   The condition in which a structure has more than one possible meaning. The source may be lexical ("She is *blue*") or structural ("*Visiting relatives* can be boring") or both ("The detective looked *hard*").

Antecedent.   The noun or nominal that a pronoun stands for.

Appositive.   A structure, often a noun phrase, that renames another structure. An appositive can be thought of as either adjectival ("My neighbor, *a butcher at Weis Market,* recently lost his job") or nominal ("It is nice *that you could come*").

Article.   One of the determiner classes, including the indefinite *a,* which signals only countable nouns, and the definite *the,* which can signal all classes of nouns.

Aspect.   A feature of the verb phrase in which auxiliaries designate whether the action of the verb is completed (*have* + *-en*) or in progress (*be* + *-ing*).

Attributive adjective.   The adjective in prenoun position: "my *new* coat"; "the *big* attraction."

Auxiliary.   One of the structure-class words, a marker of verbs. Auxiliaries include forms of *have* and *be,* as well as the modals, such as *will, shall,* and *must.*

Base form of the verb.   The uninflected form of the verb. In all verbs except *be,* the base form is the present tense: *go, help.* The base form also serves as the infinitive, usually preceded by *to.*

Base morpheme.   The morpheme that gives a word its primary lexical meaning: *help*ing, re*flect.*

Bound morpheme.   A morpheme that cannot stand alone as a word. Most affixes are bound (help*ing;* re*act*); some base morphemes are also bound (con*cise; leg*al).

Case.   A feature of nouns and certain pronouns that denotes their relationship to other words in a sentence. Pronouns have three case distinctions: subjective (e.g., *I, they, who*); possessive (e.g., *my, their, whose*); and objective (e.g., *me, them, whom*). Nouns have only one case inflection, the possessive (*John's*, the *cat's*). The case of nouns other than the possessives is sometimes referred to as common case.

Catenative verb. A transitive verb that can take another verb as its object: "I *like* to jog"; "We *enjoy* jogging."

Clause. A structure with a subject and a predicate. The sentence patterns are clause patterns.

Cleft sentence. A sentence variation that provides a way of shifting the stress or focus of the sentence: "A careless bicyclist caused the accident" → "It was a careless bicyclist who caused the accident."

Collective noun. A noun that is singular in form, whose referent is a collection of individuals: *group, team, family*. Collective nouns can be replaced by both singular and plural pronouns, depending on the meaning.

Command. See *Imperative.*

Common case. See *Case.*

Common noun. A noun with general, rather than unique, reference (in contrast to proper nouns). Common nouns may be countable (*house, book*), noncountable (*water, oil*); they may be concrete (*house, water*) or abstract (*justice, indifference*).

Comparative degree. See *Degree.*

Complement. A structure that "completes" the sentence. The term includes those slots in the predicate that complete the verb: direct object, indirect object, subjective complement, and objective complement. Certain adjectives also have complements—clauses and phrases that pattern with them: "I was *certain that he would come;* I was *afraid to go.*"

Complementary infinitive. An infinitive that functions as the main verb. "I'm going *to move* next week"; "I have *to find* a new apartment." There is a modal-like quality in "going to" and "have to."

Complex sentence. A sentence that includes at least one dependent clause.

Compound sentence. A sentence with two or more independent clauses.

Conditional mood. The attitude of probability designated by the modal auxiliaries *could, may, might, would,* and *should.*

Conjunction. One of the structure classes, which includes connectors that coordinate ideas (e.g., *and, or*), subordinate ideas (e.g., *if, because, when*), and connect them with an adverbial emphasis (e.g., *however, therefore*).

Conjunctive adverb. A conjunction that connects two sentences with an adverbial emphasis, such as *however, therefore, moreover,* and *nevertheless.*

Coordinating conjunction. A conjunction that connects two or more sentences or structures within a sentence as equals: *and, but, or, nor, for,* and *yet.*

Coordination. A way of expanding sentences in which two or more structures of the same form function as a unit. All of the sentence slots and modifiers in the slots, as well as the sentence itself, can be coordinated. See Chapter 13.

Correlative conjunction. A two-part conjunction that expresses a relationship between the coordinated structures: *either—or, neither—nor, both—and.*

Countable noun. A noun whose referent can be identified as a separate entity; the countable noun can be signaled by the indefinite article, *a,* and numbers: *a house; an experience; two eggs; three problems.*

Declarative sentence.   A sentence in the form of a statement (in contrast to a command, a question, or an exclamation).

Deep structure.   A term from transformational-generative grammar that refers to the underlying semantic and syntactic relationships of the sentence (in contrast to surface structure, the sentence as it is actually written or spoken).

Definite article.   The determiner *the,* which generally marks a specific or previously mentioned noun: *"the* man on the corner"; *"the* blue coat I want for Christmas."

Degree.   The variations in adjectives that indicate the simple quality of a noun, or positive degree ("Bill is a *big* boy"); its comparison to another, the comparative degree ("Bill is *bigger* than Tom"); or to two or more, the superlative degree ("Bill is the *biggest* person in the whole class"). Certain adverbs also have degree variations, usually designated by *more* and *most.*

Demonstrative pronoun.   The pronouns *this* (plural *these*) and *that* (plural *those*), which function as nominal substitutes and as determiners. They include the feature of proximity: near (*this, these*); distant (*that, those*).

Dependent clause.   A clause that functions as an adverbial, adjectival, nominal, or sentence modifier (in contrast to an independent, or main, clause).

Derivational affix.   A morpheme that is added to a form-class word, either to change its class (*friend* → *friendly; act* → *action*) or to change its meaning (*legal* → *illegal; boy* → *boyhood*).

Determiner.   One of the structure-class words, a marker of nouns. Determiners include articles (*a, the*); possessive nouns and pronouns (e.g., *Chuck's, his, my*); demonstrative pronouns (*this, that*); quantifiers (e.g., *many, several*); indefinite pronouns (e.g., *each, every*); and numbers.

Direct object.   A nominal slot in the transitive sentence patterns.

The direct object names the objective or goal or the receiver of the verb's action: "We ate *the peanuts*"; "The boy hit *the ball*"; "I enjoy *playing chess.*"

Do transformation.   The addition of the "stand-in auxiliary" *do* to a verb string that has no other auxiliary. The question, the negative, and the emphatic transformation all require an auxiliary.

Elliptical clause.   A clause in which a part has been left out but is "understood": "Chester is older *than I* (*am old*)"; "Bev can jog farther *than Otis* (*can jog*)"; "*When* (*you are*) *planning your essay,* be sure to consider the audience."

Emphatic statement.   A statement in which the main stress has been shifted to the auxiliary: "I AM trying." When there is no auxiliary, the "stand-in auxiliary" *do* is added to carry the stress: "I DO want to go."

Exclamatory sentence.   A sentence that is an exclamation. It includes a shift in the word order of a basic sentence that focuses on a complement: "What a beautiful day we're having!" It is often punctuated with an exclamation point.

Expletive.   A word that enables the writer or speaker to shift the stress in a sentence or to embed one sentence in another: "A fly is in my soup → *There*'s a fly in my soup"; "I know *that* he loves me." The expletive is sometimes called an "empty word" because it plays a structural rather than a lexical role.

Finite verb.   The main verb of the clause together with its auxiliaries, if any, sometimes called the predicating verb. A finite verb can be marked for tense, mood, aspect, and voice (in contrast to gerunds, participles, and infinitives, which can be marked only for aspect and voice).

Flat adverb.   A class of adverb that is the same in form as its corresponding adjective: *fast, high, early, late, hard, long,* etc.

Form classes.   The large, open classes of words that provide the lexical content of the language: nouns, verbs, adjectives, and adverbs. Each has characteristic derivational and inflectional morphemes that distinguish its forms. See Chapter 5.

Free morpheme. A single morpheme that is also a complete word (in contrast to a bound morpheme, which is not).

Gender. A feature of personal pronouns and certain nouns that distinguishes masculine (*he*), feminine (*she*), and neuter (*it*). Nouns with gender distinctions include *waiter, waitress, actor, actress, girl, boy, man, woman, mare, ram.*

Genitive case. The Latin term for possessive case.

Gerund. An *-ing* verb functioning as a nominal: "I enjoy *jogging*"; "*Playing tennis* is good exercise."

Headword. The word that fills the noun slot in the noun phrase: "the little *boy* across [the *street*]."

Homophones. Morphemes, both bases and affixes, that sound alike but have different meanings: *sale/sail;* farmer/brighter.

Idiom. A combination of words whose meaning cannot be predicted from the meaning of the individual words.

Immediate-constituent (I-C) analysis. A system of sentence analysis that is based on the binary nature of the sentence and its parts. See Appendix B.

Imperative. The sentence—and also the verb—in the form of a command. The imperative sentence includes the base form of the verb and usually an understood subject (*you*): "*Eat* your spinach"; "*Finish* your report as soon as possible"; "You *go* on without me."

Indefinite article. The determiner *a,* which marks an unspecified count noun. See also *Definite article.*

Indefinite pronoun. A large category that includes quantifiers (e.g., *enough, several, many, much*), universals (*all, both, every, each*), and partitives (*any, either, neither, no, some*). Many of the indefinite pronouns can function as determiners.

Indefinite relative pronoun. The relative pronouns with *-ever* added, which have indefinite referents; they introduce adjectival clauses: "I will give a bonus to *whoever* works the hardest" (i.e., to the person who works the hardest).

Independent clause. The main clause of the sentence; a compound sentence has more than one independent clause.

Indicative mood. The expression of an idea as fact (as opposed to probability). Verb phrases without modal auxiliaries and those with *will* and *shall* are considered the indicative mood: "We *will go* soon"; "We *are going* tomorrow." "When *are* you *going*?" See also *Subjunctive mood* and *Conditional mood.*

Indirect object. The nominal slot following the verb in a Pattern VIII sentence. In a sentence with a verb like *give,* the indirect object is the recipient; the direct object is the thing given: "We gave *our friends* a ride home."

Infinitive. The base form of the verb (the present tense), usually expressed with *to,* which is called the "sign of the infinitive." The infinitive can function adverbially ("I stayed up all night *to study for the exam*"); adjectivally ("That is no way *to study*"); or nominally ("*To stay up all night* is foolish"). The only verb with an infinitive form separate from the present tense is *be.*

Inflectional morpheme. Morphemes that are added to the form classes (nouns, verbs, adjectives, and adverbs) to change their grammatical role in some way. Nouns have two inflectional suffixes (*-s* plural and *-'s* possessive); verbs have four (*-s, -ing, -ed,* and *-en*); adjectives and some adverbs have two (*-er* and *-est*).

Intensifier. See *Qualifier.*

Intensive pronoun. A pronoun that serves as an appositive to emphasize a noun or pronoun. It is formed by adding -*self* or -*selves* to a personal pronoun: "I *myself* prefer chocolate."

Interjection. A word considered independent of the main sentence, often punctuated with an exclamation point: "*Ouch!* My shoe pinches"; "*Oh!* Is that what you meant?"

Interrogative. A sentence that is a question in form: "Are you leaving now?" "When are you leaving?" The term interrogative also refers to the "*wh*-words" that introduce questions and nominal clauses: "*Where* are you going?" "I wonder *where* he is going."

Intonation. The rhythmic pattern of a spoken sentence, affected by its stress and pitch and pauses.

Intransitive verb. The verbs of Pattern VI sentences, which require no complement to be complete.

Irregular verb. Any verb in which the -*ed* and -*en* forms are not that of the regular verb; in other words, a verb in which the -*ed* and -*en* forms are not simply the addition of -*d*, -*ed*, or -*t* to the base form.

Lexicon. The store of words—the internalized dictionary—that every speaker of the language has.

Linking verb. The verbs of Patterns IV and V, which require a subjective complement to be complete.

Manner adverb. An adverb that answers the question of "how" or "in what manner" about the verb. Most manner adverbs are derived from adjectives with the addition of -*ly: quickly, merrily, candidly.*

Mass nouns. See *Noncountable nouns.*

Modal auxiliary. The auxiliary that occupies the opening slot in the verb-expansion rule and may affect what is known as the mood of the verb, conveying probability, possibility, obligation, and the like.

Mood. A quality of the verb denoting fact (indicative), a condition contrary to fact (subjunctive), and probability or possibility (conditional).

Morpheme.   A sound or combination of sounds with meaning.

Morphology.   The study of morphemes. See Chapter 4.

Nominal.   Any structure that functions as a noun phrase normally functions. See Chapter 11.

Nominal clause.   A clause that fills an NP slot.

Nominative case.   The Latin term for subjective case.

Noncountable noun.   Nouns referring to what might be called an undifferentiated mass—such as *wood, water, sugar, glass*—or an abstraction—*justice, love, indifference.* Whether or not you can use the indefinite article, *a,* is probably the best test of countability: If you can, the noun is countable.

Nonfinite verb.   A verb that functions other than as the main (finite) verb. Verbs and verb phrases acting as adjectivals, adverbials, and nominals within the sentence are called nonfinite verbs.

Nonrestrictive modifier.   A modifier in the noun phrase that comments about the noun rather than defines it. Nonrestrictive modifiers following the noun are set off by commas.

Noun.   One of the four form classes, whose members fill the headword slot in the noun phrase. Most nouns can be inflected for plural and possessive (*boy, boys, boy's, boys'*). Nouns have characteristic derivational endings, such as *-ion* (*action, compensation*), *-ment* (*contentment*), and *-ness* (*happiness*).

Noun clause.   See *Nominal clause.*

Noun phrase.   The noun headword with all of its attendant pre- and postnoun modifiers.

Number. A feature of nouns and pronouns, referring to singular and plural.

Objective case. The role in a sentence of a noun phrase or pronoun when it functions as an object—direct object, indirect object, objective complement, or object of the preposition. Although nouns do not have a special form for objective case, many of the pronouns do; personal pronouns and the relative pronoun *who* have separate forms when they function as objects. See Chapter 7.

Objective complement. The slot following the direct object, filled by an adjectival (Pattern IX) or a nominal (Pattern X). The objective complement has two functions: (1) It completes the idea of the verb; and (2) it modifies (if an adjective) or renames (if a nominal) the direct object: "I found the play *exciting*"; "We consider Pete *a good friend.*"

Parallel structure. A coordinate structure in which all of the coordinate parts are of the same grammatical form.

Participle. The *-ing* and *-en* verb (or verb phrase) functioning as an adjectival. See also Present Participle and Past Participle.

Particle. A word that combines with a verb to form a phrasal verb: look *up;* look *into;* put *up with.*

Passive voice. A feature of transitive sentences in which the direct object (the objective or goal) is shifted to the subject position and *be* + *-en* is added to the verb. The term passive refers to the relationship between the subject and the verb: "Ed ate the pizza" → "The pizza *was eaten* by Ed." See Chapter 2.

Past participle. The *-en* form of the verb.

Past tense. The *-ed* form of the verb, usually denoting a specific past action.

Person. A feature of personal pronouns that distinguishes the speaker or writer (first person), the person or thing spoken to (second person), and the person or thing spoken of (third person).

Phoneme. The smallest unit of sound that makes a difference in meaning.

Phonology. The study of phonemes. See Appendix A.

Phrasal preposition. A preposition of more than one word that acts as a unit: *according to, because of, out of.*

Phrasal subordinator. A subordinating conjunction of more than one word that acts as unit to subordinate one clause to another: *as if, even though, provided that.*

Phrasal verb. A verb together with a particle that produces a meaning that cannot be predicted from the meaning of the parts: *look up; put up with; make up.*

Phrase. A combination of words that constitutes a unit of the sentence.

Plural. A feature of nouns and pronouns denoting more than one, usually signaled in nouns by the inflectional ending -*s* (or -*es*).

Positive degree. See *Degree.*

Possessive case. The inflected form of nouns (*John's, the dog's*) and pronouns usually indicating possession (*my, his, your, her, their,* etc.).

Predicate. One of the two principal parts of the sentence, the comment made about the subject. The predicate includes the verb, together with its complements and modifiers.

Predicate adjective. The adjective that functions as a subjective complement.

Predicate nominative.   The noun or nominal that functions as a subjective complement.

Predicative adjective.   The adjective that occupies a complement slot in the sentence as subjective or objective complement.

Prefix.   An affix added to the beginning of a word to change its meaning (*un*likely, *il*legal, *pre*scribe, *re*new) or its class (*en*able, *be*little).

Preposition.   A structure-class word found in pre-position to—that is, preceding—a noun phrase. Prepositions can be classed according to their form as simple (*above, at, in, of,* etc.) or phrasal (*according to, instead of,* etc.).

Prepositional phrase.   The combination of a preposition and a nominal, which is known as the object of the preposition.

Present participle.   The *-ing* form of the verb.

Present tense.   The base form and the *-s* form of the verb: *help, helps.* The present tense denotes a present point in time ("I *understand* your position"), a habitual action ("I *jog* five miles a day"), or the "timeless" present ("Shakespeare *helps* us understand ourselves").

Pronoun.   A word that substitutes for a noun—or, more accurately, for a nominal—in the sentence.

Pronoun–antecedent agreement.   See *Agreement.*

Proper noun.   A noun with individual reference to a person, a place, a historical event, or other name. Proper nouns are capitalized.

Qualifier.   A structure-class word that qualifies or intensifies an adjective or adverb: "We worked *rather* slowly"; "We worked *very* hard."

Reciprocal pronoun.   The pronouns *each other* and *one another,* which refer to previously named nouns.

Referent.   The thing (or person, event, concept, action, etc.)—in other words, the reality—that a word stands for.

Reflexive pronoun.   A pronoun formed by adding *-self* or *-selves* to a form of the personal pronoun, used as an object in the sentence.

Regular verb.   A verb in which the *-ed* form (the past tense) and the *-en* form (the past participle) are formed by adding *-ed* (or, in some cases, *-d* or *-t*) to the base. These two forms of a regular verb are always identical. "I *walked* home"; "I have *walked* home every day this week."

Relative adverb.   The adverbs *where, when,* and *why,* which introduce adjectival and adverbial clauses.

Relative clause.   A clause introduced by a relative pronoun (*who, which, that*) or a relative adverb (*when, where, why*) that modifies a noun.

Relative pronoun.   The pronouns *who* [*whom, whose*], *which,* and *that* in their role as introducers of a relative (adjectival) clause.

Restrictive modifier.   A modifier in the noun phrase whose function is to restrict the meaning of the noun. A modifier is restrictive when it is needed to identify the referent of the headword. The restrictive modifier is not set off by commas.

Retained object.   The direct object of a Pattern VIII sentence that is retained in its original position when the sentence is transformed into the passive voice: "The judges awarded Mary the prize" → "Mary was awarded *the prize.*"

Sentence.   A word or group of words based on one or more subject–predicate, or clause, patterns. The written sentence begins with a capital letter and ends with terminal punctuation—a period, question mark, or an exclamation point.

Sentence modifier.   A word or phrase or clause that modifies the sentence as a whole. See Chapter 12.

Sentence patterns.   The simple skeletal sentences, made up of two or three or four required elements, that underlie our sentences, even the most complex among them. Ten such patterns will account for almost all the possible sentences of English.

Singular.   A feature of nouns and pronouns denoting one referent.

Standard written English.   The level of English usage that is widely accepted as the norm for the edited public writing of newspapers and magazines and books.

"Stand-in" auxiliary.   The auxiliary *do* (*does, did*), which we add to sentences when we transform them into questions, negatives, and emphatic statements when there is no auxiliary in the original.

Structure classes.   The small, closed classes of words that explain the grammatical or structural relationships of the form classes. See Chapter 6.

Subject.   The opening slot in the sentence patterns, filled by a noun phrase or other nominal, that functions as the topic of the sentence.

Subjective case.   The role in the sentence of a noun phrase or a pronoun when it functions as the subject of the sentence. Personal pronouns have distinctive forms for subjective case: *I, he, she, they,* etc.

Subjective complement.   The nominal or adjectival in Pattern II, III, IV, and V sentences following the verb, which renames or modifies the subject.

Subject–verb agreement.   See *Agreement.*

Subjunctive mood.   An expression of the verb in which the base form, rather than the inflected form, is used (1) in certain *that* clauses conveying strong suggestions or resolutions or commands ("We suggest that Mary *go* with us"; "I move that the meeting *be* adjourned"; "I demand that you *let* us in"), and (2) in the expression of wishes or conditions contrary to fact ("If I *were* you, I'd be careful"; "I wish it *were* summer"). The subjunctive of the verb *be* is expressed by *were*, or *be*, even for subjects that normally take *is* or *was*.

Subordinate clause. A dependent clause introduced by a subordinating conjunction, such as *if*, *since*, *because*, and *although*.

Subordinator. A subordinating conjunction that turns a complete sentence into a subordinate clause.

Substantive. A structure that functions as a noun; a nominal.

Suffix. An affix added to the end of a form-class word to change its class (*act* → *action; laugh* → *laughable*) with derivational suffixes or to change its grammatical function (*boy* → *boys; walk* → *walking*) with inflectional suffixes. See also *Derivational affixes* and *Inflectional suffixes*.

Superlative degree. See *Degree*.

Surface structure. A term used by transformational grammarians to designate the sentences of the language as they are spoken and written. See also *Deep structure*.

Syntax. The structure of sentences; the relationship of the parts of the sentence.

Tense. A feature of verbs and auxiliaries relating to time. Tense is designated either by an inflectional change (*walked*), by an auxiliary (*will walk*), or both (*am walking, have walked*). Note that "tense" in relation to the modal auxiliaries refers to form, not to time.

***There* transformation.** A variation of a basic sentence in which the expletive *there* is added at the beginning and the subject is shifted to a position following *be:* "A fly is in my soup" → *"There is a fly in my soup."*

Third person singular. The personal pronouns *he*, *she*, and *it*. The term is also used in reference to the *-s* form of the verb.

Transformational grammar (also called Transformational-Generative, or T-G). A theory of grammar that attempts to account for the ability of native speakers to generate and process the sentences of their language.

Transitive verb. The verbs of Patterns VII through X, which require at least one complement, the direct object, to be complete. With only a few exceptions, transitive verbs are those that can be transformed into the passive voice.

Verb. One of the four form classes, traditionally thought of as the action word in the sentence. A better way to recognize the verb, however, is by its form. Every verb, without exception, has an *-s* and an *-ing* form; every verb also has an *-ed* and an *-en* form, although in the case of some irregular verbs these forms are not readily apparent. And every verb, without exception, can be marked by auxiliaries. Many verbs also have characteristic derivational forms, such as *-ify* (*typify*), *-ize* (*criticize*), and *-ate* (*activate*).

Verb phrase. The main verb with all of its complements and modifiers, constituting the predicate of the sentence.

Verb-expansion rule. The formula that describes our system for expanding the verb with auxiliaries to express variations in meaning: T + (M) + (have + -en) + (be + -ing) + V. See Chapter 2.

Vocative. The noun or noun phrase of direct address, considered a sentence modifier: *"Mike,* is that you?"

APPENDIXES

APPENDIX

A

PHONOLOGY

For the structural linguist, the study of language begins not with the grammar of sentences nor even with the parts of speech. It begins with the study of sounds, the smallest units of language. We call these sounds *phonemes* and the study of them *phonology*.

PHONEMES

An important first step in the study of phonology is to recognize the parts of words and syllables as sounds rather than as letters of the alphabet and to hear these sounds separately. If you can isolate the sounds, you should have no trouble in learning the system of phonemes that make up the morphemes and words and sentences of English.

First, let's define *phoneme*. A phoneme is not just any sound: It is a sound that can make a difference in meaning. In English the inventory of distinctive sounds numbers around three dozen. Our vocal apparatus is capable of making many more sounds than this, of course; we make many more than this every day. We whistle and hum and groan and hiss and click our tongues and giggle and howl with laughter. All such sounds, of course, convey messages, so in that sense they are meaningful. However, when we say that sounds are distinctive, or that they distinguish meaning, we are referring to their role in the production of words.

Every language has its own inventory of distinctive sounds, or phonemes. Many of our three dozen phonemes are the same as those of other languages, but the sets for even closely related languages are not identical. For example, imagine the following conversation with a student from Venezuela:

> *Joe:* How was your trip, José? Did you fly?
> *José:* No, I came by sheep.
> *Joe:* You mean "ship."
> *José:* That's what I said—"sheep."

In pronouncing *ship* exactly like *sheep,* José is imposing the phonemes of Spanish on his pronunciation of English. In English the vowel sound in *ship,* /I/, is different from the vowel in *sheep,* /i/. But Spanish does not have both of these vowels, so the difference between them makes no difference in meaning. In English the difference between /I/ and /i/ is what is known as a *phonemic difference;* that is, it makes a difference in meaning because *ship* and *sheep* are different words. In Spanish the difference is not phonemic because /I/ and /i/ are not separate phonemes. In fact, Spanish speakers may not even hear the two sounds as different, as the conversation with José demonstrates.

Another example illustrates a difference between Norwegian and English. The Norwegian speaker may have a hard time distinguishing between *yam* and *jam;* to the Norwegian they may sound alike. In English, of course, /ǰ/ and /y/ are separate phonemes, but Norwegian has no /ǰ/, only a /y/; consequently, Jack's Norwegian friend calls him "Yak" most of the time.

(Note: Because we have to deal with sounds in the written language, we use the convention of slashes to represent phonemes. /I/ represents the vowel sound in *ship.* When you see a symbol written between slashes, remember that it represents a sound, not a letter of the alphabet.)

THE PRODUCTION OF SOUNDS

Speech sounds are actually disturbances of the air as it travels from the lungs through the larynx and out of either the mouth or the nose. Differences in these disturbances—along with variations in the size and shape of the mouth, the resonating chamber—create the differences in the sounds. The following diagram shows the various parts of the speech apparatus.

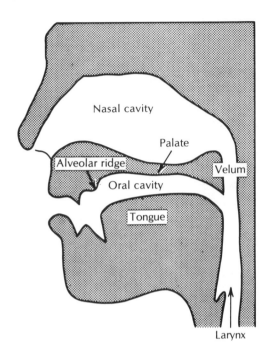

Larynx

THE INVENTORY OF PHONEMES

It is not possible to pin down our inventory of phonemes with absolute precision; certainly, the description we are using here is not the only way of categorizing the sounds of English. The vowels are especially elusive, as you will discover in trying to distinguish between *ham* and *hem* or *fear* and *fair* and *fire*. It is important to recognize that each of the phonemes represents a range of sound. For example, the positions of the vowels on the vowel chart represent the actual physical feature of tongue and lip placement, so there are bound to be differences among speakers. Especially obvious are the differences that we hear in different parts of the country.

This inventory of thirty-five phonemes includes eleven vowels and twenty-four consonants, including two glides; the three diphthongs are combinations of a vowel and a glide. We will begin our description with the consonants, which are categorized on the basis of three physical features: the manner of articulation, the place of articulation, and voicing. These are the features you will be able to recognize—to hear and to feel—as you pronounce the consonants.

CONSONANTS

We will first classify the consonant phonemes on the basis of their manner of articulation—that is, the way in which the air is disturbed. The two main classes are *stops,* where the air is completely stopped in its passage, and *fricatives,* where the air is only partially obstructed. We can further subdivide the consonants by noting if they are *voiced* or *voiceless*—that is, whether or not the vocal cords vibrate as the air passes through the larynx, or voice box.

Stops. /b/ and /p/—The Bilabial Stops. In the production of these two sounds, the air is stopped at the lips. The only difference between them is voicing: /b/ is voiced; /p/ is voiceless. When you say the following pairs of words aloud, you can probably feel the vibration in those with /b/:

tab	tap
bit	pit
bub	pup
cub	cup

You will detect the difference between /b/ and /p/ even more clearly if you put your fingers over your ears when you say the words.

You'll probably notice another difference besides voicing as you listen to these two sounds. The pitch of your voice drops as you go from /p/ to /b/. For example, say the word *pub.* You'll notice that your voice ends up lower than it began; compare the pitch pattern of *pub* with that of *pup,* in which your voice stays at one level.

/d/ and /t/—The Alveolar Stops. In the production of this pair of stop consonants, the tip of the tongue stops the air at the alveolar ridge, the ridge you can feel just behind your upper teeth. Again the difference between the two sounds is voicing—with its attendant pitch change. Say the following pairs aloud:

pad	pat
drip	trip
dad	tat

/g/ and /k/—The Velar Stops. In the production of these two sounds, the back of the tongue stops the air at the velum, or soft

palate. When you say the following words, you can feel the closure in the back of your throat as the air is being stopped. You can also feel the difference between the voiced /g/ and the voiceless /k/:

tag   tack
gore   core
pig   pick

These three pairs comprise the stop consonants. They are easy to differentiate and, except for /k/, which is not always spelled with the letter k, the stops also correspond to the written alphabet. (Notice that in the word *core* the /k/ sound is represented by the letter c and in *tack* by ck.)

Fricatives. In the production of fricative consonants, the air is not completely stopped, but it is obstructed in some way on its passage through the oral cavity, the mouth. One obvious difference between this class and the stops is that the sound of a fricative can be sustained, whereas a stop cannot. Because fricatives, like the stops, are either voiced or voiceless, we will look at them in pairs.

/v/ and /f/—The Labio-Dental Fricatives. In the production of these two sounds, the air passes freely until it reaches the front of the mouth, where it is obstructed by the lower lip and upper teeth. Say the following pair of words, sustaining the last sound:

leave   leaf

You should be able to hear the difference between the voiced /v/ and the voiceless /f/. Here are some other pairs that show the contrast between these two sounds:

vat   fat
veal   feel
five   fife

/ð/ (eth) and /θ/ (theta)—The Interdental Fricatives. You can think of these two fricatives, in which the air is obstructed with the tongue between the teeth, as the "th" sounds. In studying the consonant sounds, you may find these two the most difficult to differentiate

since you are used to seeing them written exactly alike. Consider the following pair:

thy   thigh

The difference you hear in their opening sound is a difference in voicing: *thy* begins with the voiced /ð/; *thigh* begins with the voiceless /θ/. The physical difference in their production is identical to the physical difference between /d/ and /t/ or between /b/ and /p/.

Say the following words aloud; then identify the "th" sound in each as either voiced or voiceless:

1. myth _____   5. both _____   9. path _____

2. mother _____   6. bother _____   10. thick _____

3. bathe _____   7. ether _____   11. stealth _____

4. thirsty _____   8. either _____   12. rather _____

In the list you should have identified 2, 3, 6, 8, and 12 as voiced, the others as voiceless. If you had a problem making the distinction, sustain the "th" in a pair such as *bath* and *bathe* and listen for the difference. You should feel the voicing as a kind of buzzing in your head.

/z/ *and* /s/—*The Alveolar Fricatives.* In the production of this pair, the air is obstructed at the alveolar ridge. In fact, the placement of the tongue for these sounds is almost identical to the placement for /d/ and /t/, with the tongue tip on the alveolar ridge. The air passes along the sides of the tongue as either a buzz, with the voiced /z/, or a hiss, with the voiceless /s/:

zip   sip
buzz   bus
zap   sap

/ž/ *and* /š/—*The Alveopalatal Fricatives.* The voiceless /š/ can be thought of as the "sh" sound, as in words like *ship* and *sheep*, although it is not always spelled with the letters sh: It appears also in *Chicago* and *sugar*. The voiced counterpart of /š/ is one of two consonants that does not appear in initial position in English words—that is, at the opening of a syllable. However, we do hear /ž/ at the opening of certain words recently borrowed from French, such as *genre* and *gendarme*. It is the second consonant sound in *measure* and *pleasure;* for some people it is the final sound in *garage.* You can hear the contrast between /ž/ and /š/ in the following pair:

/ž/	/š/
pleasure	pressure

/h/—The Voiceless Glottal Fricative. This fricative, the sound at the beginning of *hot, hear,* and *ham,* is caused by the air rushing through the glottis, the space between the vocal cords. It alone of the fricatives has no voiced counterpart in English.

Affricates. A third group of consonant phonemes is that of the affricates, a combination of a stop and a fricative:

/ǰ/ *the voiced alveopalatal affricate,* combines the voiced alveolar stop /d/ and the voiced alveopalatal fricative /ž/;

/č/, *the voiceless alveopalatal affricate,* represents the "ch" sound, a combination of the voiceless counterparts of those two phonemes: /t/ and /š/.

/ǰ/	/č/
badge	batch
ridge	rich
jug	chug

Exercise 1: Consonants. Identify the opening and closing consonant sound in each of the following words:

1. shrug	4. tax	7. pledge	10. that
2. circus	5. cards	8. huff	11. judge
3. Thomas	6. thatch	9. dropped	12. bored

(You can check your answers on page 378.)

Nasals. The consonants described so far are all oral sounds; that is, the air passes through the oral cavity. But we articulate three consonants by allowing the air to pass through the nasal cavity. (The diagram on page 366 shows a clear passage behind the velum; this passage is closed for the production of the oral consonants you have just been studying.)

/m/, /n/, and /ŋ/—The Nasal Consonants. You can easily demonstrate the physical difference between oral and nasal sounds: First say the word *ham,* sustaining the /m/; then pinch your nose, cutting off the air. You have also cut off the sound.

The three nasals, all of which are voiced, are articulated exactly as the three pairs of stops are: /m/ is bilabial, corresponding to /b/; /n/ is alveolar, corresponding to /d/; and /ŋ/ is velar, corresponding to /g/:

tam   tan   tang

The letters m and n, of course, represent the sounds /m/ and /n/. The combined letters ng, in such words as *tang* and *sing,* stand for the velar nasal sound, /ŋ/, even though it is a single sound; in words like *finger, linger,* and *wink,* however, /ŋ/ is spelled with n. Incidentally, /ŋ/ is the other phoneme (along with /ž/) that does not appear in initial position. Other words with /ŋ/ are *think, ink,* and *mingle.*

Liquids. The two liquids are /l/, the lateral consonant, so called because the air escapes at the sides of the tongue, and /r/, called the retroflex, because of the backward, or bending, movement of the tongue tip:

late   rate
leer   reel

Glides. The glides, /w/ and /y/, are characterized by lip and tongue movement:

wet   yet

The difference between the following pair is the presence of the /y/ glide in *cue:*

coo /ku/   cue /kyu/

Glides also combine with vowels in the formation of diphthongs; we will take these up after the discussion of vowels.

The following chart shows the consonants according to their place and manner of articulation.

	BILABIAL	LABIO-DENTAL	INTER-DENTAL	ALVEOLAR	ALVEOLAR-PALATAL	VELAR	GLOTTAL
Stops							
voiced	b			d		g	
voiceless	p			t		k	
Fricatives							
voiced		v	ð	z	ž		
voiceless		f	θ	s	š		h
Affricates							
voiced					ǰ		
voiceless					č		
Nasals							
voiced	m			n		ŋ	
voiceless							
Liquids							
lateral				l			
retroflex				r			
Glides					y	w	

(The broken line encloses those consonants known as sibilants.)

SIBILANTS

The consonants identified on the chart as *sibilants,* you'll notice, are s-like or z-like sounds. This feature makes a difference when the sibilant comes at the end of a noun or verb; the sibilant determines both pronunciation and spelling of the plural and possessive morphemes for nouns and the *s*-form of verbs. When a word ends in a sibilant, we add a complete syllable for the "s" endings:

church → churches   garage → garages
kiss → kisses   judge → judges
splash → splashes   buzz → buzzes

Notice also that when these "s" morphemes are added to other nouns and verbs (run → runs; dog → dogs; cat → cats; hit → hits; walk → walks; head → heads; sofa → sofas) they are not always pronounced /s/, no matter how they are written. Following vowels (which are always voiced) and following voiced consonants, the letter s is pronounced /z/; it is only after voiceless consonants that the s is actually pronounced /s/. However, when the ending is added to sibilants, as described in the preceding paragraph, the sound is never /s/, because we add a complete syllable, including the voiced vowel; the voicing of the vowel carries over to the s, producing a /z/ sound.

VOWELS

With few exceptions, every syllable has a vowel; to count the syllables in a word, you can count the vowel sounds, which form the peaks of loudness in the syllable. The vocal cords vibrate in the production of all English vowels, so they are all voiced phonemes.

The differences in the vowel sounds are caused by the differences in the size and shape of the mouth, which acts as a resonance chamber for the sound. These differences are caused by changes in the placement of the tongue, in the action of the lips, and in the opening and closing of the mouth.

The vowels are classified as to position—from front to central to back and from high to mid to low. The position labels refer to tongue placement. For example, a designation such as "high front vowel" or "low back vowel" refers to the sound produced when the highest part of the tongue is in that position.

The easiest way to differentiate and to remember the vowels is to learn a sample word for each:

	FRONT	CENTRAL	BACK
HIGH	/i/ (beat)		/u/ (boot)
	/I/ (bit)		/ʊ/ (put)
MID	/e/ (bait)	/ə/ (but)	/o/ (boat)
	/ɛ/ (bet)		/ɔ/ (bought, caught)
LOW	/æ/ (bat)		/a/ (father, cot)

As you say the front vowels, from high to low—from *beat* to *bat*—you can feel your mouth opening wider and your tongue lowering. As you say the vowels from front to back—from *bait* to *but* to *boot*—you can feel your lips rounding.

Before going on, we should note some common variations in the pronunciation of vowels among people from different parts of the country. One difference occurs in the following pairs:

cot	collar	don	hock
caught	caller	dawn	hawk

For many speakers the vowel sounds in these pairs represent the contrast between /a/ (the first member of each pair listed) and /ɔ/, sometimes called the "open o"; but for other speakers these pairs of words are homophones, words that sound identical. For this latter group, in fact, the open o is not a phoneme (except for its occurrence in the diphthong /ɔy/, described in the next section); in other words, it is not a sound that makes a difference in meaning. People who live in Washington, Oregon, and parts of northern California, for example, do not make the distinction between /a/ and /ɔ/; this is also true of an area extending several hundred miles with Pittsburgh at its center. For these speakers the vowels in the words *cot, caught, don, dawn, law,* and the first syllable of *father* are all pronounced the same. There are a great many other regional differences in the production of vowel sounds. New Englanders and Southerners, for example, have very distinct accents to people outside of their regions, caused mainly by differences in vowels.

DIPHTHONGS

In addition to the simple vowel sounds, we produce diphthongs by combining a vowel and a glide:

$$/ay/ \quad \text{bite}$$
$$/aw/ \quad \text{bout}$$
$$/ɔy/ \quad \text{boy}$$

The diphthong is a vowel sound combined with lip and tongue movement to produce a new sound. In the production of /ay/, for example, we begin with the low back vowel, /a/, and move the position of the tongue and lips toward the position for the high front vowel, /i/, which is the region of the /y/ glide. Likewise, in producing /aw/, we begin with the same sound, /a/, and move to the position for the high back sound, the region of /w/. The diphthongs are characterized by this movement toward closure from the open position of the vowel.

The following exercises will give you practice with vowels and diphthongs. To transcribe the sounds in the word, say the word aloud and listen for the sound of the vowel—and try to disregard spelling. If you have trouble identifying a vowel, isolate it by dropping the sounds before and after it, one at a time. For example, to identify the vowel sound in *mad,* pronounce the word; then say it without the /d/, sustaining the vowel; then drop the /m/. You're left with the vowel. Now match it with the chart on page 374; you'll probably decide that the vowel in *mad* is most like the vowel in *bat.*

Exercise 2: Vowels and Diphthongs. Transcribe the following words as you pronounce them.

1. deep _____	5. pout _____	9. gripe _____
2. drop _____	6. pest _____	10. grip _____
3. chug _____	7. food _____	11. laid _____
4. good _____	8. feud _____	12. lad _____

(You can check your answers on page 378.)

The following exercise will give you practice with longer words. Each of the words listed has two or more vowel sounds, one for each syllable. You'll find that the loudest syllable, the one that gets the main stress, will be the easiest to identify. You'll also discover that the mid central vowel on the vowel chart, /ə/, the sound in *but* (called the schwa), turns up frequently in syllables without main stress. This "uh" sound is our most common vowel.

Exercise 3: Vowels and Diphthongs. Transcribe the following words as you pronounce them. (Note: The "er" sound in such words as *consider, mother,* and *bird* is conventionally transcribed /ər/.)

1. meadow	_____	7. easy	_____
2. consider	_____	8. consent	_____
3. female	_____	9. Idaho	_____
4. common	_____	10. loudest	_____
5. persecute	_____	11. teacup	_____
6. paranoid	_____	12. flowers	_____

As you have probably discovered, the vowel sounds are harder to pin down than the consonants. And some of your answers were probably different from those given on page 378. That's understandable. Each of the phonemes actually represents a range of sounds, with variations depending on the environment—on the sounds that surround another particular sound—and on the individual speaker.[1] Certain consonants, especially /r/ and /l/, often make the vowel sounds hard to identify. For example, pronounce the following words; then identify the vowel in each:

fit	_____	pet	_____
fear	_____	pair	_____

---

[1] These variations in phonemes—differences that make no difference in meaning—are called allophones. The distinction between phonemes and allophones is comparable to the distinction between morphemes and allomorphs.

The /r/ has the effect of a glide, causing movement during the production of the vowel, thus making the sound difficult to identify precisely. (In fact, in some descriptions of phonology the /r/ is included with the glides.) You probably had no problem with the vowels in *fit* /fɪt/ and *pet* /pɛt/, but for *fear* and *pair* the /ɪ/ and /ɛ/ are not as clear. In fact, you may have made a different decision—perhaps /fir/ and /per/.

ASSIMILATION

The pronunciation of words in isolation is often quite different from the pronunciation in connected speech. Say the following sentences aloud:

> I have to leave now.
> I have two dollars.

You'll notice that *have to* /hæftə/ in the first sentence is quite different from *have two* /hævtu/ in the second. Now say the following:

> I must tell Lucy about Tom.

You probably said something like this:

> /ay məstɛlusi əbawtam/

Notice how the t's and l's run together. These changes in the pronunciation of connected speech are called *assimilation*. Here are some further examples:

> He bought it for me.
> Bill and Pam left town.
> Did you make it yourself?
> Would you give me a cup of coffee?

If you first pronounce the words in the sentences separately, as though they were in a list, and then say the sentences as you would in conversation, you'll notice the difference that assimilation produces. Here's how your conversational sentences might be transcribed:

/hi bat It fər mi/
/bIl ən pæm lɛftawn/
/dIǰu mek It yərsɛlf/ or /ǰumekičərsɛlf/
/wuǰu gImi ə kəp əv kafi/ or /ju gImi ə kəp əv kɔfi/

SUMMARY

An understanding of phonemes—the smallest meaningful units of our language—helps make us sensitive to the wonder of speech and the wonderful variety of speech that we hear all around us.

ANSWERS TO EXERCISES

Exercise 1		*Exercise 2*	*Exercise 3*
1. /š/ /g/		1. /dip/	1. /mɛdo/
2. /s/ /s/		2. /drap/	2. /kənsIdər/
3. /t/ /s/		3. /čəg/	3. /fimel/
4. /t/ /s/		4. /gʊd/	4. /kamən/
5. /k/ /z/		5. /pawt/	5. /pərsəkyut/
6. /θ/ /č/		6. /pɛst/	6. /pɛrənɔyd/
7. /p/ /ǰ/		7. /fud/	7. /izi/
8. /h/ /f/		8. /fyud/	8. /kənsɛnt/
9. /d/ /t/		9. /grayp/	9. /aydəho/
10. /ð/ /t/		10. /grIp/	10. /lawdəst/
11. /j/ /ǰ/		11. /led/	11. /tikəp/
12. /b/ /d/		12. /læd/	12. /flawərz/

B

Immediate-Constituent (I-C) Analysis

Immediate-constituent analysis, like traditional diagramming, provides a visual representation of the way the parts of the sentence are related to one another. The term *immediate constituent* refers to the binary method on which this system is based: What are the *two parts* of the structure that constitute the *whole*? In the following sentence, the subject (*the boy*) and the predicate (*hit the ball*) are the two constituents immediately related, or related on the same level:

The boy | hit the ball

The next level of analysis shows the two immediate constituents of each of these:

the | boy   hit | the ball

The complete I-C analysis looks like this:

The | boy | hit | the | ball

You have two important preliminary steps at each level of the analysis before dividing a particular structure into its constituents:

1. Underline the construction to be analyzed.
2. Identify its form.

Following is a step-by-step I-C analysis of an expanded version of the previous sample sentence:

STEP 1:
Q. What is the form of the following construction?

THE LITTLE BOY WHO LIVES DOWN THE STREET	HAS HIT HIS BALL INTO MY YARD

A. Sentence.
Procedure: Cut the sentence into its two parts: the subject and the predicate.

STEP 2:
Q. What is the form of the following construction?

$$\overset{\times}{\text{HAS HIT HIS BALL}} \mid \text{INTO MY YARD}$$

A. Verb phrase.
Procedure: In analyzing the verb phrase,

1. Identify the main verb. (In this case, *hit*.)
2. Next, cut off any adverbials in preverb position. (In this case there are none.)
3. Now determine the number of complements and/or adverbials following the verb. (In this case, two.)
4. Cut them off, beginning with the most remote.

    (Note: The vertical line in the verb phrase above, the "cut," shows that the two parts of the verb phrase immediately related to one another are *has hit his ball* and *into my yard*. That is, the prepositional phrase modifies the entire phrase *has hit his ball*, not simply *hit*.) Continue cutting complements and/or modifiers up to the verb:

    HAS HIT | HIS BALL

5. Cut off auxiliaries, beginning with the most remote.

    HAS | HIT

In a verb string with three or more auxiliaries, they are cut off one at a time:

```
HAS | BEEN | HIT
       |_____
   _____
```

So far, the I-C analysis looks like this:

```
THE LITTLE BOY WHO LIVES DOWN THE STREET | HAS | HIT | HIS BALL | INTO MY YARD
                                            |  |
                                            _____
                                          _____
_____
```

Now we will analyze the subject noun phrase, following the same procedure, first underlining the structure:

STEP 3:
Q. What is the form of the underlined construction?

```
                    X
THE LITTLE BOY | WHO LIVES DOWN THE STREET
                 |
   _____
```

A. Noun phrase.
Procedure: In analyzing the noun phrase,

1. Identify the noun headword. (In this case, *boy.*)
2. Determine how many modifiers follow the headword, then cut them off, beginning with the most remote. (In this case, one.)
   (Note: This analysis shows that *who lives down the street* is immediately related to the noun phrase *the little boy,* not simply to the headword *boy.*)
3. Determine the number of preceding modifiers, including the determiner, and cut them off, beginning with the most remote. After drawing each vertical line, underline the remaining structure before drawing another vertical line. You'll notice that every vertical line bisects a horizontal line.

```
THE | LITTLE | BOY
       |_____
   _____
```

So far, the I-C analysis looks like this:

| THE | LITTLE | BOY | WHO LIVES DOWN THE STREET | HAS | HIT | HIS BALL | INTO MY YARD |

STEP 4:

Analyze into its immediate constituents any complement or modifier of two or more words:

Q. Form?

A. Prepositional phrase.

| INTO | MY YARD |

Procedure: Cut the prepositional phrase into its two parts: the preposition and the noun phrase. After cutting the prepositional phrase, follow the procedure for analyzing the object of the preposition, the noun phrase: Step 3 above.

| MY | YARD |

| WHO | LIVES | DOWN | THE | STREET |

Q. Form?

A. Clause (i.e., sentence).

Procedure: Because the clause is a sentence in form, begin with Step 1 above.

The complete I-C analysis looks like this:

| THE | LITTLE | BOY | WHO | LIVES | DOWN | THE | STREET | HAS | HIT | HIS | BALL | INTO | MY | YARD |

As a method for understanding syntax, I-C analysis has both advantages and disadvantages compared with traditional diagramming. Two structures that I-C analysis renders more accurately are the noun phrase and the sentence modifier. Here is the sample noun phrase done in both ways:

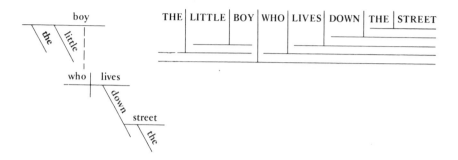

Both methods require an understanding of such concepts as headwords and pre- and postmodifiers. The traditional diagram creates a clearer picture of the headword with its three modifiers. What the I-C analysis can show that the traditional diagram cannot, however, is the "nesting" relationship of the modifiers to the headword. For example, the *who* clause modifies *the little boy,* not simply *boy;* the determiner signals *little boy,* not simply *boy.*

In the following example, the determiner *my* signals *old blue Ford;* the traditional diagram shows *my* and *old* and *blue* as independent signalers of the headword.

In the predicate, too, the I-C analysis shows *into my yard* related to *hit the ball,* not just to *hit,* as the traditional diagram does.

Another advantage of I-C analysis occurs when a whole sentence has a modifier:

Clearly, he did not explain his idea.
He did not explain his idea clearly.

With the I-C analysis, these two sentences are quite different. The first shows that the two constituents of the structure are the sentence and the sentence modifier:

CLEARLY	HE DID NOT EXPLAIN HIS IDEA

The second shows *clearly* as an adverbial:

HE | DID NOT EXPLAIN HIS IDEA | CLEARLY

Because the traditional diagram has no system for diagramming the structure that modifies the entire sentence, both versions of this sentence would look the same:

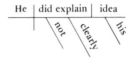

Another difference between the two methods is that I-C analysis retains the original word order of the sentence. Because the purpose of analysis is to show the relationship of the parts no matter what their order, maintaining the word order is really not an advantage. This feature of I-C analysis, in fact, includes a disadvantage: The length of a sentence to be analyzed is limited by the width of the page.

Because sentence transformations so frequently include shifts in word order, I-C analysis is at a disadvantage in many circumstances. For example, it cannot show the immediate constituents of the *there* transformation in any meaningful way:

THERE | 'S | A FLY IN MY SOUP

The traditional diagram shows the subject–verb relationship clearly:

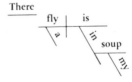

Even a simple question transformation is a problem for I-C analysis:

WHY | ARE | YOU DOING THIS?   IS | HE | COMING WITH YOU?

Because I-C analysis is based on the binary nature of the sentence and its parts, it does not work efficiently in circumstances where that binarity is either altered or simply not evident.

Another drawback of I-C analysis is the absence of any signals relating to either the form or the function of a structure. For example, the analyses of Patterns I through VII are all the same:

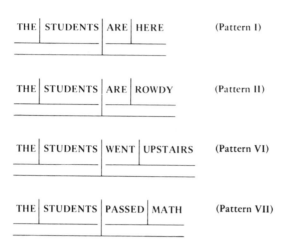

| THE | STUDENTS | ARE | HERE | (Pattern I) |

| THE | STUDENTS | ARE | ROWDY | (Pattern II) |

| THE | STUDENTS | WENT | UPSTAIRS | (Pattern VI) |

| THE | STUDENTS | PASSED | MATH | (Pattern VII) |

The finished product makes no distinctions between adverbials and complements, nor between direct objects and subjective complements, nor between adjectives and noun phrases as subjective complements.

Further, the I-C analysis makes no distinction between a gerund and a participle. It cannot show the ambiguity of a sentence such as this:

| VISITING | RELATIVES | CAN | BE | BORING |

A traditional diagram, on the other hand, identifies the subject—verb relationship in the gerund phrase and the modifier—subject relationship of the participle; and it identifies *boring* as a subjective complement.

I-C analysis can, of course, show ambiguity in many cases:

| JOHN | DISCUSSED | HIS | PROBLEM | WITH | THE | TEACHER |

| JOHN | DISCUSSED | HIS | PROBLEM | WITH | THE | TEACHER |

But these two diagrams also illustrate the biggest drawback of I-C analysis; the end result is not accessible in the way that a traditional diagram is:

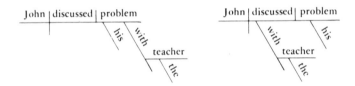

The traditional diagram enables you to picture the relationships, to see at a glance the difference between the two. In the sentences above, you see immediately that the prepositional phrase modifies either *discussed* or *problem*. That message is not nearly as easy to read in the I-C diagram.

I-C analysis does a good job in showing the levels of sentences, the nesting of small structures within larger ones. In that limited way, it can be a useful tool in understanding the system of syntax.

Further
Notes on Diagramming

1. Prenoun modifiers: The traditional diagram treats hyphenated modifiers as single words:

an out-of-the-way place   a cheese-tasting party

An alternative method can show the underlying deep structure of the modifiers:

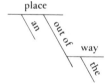   

Many *-ing* modifiers are gerunds in the deep structure, although the traditional diagram generally treats them as adjectives:

the dining room   the drinking fountain

387

Again, the diagram could easily show the underlying structure:

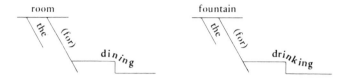

2. Proper nouns of more than one word are generally treated as a single word:

President Lincoln wrote "The Gettysburg Address" on the back of an envelope.

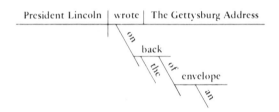

Harriett Smith lives on Center Street.

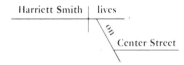

3. Contractions can be shown either connected to or separated from the word they are attached to:

I haven't voted yet.

He's a pest.

She'll be leaving soon.

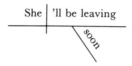

4. The relative adverb that introduces an adverbial or adjectival clause is more conveniently diagrammed on the broken line that connects the two clauses than attached as an adverb in the subordinate clause. But that's just a matter of convenience; both ways are acceptable:

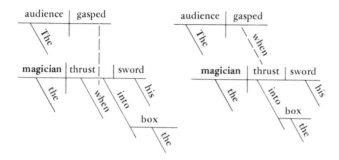

5. Traditional diagramming does not include a method for showing adverbs and clauses as sentence modifiers:

Clearly, he did not explain his idea.
As we were leaving, he began to laugh.

Both of these are generally diagrammed under the verb, as any modifier of the verb would be. This is a weakness of traditional diagramming. Some sentence modifiers, however, can be shown as separate structures:

To tell the truth, I have never read *Silas Marner*.

Speaking of the weather, the picnic has been canceled.

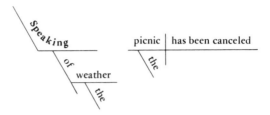

The absolute phrase is another structure that is shown as independent in the diagram:

Julie fit the key into the rusty lock, her hands trembling.

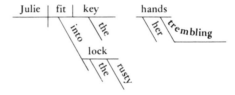

6. In some sentences the appositive, a noun phrase in form, re-names the idea of the whole sentence; it is in apposition to an idea, not simply to a noun phrase. In this case, the appositive is diagrammed by itself, very much like the absolute:

A pair of cardinals has settled in our pine tree—an unexpected but welcome surprise.

ANSWERS
TO THE EXERCISES

CHAPTER 1

Exercise 1, Page 10

1. Pattern III

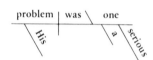

2. Pattern II

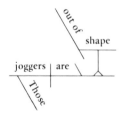

3. Pattern II

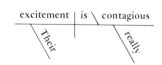

4. Pattern I

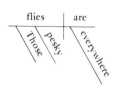

5. Pattern II

6. Pattern II

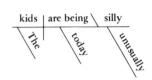

7. Pattern III

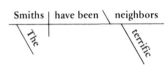

8. Pattern I

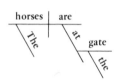

9. Pattern II

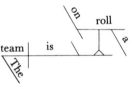

10. Pattern I

Exercise 2, Page 11

1. Pattern IV

2. Pattern V

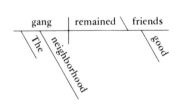

3. Pattern IV

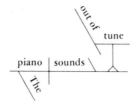

4. Pattern V

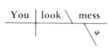

5. Pattern IV

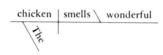

6. Pattern IV

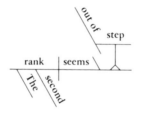

Exercise 3, Page 14

1. Pattern VI

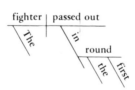

2. Pattern VI

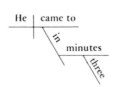

3. Pattern VI

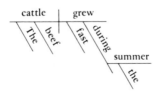

4. Pattern IV

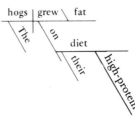

5. Pattern VI

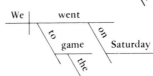

6. Pattern IV

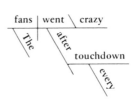

7. Pattern VI

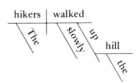

8. Pattern VI

Exercise 4, Page 17

1. Pattern VII

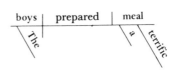

2. Pattern VII

3. Pattern VII

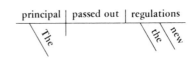

4. Pattern VII

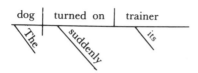

5. Pattern VI

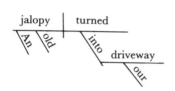

6. Pattern VII

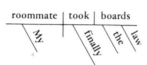

7. Pattern VII

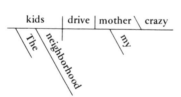

Exercise 5, Page 20

1. Pattern IX

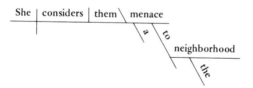

2. Pattern X

3. Pattern VIII

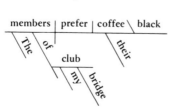

4. Pattern IX

5. Pattern IX

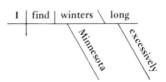

6. Pattern VIII

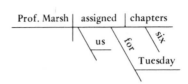

7. Pattern IX

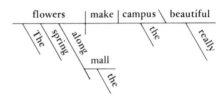

8. Pattern VIII

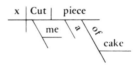

CHAPTER 2

Exercise 6, Page 36

1. go	goes	went	gone	going
2. break	breaks	broke	broken	breaking
3. come	comes	came	come	coming
4. move	moves	moved	moved	moving
5. expect	expects	expected	expected	expecting
6. put	puts	put	put	putting
7. drink	drinks	drank	drunk	drinking
8. think	thinks	thought	thought	thinking
9. like	likes	liked	liked	liking
10. feel	feels	felt	felt	feeling
11. lose	loses	lost	lost	losing
12. pass	passes	passed	passed	passing
13. meet	meets	met	met	meeting

14. beat	beats	beat	beat (en)	beating
15. lead	leads	led	led	leading
16. read	reads	read	read	reading
17. say	says	said	said	saying
18. drive	drives	drove	driven	driving

Exercise 7, Page 40

1. has worked
2. was working
3. has been playing
4. was being
5. is having
6. has had
7. had had
8. had been being

Exercise 8, Page 42

1. shall be going
2. should have gone
3. would come
4. may have been playing
5. might play
6. could have drunk

Exercise 9, Page 47

1. The lead article in today's *Collegian* was written by my roommate.
2. Some of our most intricate fugues were composed by Bach.
3. The most expensive houses in town are built by my brother-in-law.
4. That expensive apartment complex on Allen Street was built by him.
5. A new tax collection system is tried out every four years by the county commissioners.

1. The cheerleaders led the football team onto the field.
2. A committee chose this year's squad last spring.
3. Someone burglarized Bill's apartment last weekend.

4. The market expects a shipment of fresh lobsters any minute.
5. We held the elections on Tuesday, as usual.

Exercise 10, Page 49

1. The people elected Mario Cuomo governor of New York in 1982. (Pattern X)
2. Someone found the kidnapping victim in the woods unharmed. (Pattern IX)
3. The neighbors painted the house next door purple. (Pattern IX)
4. Someone finally gave Marylou the recognition she deserves. (Pattern VIII)
5. People mistakenly call women the weaker sex. (Pattern X)

Exercise 11, Page 51

1. A Republican will probably be elected as mayor next year.
2. Prospectors had found gold in Alaska long before the Gold Rush in California.
3. The federal government is now giving help in the form of a fuel allowance to the poor.
4. A big batch of cookies was being mixed up this morning by my son and his friends.
5. The subway fare is being raised to sixty cents next week.
6. The play has been called witty and warm by well-known and knowledgeable critics.
7. The weatherman has expected a snowstorm since Monday.
8. You should study six chapters before the next exam.

Exercise 12, Page 56

Here are some possibilities; you may think of some others.

1. The house was under construction for five years.
2. Angry demonstrators crowded the front steps.
3. Rare postage stamps have arrived from all over the world.
4. All of my computer cards disappeared in the rush of registration.
5. Good family programs rarely appear on the commercial networks.
6. Wood has become popular as fuel in homes throughout the country.

CHAPTER 3

Exercise 13, Page 66

1. Pattern VI

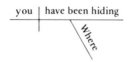

2. Pattern VI

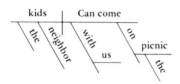

3. Pattern VII

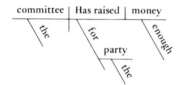

Note: *For the party* could also be considered a modifier of *money.*

4. Pattern VII

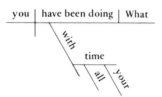

5. Pattern IV

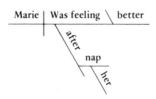

6. Pattern VII

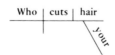

7. Pattern VI

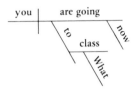

8. Pattern I

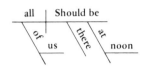

Exercise 14, Page 69

1. Do most of the children on the block own roller skates?
2. Does the girl next door skate all evening long?
3. Did Helen's children want skates for Christmas?

1. Most of the children on the block don't own roller skates.
2. The girl next door doesn't skate all evening long.
3. Helen's children didn't want skates for Christmas.

1. Most of the children on the block do own roller skates.
2. The girl next door does skate all evening long.
3. Helen's children did want skates for Christmas.

Exercise 15, Page 73

1. Pattern VI

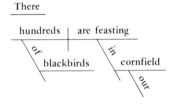

2. Pattern VII; They do a great deal of damage there. . . .

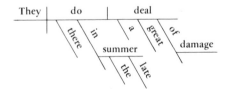

3. Pattern I; There was a serious bird problem <u>there</u>. . . .

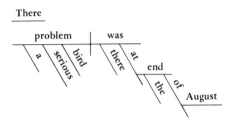

4. Pattern VII

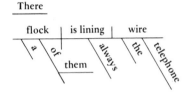

5. Pattern I; <u>There</u> they are now.

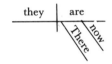

Exercise 16, Page 75

Here is a sampling of the possibilities:

1. It was Bill's grandmother who nicknamed him Buzz when he was in third grade.
2. It's Glenda who loves break dancing.
   What Glenda loves is break dancing.
3. It was seventy years before Edison's first incandescent lamp that Sir Humphrey . . . .
4. It was in 1983 that Sally Ride became the first . . . .
5. It was the San Diego Padres who won the . . . .
6. What made Brenda furious was Tom's casual remark . . . .

CHAPTER 4

Exercise 17, Page 86

n o v|a   a u d|i t|o r
r e|n o v|a t i o n   a u d|i e n c e
i n|n o v|a t e   i n|a u d|i b l e
n o v|i c e   a u d|i t|o r|i u m
n o v|e l|i s t   a u d|i o
   nov = new   aud = hear

    d u r|a b l e   c o n|c e i v e
    e n|d u r e   c a p|a b l e
    d u r|a t i o n   s u s|c e p t|i b l e
    d u r|i n g   c a p|t u r e
    e n|d u r|a n c e   i n t e r|c e p t
     dur = hard   cap (cept) = take

Exercise 18, Page 87

Check your answers with the dictionary and/or your instructor.

Exercise 19, Page 91

1. pre cis ion (bound + bound + bound; affix, base, affix)
   d   d
   (Note: d = derivational; i = inflectional)

2. candid ate (free + bound; base, affix)
          d

3. de tour ed (bound + free + bound; affix, base, affix)
   d   i

4. ex cess ive ly (bound + bound + bound + bound; affix,
   d   d d base, affix, affix)

5. un a ware (bound + bound + free; affix, affix, base)
   d d

6. money (free; base)

7. side walk s (free + free + bound; base, base, affix)
           i

8. pro mot ion (bound + bound + bound; affix, base, affix)
    d   d

9. il leg al (bound + bound + bound; affix, base, affix)
   d   d

10. weal th y (free + bound + bound; base, affix, affix)
       d d

11. tele vis ion (bound + bound + bound; affix, base, affix)
    d   d

12. re vis es (bound + bound + bound; affix, base, affix)
   d   i

CHAPTER 5

Exercise 20, Page 96

1. pleasure
2. regulation, regulator
3. stealth
4. health, healer
5. derivation
6. inflection
7. formula, formation, formant
8. revival
9. seizure
10. retirement, retiree

Exercise 21, Page 98

1. teacher's, teachers'
2. horse's, horses'
3. sister's husband's, sisters' husbands'
4. American's, Americans'
5. son's, sons'

Exercise 22, Page 99

1. Price's
2. Hedges'
3. James's (or James')
4. Massachusetts'
5. Linus's
6. neighbor's
7. neighbors'
8. Miss Piggy's
9. women's
10. Confucius'

Exercise 23, Page 106

truth *s* (i)
m*en* (The plural inflection is irregular.)
creat *or* (d)
right *s* (i)
life (no inflectional or derivational)
liber *ty* (d)
pursuit (noun form of *pursue*)
happi *ness* (d)

Those nouns without obvious clues of form can be recognized as nouns
by their position in the sentence.

Exercise 24, Page 108

tree, trees, treed, treeing, treed (We treed the coon.)
water, waters, watered, watering, watered (Joe waters the plants every
day.)
rock, rocks, rocked, rocking, rocked (She has rocked the baby to
sleep.)
air, airs, aired, airing, aired (They are airing their grievances in public
again.)
fire, fires, fired, firing, fired (The foreman has fired the entire crew.)

Exercise 25, Page 111

friendly	friendlier	friendliest
helpful	more helpful	most helpful
staunch	stauncher	staunchest
wise	wiser	wisest
awful	more awful	most awful
rich	richer	richest
mellow	mellower	mellowest
expensive	more expensive	most expensive
valid	more valid	most valid
pure	purer	purest
able	abler (more able)	ablest (most able)
cheap	cheaper	cheapest

Exercise 26, Page 115

launch (*noun:* launches, launch's) (*verb:* launches, launched, etc.)
staunch (*adj:* stauncher, staunchest) (*verb,* variation of stanch: staunches, staunched, etc.)
paunch (*noun:* paunches, paunch's)
deep (*adj:* deeper, deepest)
keep (*verb:* keeps, kept, keeping, etc.) (The noun *keep* does not inflect except in idioms such as "for keeps.")
jeep (*noun:* jeeps, jeep's)
nice (*adj:* nicer, nicest)
rice (*noun:* rices—in the sense of "varieties of rice"; rice's)
     (*verb:* rices, riced, etc.—"to put through a ricer")
splice (*noun:* splices, splice's) (*verb:* splices, spliced, etc.)

Exercise 27, Page 116

grief	grieve	grievous	grievously
variation	vary	variable	variably
variance		various	variously
variety			

ability	enable	able	ably
defense	defend	defensive	defensively
economy	economize	economical economic	economically
pleasure	please	pleasant	pleasantly
type	typify	typical	typically
prohibition	prohibit	prohibitive	prohibitively
length	lengthen	long	long
validation validity	validate	valid	validly
appreciation	appreciate	appreciative	appreciatively
beauty	beautify	beautiful	beautifully
acceptance	accept	acceptable	acceptably
purity	purify	pure	purely
continuation continuity	continue	continuous continual	continuously continually

(Note: You may think of other possibilities.)

CHAPTER 6

Exercise 28, Page 126

1. my, enough, her
2. John's, the
3. Every, this, a
4. more, the week's
5. less, last
6. either, no

Exercise 29, Page 128

1. only one (one = number)
2. all of my (my = possessive pronoun)
3. The first two (The = article)
4. The next three (The = article)
5. Only that last (that = demonstrative pronoun)

Exercise 30, Page 130

1. have been having
2. don't dare walk
3. should eat
4. can't look
5. will be helping
6. has to leave
7. are frustrating
8. can be
9. didn't register
10. has been registered

Exercise 31, Page 132

1. tired (adj)
2. fast (adv)
3. ridiculous (adj)
4. Frankly (adv)—either *quite* or *very*
5. intelligent (adj)
6. well (adv)

All three qualifiers will work in all of the sentences except number six, where *rather* would probably not be used.

Exercise 32, Page 135

1. in, since
2. because of

3. in spite of
4. According to, of, to, during
5. with (*on* = particle)

Exercise 33, Page 144

1. and—coordinating conjunction; on—preposition; an—determiner; in—preposition
2. Four—determiner; from—preposition; for—preposition; for—coordinating conjunction
3. As—subordinating conjunction; an—determiner; as—expletive; at—preposition
4. be—auxiliary; by—preposition; but—coordinating conjunction
5. of—preposition; off—particle (part of verb); if—subordinating conjunction
6. are—auxiliary; of—preposition; or—expletive; our—determiner
7. will—auxiliary; with—preposition; while—subordinating conjunction
8. too—qualifier; two—determiner; to—preposition

CHAPTER 7

Exercise 34, Page 149

1. They
2. We, him
3. it
4. them
5. us
6. him, it
7. us
8. He

Exercise 35, Page 151

1. herself
2. themselves
3. itself

4. ourselves
5. herself
6. ourselves

Exercise 36, Page 152

1. Claudia herself composed the music for the show.
2. I myself never read the comic page.
3. Gil and Kim wrote their wedding ceremony themselves.
4. I will pay for the cost of the trip itself but not extras. (or I myself will pay. . . .)
5. Harold gave the tip to the waitress himself. (or . . . to the waitress herself.)

Note: Other variations are possible.

Exercise 37, Page 158

1. everything—indefinite; I—personal; one—indefinite
2. any—indefinite; they—personal
3. Someone—indefinite; we—personal; who—interrogative; it—personal
4. All—indefinite; that—relative; I—personal
5. much—indefinite; they—personal; both—indefinite; more—indefinite; I—personal
6. I—personal; whatever—relative; you—personal
7. enough—indefinite; me—personal
8. themselves—reflexive; one another's—reciprocal
9. me—personal; what—interrogative; I—personal; your—personal
10. whoever—relative; one—indefinite

CHAPTER 8

Exercise 38, Page 171

Here are some possible variations; you may find others.

1. Now the leaves are steadily falling.

2. The snow will be everywhere very soon.
3. Here winter often arrives suddenly. Often winter suddenly arrives here.
4. Winter sneaks in quietly sometimes. Sometimes winter quietly sneaks in.

Exercise 39, Page 174

1. In winter, for our heat (Both are movable.)
2. in homes, throughout the country, for fuel (All are movable.)
3. on Saturday (movable)
4. on the back porch, under the eaves (probably not movable)
5. According to the latest reports, before January (Both are movable.)

Note: In number two, *throughout the country* could be considered a modifier of *homes;* if so, it would not be movable; it would stay with *homes.*

Exercise 40, Page 176

1. I'm going to wax the car parked in the garage.
   I'm going into the garage to wax the car.

2. Tim chopped the wood that was on the porch.
   Tim did the wood chopping on the porch.

3. I hid from the neighbors who live upstairs.
   I went upstairs to hide from the neighbors.

4. Fred tripped his teammate who was holding the bat.
   Fred stuck the bat out and tripped his teammate.

5. Susan washed the stones she found in the riverbed.
   Susan went to the river to wash the stones she found.

Exercise 41, Page 178

1. Pattern VI
2. Pattern VII
3. Pattern VII
4. Pattern VII

5. Pattern I
6. Pattern VII
7. Pattern VI
8. Pattern I
9. Pattern II
10. Pattern VII

Exercise 42, Page 181

1. Our cat <u>often</u> jumps <u>up</u> on the roof <u>to reach the attic window.</u>

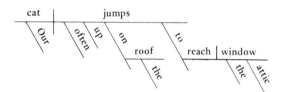

(main clause: Pattern VI; infinitive: Pattern VII)
2. <u>Sometimes</u> she <u>even</u> climbs the ladder <u>to get there.</u>

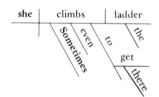

(main clause: Pattern VII; infinitive: Pattern VI)
3. <u>Last night</u> the television set buzzed <u>strangely</u> <u>after the ten o'clock news.</u>

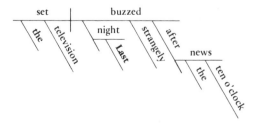

(Pattern VI)

4. We were in the kitchen at the time.

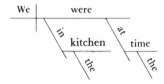

(Pattern I)

5. We went downtown last Saturday to take advantage of the side-walk sales.

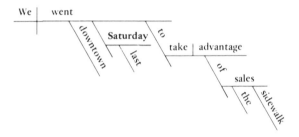

(main clause: Pattern VI; infinitive: Pattern VII)

6. First I bought the children winter boots at the new shoe store.

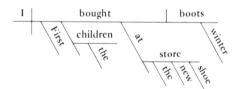

(Pattern VIII)

7. Afterwards we stayed home to watch the playoff game with Uncle Dick.

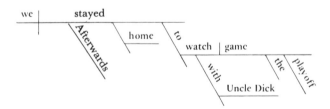

(main clause: Pattern VI; infinitive: Pattern VII)

Exercise 43, Page 185

1. On Halloween—prepositional phrase; out—adverb; trick-or-treating—verb phrase
2. expectantly—adverb; to fill . . . goodies—infinitive phrase; with goodies—prepositional phrase
3. slowly—adverb; in the park—prepositional phrase; last night—noun phrase
4. on crutches—prepositional phrase; with difficulty—prepositional phrase
5. after their divorce—prepositional phrase
6. home—noun; for the holidays—prepositional phrase; for . . . years—prepositional phrase
7. beautifully—adverb; at the . . . season—prepositional phrase
8. After . . . beautifully—clause; so beautifully—qualified adverb
9. to graduate this term—infinitive phrase; this term—noun phrase
10. Where—interrogative; when . . . repairs—clause; to get . . . repairs—infinitive phrase; for repairs—prepositional phrase

CHAPTER 9

Exercise 44, Page 196

1. The department's personnel committee
   (determiner) (adjective) (headword)

   the main office   Monday night
   (d) (adj) (H)   (n) (H)

2. the new Sunday brunch menu   the Country Club
   (d) (adj) (n) (n) (H)   (d) (n) (H)

3. an expensive-looking copper-colored bracelet
   (d) (adj) (part) (n) (part) (H)

   the subway station
   (d) (n) (H)

4. The committee   this year's homecoming celebration
   ‾(d)‾ ‾(H)‾   ‾(d)‾   (n)   ‾(H)‾

   a   really festive   occasion
   ‾(d) (qualified adj)‾   ‾(H)‾

5. The bicycle safety commission   the new regulations
   ‾(d)‾ (n)   (n)   ‾(H)‾   ‾(d) (adj)‾ ‾(H)‾

   their regular meeting   this noon
   ‾(d)‾ (adj) ‾(H)‾   ‾(d) (H)‾

6. Her lovely, gracious manner
   ‾(d)‾ (adj)   (adj)   ‾(H)‾

7. My poor old cat   another extreme winter
   ‾(d) (adj) (adj) (H)‾   ‾(d)‾   (adj)   ‾(H)‾

8. a splendid old table   the auction
   (d) (adj) (adj) ‾(H)‾   ‾(d)‾ ‾(H)‾

9. delicious, refreshing iced tea
    (adj)   (adj)   (part) ‾(H)‾

10. A commonly held notion   my cynical friends
    ‾(d)‾ (adv) (part) ‾(H)‾   ‾(d)‾ (adj) ‾(H)‾

    big-business lobbyists
    (adj)   (n)   ‾(H)‾

Exercise 45, Page 200

1. with a cast on his left foot
2. of the museum (*Near the visitors' information booth* could modify
   either *museum* or *meet.*)
3. after the game (*At Bob's* could modify either *party* or *game.*)
4. across the street
5. of spring
6. for my science course, from Stanford

Exercise 46, Page 203

1. Bill owns that expensive sports car standing in the driveway.
   (Note that the indefinite *an* becomes definite with *that.*)

2. There will be no sleep tonight for <u>the students cramming for their history test</u>.
3. I am babysitting for <u>the baby sleeping upstairs in the crib</u>.
4. Some of <u>the fans lining up at the ticket office</u> will probably be disappointed.
5. A hush settled over <u>the huge crowd watching the parade</u> when the magnificent Percherons pranced by.

Exercise 47, Page 205

1. We raised <u>our mugs, filled to the brim</u>, and toasted the bartender.
2. The <u>costumes, made by Betty</u>, were the best part of the play.
3. <u>The murderer's name scrawled on the floor in lipstick</u> was the victim's last message in this world.
4. <u>Mary, awarded first prize for her charcoal sketch of an albatross</u>, donated half the money to the local bird-watching club.

Exercise 48, Page 208

Here are some possibilities; you will probably think of others.

1. Having endured rain all week, we weren't surprised at the miserable weather on Saturday.
2. Having hiked five miles uphill, I was sure my backpack weighed a ton.
3. Hoping for the sixth win in a row, the fans in the grandstand could not contain their excitement as the band played "The Star Spangled Banner."
4. The dog's reaction to strangers was fascinating to watch; he guarded his bone as if it were his very last meal.
5. Working ten hours a day six days a week, John completely finished his first novel in six months.
6. Exhausted by the hot weather, we could do nothing but lie in the shade.
7. Wearing their new uniforms proudly, the band marched across the field and formed a huge "O."
8. Having spent nearly all day in the kitchen, I nevertheless decided that my superb gourmet dinner was worth the effort.

or

Even though I spent nearly all day in the kitchen, that superb gourmet dinner was worth the effort.

Exercise 49, Page 209

1. Our visitor snores.
2. The dog is barking.
3. The hinge broke. (*or* Someone broke the hinge.)
4. Strangers are passing.
5. Our visitor snores (*or* is snoring) loudly.
6. The baby is sleeping peacefully.

Exercise 50, Page 212

1. (whom) I love. (whom = direct object; Pattern VII)
2. that we bought. (that = direct object; Pattern VII)
3. whose farm we rent (whose = determiner; Pattern VII)
4. which . . . cold (which = direct object; Pattern X)
5. who . . . brothers (who = subject; Pattern VI)
6. whom . . . loved (whom = direct object; Pattern VII)
7. who . . . conference (who = subject; Pattern I)
8. that . . . lawn (that = direct object; Pattern VII)

Exercise 51, Page 214

1. whom
2. whomever
3. whom
4. whomever
5. Whoever
6. whom

Exercise 52, Page 220

1. My parents, who retired to Arizona in 1975, love . . . .
2. My favorite teacher, who always celebrates Fridays with cookies for the class, will . . . .
3. (no commas)

4. After our first assignment in economics class, which everyone complained about, I'm not . . . .
5. (no commas)
6. That little house is occupied by our county's only known recluse, whom I often see . . . .

Exercise 53, Page 226

1. My sister Susan's husband, Bill, Wednesday, his bowling night
2. proposal, a crackpot plan from the word go
3. monsters, sixteen-wheelers . . . machinery
4. novel, The Floating Opera   one, an exercise . . . gymnastics
5. Snoots, his . . . pig
6. Black lung, an incurable . . . system

Exercise 54, Page 232

1.

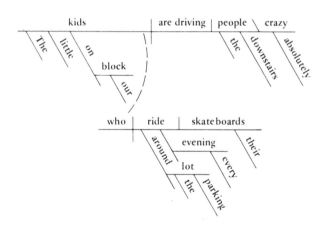

(main clause: Pattern IX; adjectival clause: Pattern VII)
Note: See Appendix, Further Notes on Diagramming, for an alternative treatment of parking (page 388).

2.

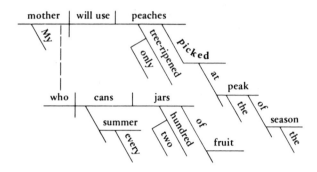

(main clause—Pattern VII; adjectival clause—Pattern VII; participial phrase—Pattern VII, passive)

3.

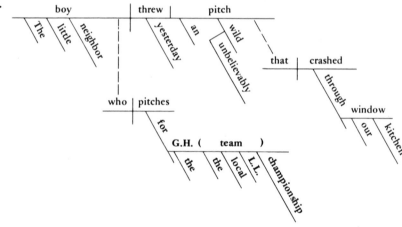

(main clause—Pattern VII; adjectival *who* clause—Pattern VI; adjectival *that* clause—Pattern VI)

4.

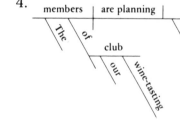

(main clause—Pattern VII; adjectival clause—Pattern X, passive)

5.

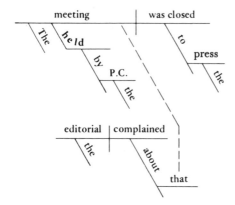

(main clause—Pattern VII, passive; adjectival clause—Pattern VI; participial phrase—Pattern VII, passive)

CHAPTER 10

Exercise 55, Page 240

1. Planes fly; people fly planes.
2. Someone shot the hunters; the hunters are shooting.
3. People burp babies; babies burp.

Exercise 56, Page 246

1. the man [the man is in the boat]
2. the man [the man is standing in the boat]
3. the people [the people live upstairs]
   the people [the people are upstairs]
4. the driver [the driver delivered our furniture]
5. the movies [Woody Allen makes the movies]
6. the people [we visited the people in Utah]
7. the park [the park is behind the school]
8. the man [I love the man]

CHAPTER 11

Exercise 57, Page 254

1. Having measles—Pattern VII; main clause—Pattern III
2. Staying . . . week—Pattern VI; main clause—Pattern IX
3. Painting . . . purple—Pattern IX; main clause—Pattern III
4. Your complaining about the schedule—Pattern VI; main clause—Pattern IX
5. Being an actor—Pattern III; main clause—Pattern IV
6. Studying math—Pattern VII; main clause—Pattern VIII
7. Jogging . . . morning—Pattern VI; main clause—Pattern IX
8. Jogging—Pattern VI; main clause—Pattern III

Exercise 58, Page 256

1. clearing the courtroom—Pattern VII; object of preposition
2. going . . . light—Pattern VI; object of preposition
3. weeding the garden—Pattern VII; direct object·
4. growing roses—Pattern VII; subjective complement
5. Finding . . . roses—Pattern VII; subject
6. (no gerund)
7. being here with you—Pattern I; appositive to *it*
8. giving people a bad time—Pattern VIII; direct object

Exercise 59, Page 258

1. <u>my</u> speaking out
2. <u>John</u> starting the car
3. (<u>dating my daughter</u> is a participial phrase)
4. <u>you</u> starting to bake a cake
5. <u>dog's</u> barking

Exercise 60, Page 259

Here are some possibilities; you may find others.

1. Before starting to bake a cake, first assemble the ingredients.
2. You should avoid heavy meals before swimming.

3. When I was making a career decision, my counselor was a big help.
4. After we stored the outdoor furniture in the garage, there was no room left for the car.

Exercise 61, Page 262

1. <u>to venture into outer space</u>—Pattern VI, direct object; main clause—Pattern VII
2. <u>to fly stand-by</u>—Pattern VI, direct object of participle; main clause—Pattern VI
3. <u>to fly to California</u>—Pattern VI, subjective complement; main clause—Pattern III
4. <u>to see myself . . . morning</u>—Pattern VII, appositive to *it;* main clause—Pattern II
5. <u>to stand . . . camera</u>—Pattern VI, direct object; main clause—Pattern VII
6. <u>To survive midterms</u>—Pattern VII, subject; main clause—Pattern III.

Exercise 62, Page 266

1.

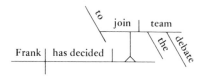

2.

3.

4.

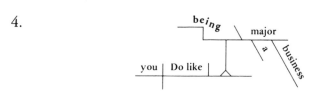

5.

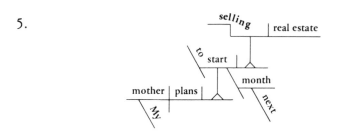

6.

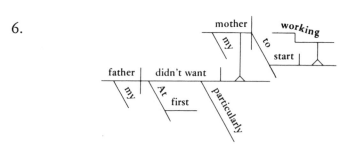

7.

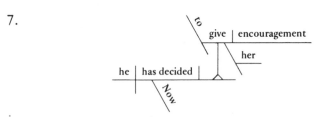

Exercise 63, Page 271

1. that lined up for concert tickets—adjectival, modifies *crowd*
2. that anyone . . . ticket—nominal, direct object

3. that Mary . . . behavior—adjectival, modifies *reason*
4. that you . . . weekend—nominal, direct object
5. that riding . . . tiring—nominal, direct object
6. that the party . . . worthwhile—nominal, direct object
   that his frat . . . Saturday—adjectival, modifies *party*

Exercise 64, Page 276

1. where . . . book—adverbial
2. How . . . money—adverbial
3. who . . . today—subject
4. (The *who* clause is adjectival.)
5. which . . . take—adjectival, determiner for *class*
6. how . . . up—adverbial (The *who* clause is adjectival.)

Exercise 65, Page 280

1.

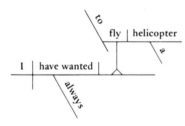

main clause—Pattern VII
infinitive—Pattern VII

2.

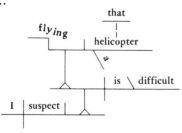

main clause—Pattern VII
gerund—Pattern VII
nominal clause—Pattern II

3.

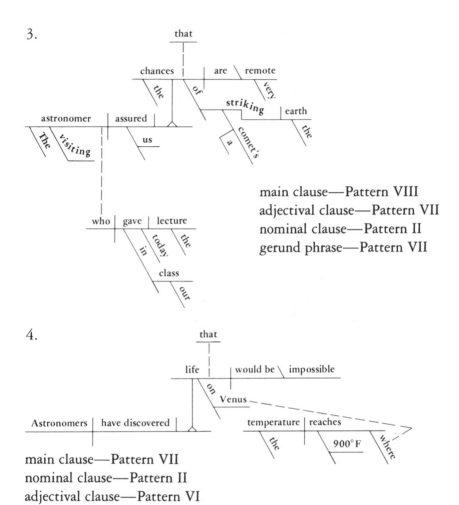

main clause—Pattern VIII
adjectival clause—Pattern VII
nominal clause—Pattern II
gerund phrase—Pattern VII

4.

main clause—Pattern VII
nominal clause—Pattern II
adjectival clause—Pattern VI

5.

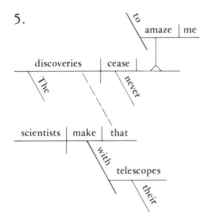

main clause—Pattern VII
infinitive—Pattern VII
adjectival clause—Pattern VII

6.

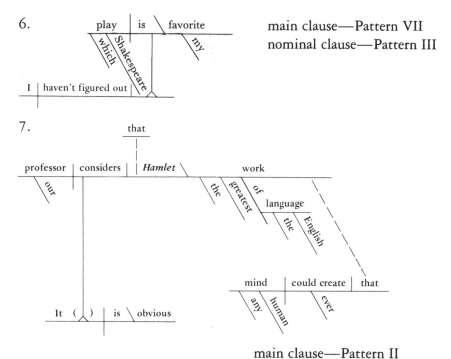

main clause—Pattern VII
nominal clause—Pattern III

7.

main clause—Pattern II
nominal clause—Pattern X
adjectival clause—Pattern VII

8.

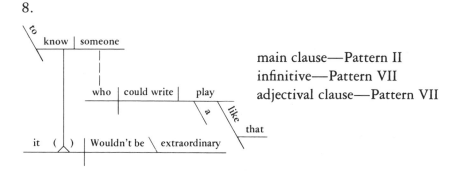

main clause—Pattern II
infinitive—Pattern VII
adjectival clause—Pattern VII

CHAPTER 12

Exercise 66, Page 290

1. <u>Amazingly</u>
2. (none)

3. <u>Well</u>
4. (none)
5. <u>Strangely</u>
6. (none)
7. <u>Without a doubt</u>
8. <u>no doubt</u>
9. (none)
10. <u>my friend</u>

Exercise 67, Page 292

1. (no commas)
2. us, although
3. over, we
4. coffee, since (optional)
5. rent, even
6. (no commas)
7. apartment, even (optional)

Exercise 68, Page 294

A. When you are late for work, the subway is better than the bus.
B. If bread is kept too long in hot weather, mold will grow on it.
C. While we were waiting for the guests to arrive, there were a lot of last minute details to take care of.

1. I picked up a Midwestern accent while *I was* living in Omaha.
2. My accent is not as noticeable as Mary's *accent is* [noticeable].
3. Holmes hit Ali harder than Norton (*hit Ali* or *Holmes hit Norton*).
4. If *it is* necessary, strain the juice before adding the sugar.
5. While *I was* waiting . . . .
6. If *your paper is* handed in late . . . .

Exercise 69, Page 299

1. <u>her tail . . . metronome</u> (participle)
2. <u>their arms . . . shoulders</u> (participle)
3. <u>The rain having . . . hour</u> (participle)
4. (no absolute phrase)

5. her eyes . . . floor (participle)
6. Hands on hips (prepositional phrase)
7. (no absolute phrase)
8. his bunched shirt . . . blades (prepositional phrase)
   his toes . . . floor (participle)
   the aunt's arms . . . shoulders (prepositional phrase)

Exercise 70, Page 301

1. Cleaning the basement this morning wasn't very much fun.
2. It surprised me that Otis didn't want to stay for the second half of the game.
3. The president criticized the Congress rather severely in his press conference; some observers considered his criticism quite inappropriate.
4. Contrary to the prediction of the weather service, the first snowstorm of the season in Denver was both early and severe.
5. Our having company for dinner three times this week probably means hot dogs for the rest of the month.

CHAPTER 13

Exercise 71, Page 310

1. (no commas)
2. now, I
3. tires, shock absorbers, and brake linings
4. 1940s, a 1929 Whippet, required
5. (no commas)
6. Corvette, the car

Exercise 72, Page 313

There's more than one possibility in each case.

1. I can't decide which activity I prefer: swimming . . . or jogging . . . .

2. I almost never watch television. Either there is nothing on that appeals to me or the picture . . . .
3. I don't enjoy flying, and I don't feel like taking the train.
4. Either the recipe was printed wrong, or I misread it.
5. Other people can become frail and can break, but not parents.
6. The coach announced an extra hour of drill on Saturday and no practice on Sunday.
7. For my birthday dinner, Aunt Rosa has promised to fix her famous lasagna and to bake my favorite cake.

Exercise 73, Page 316

1. The library closes at noon on Thursdays but stays open until 9:00 P.M. on Fridays.
2. The food at the new French restaurant may be exceptionally good, but the prices are exceptionally high.
3. I am going to take piano lessons this fall, and I may take guitar lessons, too.
4. My first-period students are not only bright, they are also wide awake at 8:00 A.M.
5. Our trip across Kansas was long and straight and uneventful, and it took an entire day.

INDEX